T0329046

*f*P

Also by John L. Nesheim

High Tech Start Up: The Complete Handbook
for Creating Successful New High Tech Companies,
Revised and Updated

The Power of Unfair Advantage

How to Create It,
Build It, and Use It to
Maximum Effect

JOHN L. NESHEIM

Free Press
New York London Toronto Sydney

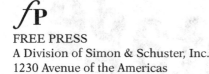

FREE PRESS
A Division of Simon & Schuster, Inc.
1230 Avenue of the Americas
New York, NY 10020

FREE PRESS and colophon are trademarks
of Simon & Schuster, Inc.
For information about special discounts for bulk purchases,
please contact Simon & Schuster Special Sales: 1-800-456-6798
or business@simonandschuster.com

Designed by Nancy Singer Olaguera

Manufactured in the United States of America

10 9 8 7 6 5 4 3 2 1

Library of Congress Cataloging-in-Publication Data

Nesheim, John L.
The power of unfair advantage: how to create it, build it, and use it to
maximum effect / John L. Nesheim
  p. cm.
Includes bibliographical references and index.
1. New business enterprises—Management. 2. Business planning.
I. Title.
HD62.5 .N472 2005
658—dc22 2005040567

ISBN 978-1-4516-2426-7

CONTENTS

PREFACE

My previous book *High Tech Start Up* focused on the process of converting an idea into a world-class business. Although it covers the full range of issues facing a new enterprise across its complete life cycle, feedback from readers showed that entrepreneurs wanted something more—something in depth about the causes of start-up winners and losers. Many had learned painfully how hard it is to get an idea funded. Even those who were funded quickly found out how rough it is to become a successful new enterprise. They wanted to learn from their painful lessons.

When entrepreneurs contacted me, I found them fixated on a quest: to find what they missed, what would "get [them] the money" next time. Engineers wanted a secret formula. Marketing people looked for "killer apps." They all desperately wanted to discover what got those other companies into the headlines and on to an initial public offering. They wanted to find the missing magic elixir, the secret sauce. That is what this book is about. In Silicon Valley, it is a well-kept public secret.

It is called *unfair advantage*. It is what was missing in most dot-coms.

Just ask Bill Gates and Michael Dell. They became the dominant giants by knowing something that others didn't. So did Google, Amazon.com, and Cisco. And Jeff Hawkins, inventor of the Palm Pilot.

Serial entrepreneurs live and breathe unfair advantage. It is what venture investors are scouring the world for. It is what talented people interview companies for. It is what reporters are searching for. Successful products have it, and so do companies, universities, governments, and countries. So do individuals. Start-ups must have it, or they should not begin the game. The trouble is, everywhere I look, I see mostly weak or nonexistent advantages in the plans for new enterprises. When I counsel start-up clients or teach students, I tell them to begin their plans by focusing on creating an unfair advantage. That is what makes start-ups thrive. That is what gets the top employees, the media buzzing, investors stuffing checks into your mailbox.

First-time entrepreneurs and fledgling venture capitalists sometimes look down on writing a comprehensive business plan. They demean it as a lowly task done only by inferior founding teams. They see it as useful only as a quasi-statutory requirement done at the last minute to close on a round of funding. Nothing could be further from the truth. The best storytellers get the money. Their tales are filled with thrilling unfair advantages. That is how I recommend a business plan be written: as an exciting narrative about your unfair advantage.

Why is this so seldom done? Because unfair advantage is such a well-kept secret. Hence the title of this book: *The Power of Unfair Advantage: How to Create It, Build It, and Use It to Maximum Effect.*

INTRODUCTION

Arnold Schwarzenegger understands unfair advantage. "I learned that you have to establish yourself in an area where there is no one else," he said in an interview. "Then you have to create a need for yourself, build yourself up. While their empire goes on, slowly, without realizing it, build your own little fortress. And all of the sudden it's too late for them to do anything about it."[1] His empire grew from bodybuilding in a tiny Austrian village to films in Hollywood and continued with investments in real estate and restaurant properties around the world. It sponsored charitable events and was instrumental in his becoming governor of the state of California with an economy the size of France's.

You come up with an idea for a new enterprise. Your goal is to become king of a new hill. You focus on a new market segment that others do not yet see. You climb to the top before your competitors do because you have an advantage. It is so strong that your competitors complain it's unfair.

Unfair advantage is the holy grail. Business fads come and go, but unfair advantage is here to stay. Always was and always will be.

Everyone needs an unfair advantage. Large corporations, universities, and nonprofit organizations, countries, governments, political parties and militaries need it, as well as entrepreneurs and venture capital firms. Reporters, students, and even you need one. Our world is intensely competitive.

The best way to learn about unfair advantage is by looking at new enterprises. They have uncovered the secret of how to create, build, and use unfair advantage to maximum effect.

For this book, the term *new enterprise* refers to any organization that is starting something from nothing. It can begin inside a giant corporation or in a nonprofit organization. It can be a high tech industrial start-up, or a new consumer product family in an existing division. I have included many examples of venture-financed companies in this book because they are the overwhelming winners of new market competitions.

A good idea for a new business can make sense for any size organization. What makes a good investment for a venture capitalist makes a good product that any company can launch. And the opposite is true too. If the idea doesn't make sense for a venture capitalist, why would it make sense at General Electric?

CONTENTS

What is unfair advantage? This book explains it and how to construct it and gives examples of how to use it to build world-class new businesses. I will show that ideas that became revered brands and industrial standards of the world were driven to success with the engine of unfair advantage. It was missing from the plans of failed new enterprises.

The stories of many brave people are included in this book. I have respected confidentialities and in some cases have disguised the material.

STRUCTURE OF THE BOOK

The book is divided into three parts:

- Part I: Chapters 1 and 2 explain what unfair advantage is and describe its elements.

- Part II: Chapters 3 through 22 show how to create and assemble an unfair advantage.

- Part III: Chapter 23 to 29 apply unfair advantage.

  - Chapter 23 discusses the boom-to-bust cycles triggered by disruptive technologies and explains how to use unfair advantage during each phase of the waves.

  - Chapter 24 gives guidelines about how a local new enterprise can become world-class using unfair advantage.

  - Chapter 25 discusses why giant corporations seldom crush new enterprises that create new markets.

- Chapter 26 reveals how venture capital firms exploit unfair advantage as they compete for the best deals.

- Chapter 27 shows how large corporations use unfair advantage to grow from infancy to gorillas.

- Chapter 28 reviews how MBA schools use unfair advantage to position themselves in crowded, intensely competitive markets.

- Chapter 29 discusses how countries use unfair advantage.

- Chapter 30 uses checklists for spotting weaknesses and opportunities in what appear to be good ideas for new enterprises.

- Chapter 31 presents conclusions and challenges.

- The appendixes contain unfair advantage checklists and other practical information.

PART I

WHAT UNFAIR
ADVANTAGE IS

1

WHAT IS AN UNFAIR ADVANTAGE?

*T*hink of an unfair advantage like a diamond. At first it is a rough, unattractive, dirty stone hidden deep below the surface of the earth, in very hard-to-get-to, sometimes dangerous places. Geologists and miners work hard to find diamonds. As polished gems, they are very valuable.

After digging one up, diamond merchants examine the rough stone and decide what they can do to make it into a beautiful gem. Their plan will be to cut and polish the stone in a special way until it sparkles so brightly that it attracts every eye. Experts know each stone is unique and there is a special way to bring out its hidden best. To do that, a diamond cutter will cut tiny faces, called facets, onto every side of the stone. An admiring person will see the gleam of the gem from any viewing angle.

That is how unfair advantage mining works. There is a special process for its discovery, extraction, planning, and polishing. When you learn it, you can do what serial entrepreneurs do: become a world-class unfair advantage miner.

Unfair advantage propels new enterprises to victory. Without it they die, sooner or later—mostly sooner. My research shows that fewer than six ideas in 1 million achieve an initial public offering (IPO). The vast majority lacks an unfair advantage. They expired while attempting to move from an idea to a world-class enterprise.

Unfair advantage attracts the money. The best investors will not fund just a raw idea. Competition for funding is intense. Fewer than six in a thousand ideas get financed. The vast majority lack what it takes to attract the attention of investors. They do not have an unfair advantage.

Unfair advantage enables corporations to become icons, like Genentech, Dell, Cisco, eBay, Amazon, and Google. They began with an idea that grew and changed over years. Their initial unfair advantage kept advancing and growing stronger. Competitors could not overcome their unfair advantages.

Unfair advantage powers the new enterprise while it focuses on achieving its number one goal: to become the leader of a new market category. That is a singular goal with a clear purpose and is the prime directive for every stakeholder of the new organization. Each employee knows the company needs an unfair advantage to attain the coveted goal. Everyone pitches in to craft it, strengthen it, and advance it. The entire organization is fixated on it, driven by it.

Every competitor complains about the unfair advantage of the market leader because it is so hard to overcome. Just ask Bill Gates how powerful unfair advantage is: he has earned his black belt in unfair advantage.

To expand your insight about unfair advantage, let's scrutinize what helped a real company move from a tiny new enterprise to a world-class icon.

CISCO

"I just don't get it!" exclaimed Bill, a managing director of a respected Wall Street firm. He stood up and continued venting. "Cisco got to be the world's most valuable company by inventing nothing more than a stripped-down personal computer. That's all they had. I saw them before they were famous. But in the end, they really had something. I missed it. So did a lot of others. You have to give them credit—and their investors—they put together one hell of a business."

I decided to ask Don Valentine, the dean of Sequoia Capital, to reflect with me on what made Cisco so successful. As a Cisco board member and its lead investor, Valentine had seen the history of the company from day one. I wanted him to tell me whether Cisco's success was attributable to one special thing. "Was it some secret?" I asked. "Perhaps a skill, or simply due to good luck? Or was it a lot more?"

Example 1-1   Unfair Advantage: Cisco

      Nesheim: How do you describe the unfair advantage of Cisco today?"

      Valentine: An unfair advantage can be different from the public perception of it. For example, Intel figured out how to become virtually the only one able to finance multibillion-dollar semiconductor factories. Cisco's advantage is now beginning to be perceived by outsiders. Cisco created a huge sales and marketing presence all over the world. That makes it very difficult for companies to compete with Cisco.

Nesheim: How did Cisco move from the original idea to a world-class business?

Valentine: We spotted Cisco in the form of two employees of Stanford University who ran the data center. They had a very serious data problem to be solved. They were encountering the real problem of data storms—all those packets of data flying around, colliding. They came up with a crude solution that eventually became the router.

To find the issues to address, I called people at Hewlett-Packard and other potential customers. I was told that the 80–20 rule would apply—namely, that 20 percent of the customers will know how to deploy the router, and 80 percent will not. The challenge to launch the company was to find the 20 percent. A new enterprise does not have the time or manpower to help the other 80 percent initially. Therefore we wanted to have a person who knew sales to run the company. Sales traction is the biggest problem start-up companies have. It is true of all of them.

We financed Cisco with the understanding that the founders would provide the science; we would provide the money, hire the management, and create a management process and the team. For a while, Sequoia was the management.

Nesheim: How did Cisco's business model strengthen its competitive advantage?

Valentine: New enterprises must first determine the key issues and then build a new business model to address those issues. Sooner or later, every business model must be changed. Competition is constantly working to make your model obsolete.

We are asked, "How can our inexperienced managers take on the complexities of managing a new business?" We tell them to simplify things.

Only do the things you have to be good at. That is what we told Steve Jobs when we helped start Apple. Which kinds of assets do you have to rely on? At Yahoo we started with two young Ph.D. candidates who relaxed by surfing the Internet with a crude form of what became a search engine. We added the people who productized it.

At inception, Cisco made the decision that it did not have to invest in factories, so it outsourced everything it could. It decided it had to be good at only two things: sales and engineering. That led to unprecedented fiscal success. Today Cisco has more cash than all its competitors' cash combined, net of debt. Cisco's conceptual commitment at the beginning was to eliminate everything from the core that was not differentiable. The resulting outstanding productivity per employee stemmed from not doing what was not differentiable.

In its early days, Cisco codified the concept of end-to-end. It convinced customers it would provide a single network solution. To serve the customers, it knew it could not do all the products and services at Cisco, so it arranged a way to partner with and invest in the service companies. At the time, service companies were spinning out from the accounting companies. Cisco did not want to own and manage them, so it invested in them and took them to the customers. Cisco outsourced the services it needed to deliver an end-to-end solution.

Nesheim: What are some of the elements that differentiated Cisco?

Valentine: We find several things come together to make a company differentiable. It is more than the people. What you choose to concentrate on depends on the business issues. We try to eliminate the areas that cannot be differentiated and then concentrate on the few that can.

We look for big intellectual property. The reason for big intellectual property is that you can get high gross margins with it. With high gross margins, young presidents can make mistakes, and the mistakes are not so punitive. We look for gross margins in the range of 70 percent. That is what Cisco does.

In the early days, we were the management. We see ourselves as the entrepreneur behind the entrepreneur. We helped hire employees to form the management. Our choices for president were sales leaders. John Morgridge at Cisco is an example.

The company culture is important for the people entering the company. Management has to believe in it. The culture must reflect the values of the president and how the company makes profits. As a result, some people fit in one company but not in another.

In the final analysis, you have to evaluate whether the advantages are differentiated or not.

After reading the interview about Cisco, Kim Cushing, a Silicon Valley critic, said, "I think that the dialogue shows from the beginning there is not one specific thing that forms unfair advantage or makes a company successful, as most people seem to think. Instead it is this process of reinvention and growth—much like people develop—over time. Focusing on unfair advantage enables a company to manage that growth."

Now let's define this new term and look at some of the elements that are used to construct an unfair advantage.

THE NEW TERM

Unfair advantage is like a unique collection of resources used to deliver so much appeal to customers that they rush to buy your products while your competitors wilt attempting to overtake your lead in the new market. An unfair advantage propels your new enterprise into the leadership position of a new market category.

Example 1-2   Definition: Unfair Advantage

Unfair advantage is a unique, consistent difference in product attributes and services arising from a company capability gap based on delivering superior value over long periods of time to the customer.[1]

It is unique to one company.

If one other company has it, it is not an unfair advantage. It has to be unique. No other organization can have it. Your unfair advantage must be distinctly different. People must be able to recognize its differences immediately. They must see it as unique, not just a little different. Uniqueness is mandatory. As soon as an experienced start-up candidate for employment senses your story is not unique, that person will no longer be interested in you and your company. The same goes for reporters and investors.

It has to be hard to duplicate.

It must not be easy for another entrepreneur to say, "I can do that too—cheaper [or better or quicker]!" You must have a response for the critical person who asks, "Why can't your idea be copied in two minutes?" You can be sure that if your idea is a surprise and if it marks the trail to a lucrative new market, a stampeding herd will rush to follow you. Me-too competitors will spring up like mushrooms after the rain. An easy-to-duplicate idea that is exciting succeeds only in attracting a large herd of me-too new enterprises, none of which has a significant competitive advantage over the others. You don't want anyone to be able to do the same thing as you do with very little effort because then the idea will become a commodity—a product that users cannot differentiate. It is very hard to make a profit selling commodities.

It must be differentiated.

Investors want to see distinctive differentiation in a new enterprise—that collection of just a few things that make your idea clearly stand out from the crowd. If the idea is very much like others, you will have to work hard to build an unfair advantage. A good place to begin differentiation is by asking potential customers how attractive your proposed product is compared with others. During these conversations, focus on finding just a few things that customers perceive as especially valuable. That will help you decide on which special attributes and services to provide. For instance, you might find it best to tell customers, "Our service makes the medical patient more comfortable." Or, "Our pediatric solution removes the fear children have when getting a vaccination with a needle." Perhaps you might discover an opportunity for your new business to become the competitor most revered for outstanding service. Semiconductor equipment supplier Applied Materials used superior service to become the dominant giant in its worldwide market. Dell Computer used superior on-call, online, customer hot-line service to outdistance the many me-too competitors that tried to leapfrog the new enterprise. Or you might find it best to become known as the company with which it is easiest to place orders for a new product. Amazon used its one-click order feature to stay ahead of copycats. Picking the most attractive attributes and services are powerful ways to differentiate your business and use to build your unfair advantage.

It is relative, especially compared to the competition.

You will be compared to many things: the competition, others in your general industry sector, technology, market size, and so on. Unfair advantage is always relative. It is not an absolute. What other companies are like yours—public and private, local and in other cities and countries? How special is your management team? What makes your strategy stronger than others in your industry? Respond with answers that are relative, always relative. Refer to other organizations and their competitive advantages. Practice and become especially skilled at comparing yourself, your team, and your idea. Investors will look for direct and indirect competitors, so have your lists and analysis ready. You have to learn a lot about the competition because there is so much of it for new enterprises with new ideas. In the Internet era, new information travels around the world in seconds, and fresh companies are formed by the minute around the globe.

New enterprises always have competition.

There is always a competitor, even if there are no direct competitors. Salespeople know that the status quo is a tough competitor. People do not like to change the way they work and live because change involves risk and danger, both personal and professional. People have to be convinced to change their ways. Some call that competitor FUD— fear, uncertainty, and doubt; together, they are a fierce competitive combination. Use competitors to your advantage. Learn to work the competition into every one of your conversations about your unfair advantage. The more you know about them, the more the important stakeholders such as the industry reporter will believe that you are the true leader in this new market. Thinking constantly about competitors will help you run scared, to remain at the leading edge of the competitive market battles. Serial entrepreneurs will tell you the only way to run the race is relative to the competition.

It is very scarce.

New enterprises with unfair advantage cannot be found easily or anywhere in the world. Several veteran venture capitalists in Silicon Valley have told me they believe there are only about a couple of dozen, perhaps forty, great start-ups to invest in during a year, and that's worldwide. All the rest will be modest successes or go bankrupt. The best new enterprises are very rare. The ones with unfair advantage are hard to find even in experienced start-up centers like Silicon Valley. Yet it is true that some cities are famous for producing many great new enterprises based on strong unfair advantages, year after year. In those places, people have become skilled at searching for and building unfair advantage. They have become experienced miners of unfair advantage. They are not "we-can-do-it-for-half-the-cost" people. They know the ideas are rare for new businesses with unfair advantages but well worth the considerable time and effort it takes to find them.

A company capability gap comes from the people who together make up your company.

The word *company* means people working together. It is much more than a legal or organizational term. A company is a collection of talking, walking human beings. It is alive. The word begins with the Latin prefix *co* which is the prefix for "together." The second part of the word is *pany*, from the Latin word meaning "bread." Combined, it means people eating bread together. We get our word *companion* from similar Latin derivatives. Together (co + pany), they form the word *company*, a word that means "people working together."

New enterprises are people-intensive organizations whose fragile future is dependent on the skills and hearts of its employees. Some observers consider picking the best people to be the number one task of the CEO—more important than raising money. Serial entrepreneurs repeatedly tell me their most vital managerial task is to assemble the best core team they can find: experienced people capable of delivering the exciting attributes and services that will bring excited customers flocking to purchase your first products. When Pen Ong reached IPO with Interwoven, he said, "My most difficult task was my commitment to hiring only the best people we could find for our company—outstanding people only. The rest make too many mistakes."

Outstanding employees create outstanding capabilities in companies, capabilities so great that there is a big gap between you and your competition. To build that gap, your people will focus their efforts, time, and creative work on building your company's unfair advantage. For instance, if your advantage is built on superior selling, then you build your advantage centered on that core capability. Oracle's people created a large selling gap that led to a nearly 50 percent share of their database software market. But if you focus on technological advantage, your people will build based on your proprietary technology. Genentech's employees focused on applying gene-splitting science and became the leader of a new industry: genetic engineering.

Giant companies use the term *core competencies* to help employees remain focused on advancing the few things that contribute the most to each company's unfair advantage. C. K. Prahalad of the University of Michigan's Business School made this term famous. His research found that returning to and focusing on core competencies was critical to large organizations that had lost their sense of direction and found they had become me-too competitors. With the core competency focus clear, employees could once again begin to build unfair advantages.

Whether you begin your new enterprise as a new product line inside a giant public corporation or as a venture-backed start-up, it will be quickly ranked and labeled (or branded) according to the degree of talent of your key people, especially its founders. Such brandings are based on perceptions by outsiders of what your people, particularly your CEO, are especially good at doing. Those perceptions are passed on to media reporters and spread around the world. For example, Oracle is branded as a selling-intensive company driven by founder Larry Ellison. Intel rose to greatness labeled as a technologically driven company directed by founder Andy Grove, a master of managerial strategy. Advanced Micro Devices is focused on selling better than Intel and gets credit for being an aggressive competitor inspired by the enthusiastic spirit of founder Jerry Sanders. Companies stand out based on the capabilities of their leaders relative to competitors. Outstanding leaders are the source of the skills that build favorable competitive gaps and differentiate the unfair advantage of an organization.

Delivery is doing what you planned on doing.

New enterprise veterans call it *execution*. It means putting your plan into action in the real world. There are countless maxims and old sayings about execution: "Plan your work and work your plan." "The proof of the pudding is in the eating." One wag quipped: "Companies must execute well or be executed." These are maxims that make the same point: many are the great plans that were poorly executed and sunk a promising new enterprise.

Execution is often cited as especially vital to a new enterprise. I found many venture investors who view execution as the most important consideration when thinking about investing in a new enterprise. They look at how difficult it might be and how skilled management must be to deliver the planned results. Other stakeholders, such as employees and the media, also want to know about the company's execution skills and experience as they ponder joining the company or writing a story about it. When observing experienced serial entrepreneurs, I found they adjust their managerial decisions based on how superior the core team was at executing business plans in prior companies. If the core team is composed of first-time managers, the CEO is more cautious during each stage of the company's development. He or she waits for results before moving on to the next stage and modifies the unfair advantage responsively, depending on results of the prior stage. But if the key employees are doing their second or third start-up, decisions are made much more rapidly, often on the fly. Such a company emerges sooner with a clear unfair advantage. It has momentum that soon leaves competitors behind. In such a case, the process of building the unfair advantage is described with this phrase: "It is like building a bicycle while you are riding it."

If this is beginning to sound like the founding leadership team is expected to be an especially important part of an unfair advantage, you are getting the right message. Some in the new enterprise community believe the core of an unfair advantage begins with one or two key people and expands to a maximum of about six or so. They will create and build the unfair advantage. The rest of the company follows. The degree of unfairness depends on the early successes or failures of the small core team. That is another reason that unfair advantage is described as a living thing.

Execution also means your idea must be practical and do-able. It must already have been moved out of the laboratory and into the preproduction room. Unproven science may be promising and exciting, but it has only a small chance of supporting an unfair advantage. For instance, a new enterprise based on a medical researcher's scientific discovery must be more than a dream. It has to be practical. The discovery must be supported by a plausible plan to convert the idea into a useful pharmaceutical drug. That will include years of risky, time-consuming clinical trials. The discovery must be close to productization in order to be funded. In the field of wireless communications and other forms of information sciences, start-up ideas must be nearly ready for engineers to start working on a prototype. Investors do not want to have to wait for white coat telecommunications laboratory scientists to attempt a world first before the engineering staff can begin building the first product. Leave the science for the universities. Bring the product ideas to the new enterprises.

Example 1-3 Not Ready for Productization: Varagenics

Biotech start-up Varagenics of Cambridge, Massachusetts, was a promising new enterprise working on new technologies for creating new drugs. Its core team included highly reputed life scientists who had been well funded. They got off to a promising start as the Internet era began its rise. By mid-November 2002, the company was acquired by Hyseq, another biotech company. Even with $61 million in cash in the bank, Varagenics was sold for $56 million. As the Internet balloon popped, funding of new biotech enterprises dried up. The big pharmaceutical companies stopping putting cash into new companies focused on delivering technologies instead of drugs. That forced companies like Varagenics to have to change, to try to find a way to develop their own products. But few small companies found that path, including Varagenics. One reason was that financing clinical trials is expensive and risky. Trials were needed to bring concrete proof to the drug makers that the new technology would lead to great new drugs. Without that, there were no sales and no financing. The result was the end to many promising new enterprises focused on delivering technologies and not products.[2]

Next comes delivering superior value.

Value is not a word meaning "the cheapest product in the market." Nor does it mean the "fastest." And it does not mean "the best." Instead, it is what the customer perceives is most valuable about what you are offering. It is what gets the targeted customer excited enough to buy your product instead of the others. You want to create a superior value compared with your competitors.

To create superior value, it must be clear what your value offering is. By using your product, will your customer get products to market nine months faster? Or is the superior value in the form of a doubling of sales per employee when your product is installed at the customer's workplace? Or is it in the form of five times the fuel economy, or four times greater safety and reliability?

Your next step is to test how superior your value offering is. It must win the respect of your customers. It must be labeled "superior" by your targeted customer—superior when compared with competing products. This is a psychological element. It is also marketing intensive and what the essence of product positioning is about (more on that later). It is where superior marketing skills can create a huge competitive advantage.

Notice how creating superior value is focused on your customers and their perception of the value of what you are offering, especially the psychological aspects. All of the unfair advantage that you have worked so hard to build—the many elements that have contributed to your unfair advantage recipe—must excite the customer, or your hard work is worthless. If the value proposition that you deliver does not get the customer eager to buy your product, you will not get the sales order. Even worse, your new enterprise will find it is unlikely to get funded. And you won't be invited to be on panels at trade shows, or on the talk shows or in magazines. Word about your products won't spread to the skilled workers you need to hire. It just won't go anywhere. But if it excites your targeted customer, a hot value proposition will ignite the engine of your unfair advantage. That is one reason that it is very important to know your customer very, very well. Superior knowledge of customers is one way to be outstanding in this intensely competitive world. That's why experienced investors want to talk to potential customers before investing their money. They insist on confirming that your value proposition gets a lot of customers very excited.

It survives over time.

The company's unfair advantage must be able to last at three to five years for new enterprises based on information science. The time must be doubled for life science start-ups. That is how long investors are locked in before they can get liquid. The liquidity event may be an IPO or the sale of the company to a large publicly traded giant corporation. It is rare that a liquidity event occurs in three years or less. That happens only for a short portion of a boom-to-bust wave. Most start-ups require five years to emerge as the leader of a new category and with enough value to compensate investors for the high risks they took.

You should plan on building and developing an unfair advantage that can persist for more than half a decade. That may sound like a long time. Start-up people are in a hurry and do not like to think in terms of portions of decades. They prefer quick success with sales ("getting sales traction") and eager investors funding growth until the big one, the IPO. To the first-time entrepreneur, success is just around the corner. But history has shown it takes more than half a decade to develop a new business large enough to go public. To go IPO on NASDAQ, your company must be worth at least $100 million. You need a big company for it to become that valuable. That means big sales. It takes years to get there. The statistics show the average time from start-up to IPO exceeds five years (see Table 1-1). That is a fact of life. It is the measure of time that your start-up must be able to sustain its unfair advantage.

Table 1-1 Number of Years to IPO

Median Number of Years from Date of Company's Founding to IPO for Venture-Backed New Enterprises

Year	Median Age at IPO
1995	7.4 years
1996	6.6
1997	7.2
1998	5.9
1999	4.5
2000	5.1
2001	5.6
2002	7.4
2003	7.8
2004	7.1*
AVERAGE	**6.5**

*Through 2004 December 10
SOURCE: *Thomson Venture Economics*

MBAs refer to unfair advantage with the term "sustainable competitive advantage." Although that term is long, dull, and boring, the MBAs got it right: your advantage must be sustainable. It cannot survive as a once-in-a-lifetime advantage (a patent or first product to ship to the new market). That is a fading moment, not an advantage that can be grown and will last. Instead, it must be able to sustain its unfairness and advantage for five long, tough years of competition.

It can be grown.

Unfair advantage is alive. It is growing, changing, moving, advancing, and getting stronger every day. Think of it as if it were a recipe improved daily by the chef. It is not merely a fixed formula. Like the sci-fi Borg, it rockets through space and time, assimilating the best elements and discarding the useless. Dreaded by competitors, it is the death star of the universe of new enterprises. It is feared by slower-moving giants and sluggish empires. Every day, unfair advantage must be able to become taller, bigger, and better, growing every moment. An instant success that is not sustainable can lead to the demise of the new enterprise. For instance, your market size cannot be so small that your first products saturate it in a year and then are limited to growing only as fast as the birthrate of the population.

eMachines is an example. In its first year of selling personal computers, this pioneer that offered a PC for less than $600 recorded an amazing $1 billion of sales that led to an IPO. Its sales-savvy core management and unusual business model (almost all department functions were outsourced) contributed to its quick sales traction and very low costs. However, in the face of intense competition, its initial unfair advantage could not be sustained. The company ran into serious operational and marketing problems that resulted in its eventual demise. If you cannot develop your unfair advantage, you do not have one.

It is expandable.

To be sustainable when competitors are going to try to copy you, your unfair advantage has to be expandable: you must be able to increase the size, volume, quantity, and scope of it. You must be able to enlarge it. It has to be able to become stronger every day. You have to alter it. It must be advanced. You have to change it. Like the chameleon, you have to modify your unfair advantage in anticipation of and in reaction to arrival of danger. Think of your initial advantage like a tiny snowball on top of the mountain: as it rolls down, the ball becomes bigger and bigger, more and more powerful, until it is an awesome avalanche, thundering down, terrifying the competitors who face its fury and cannot get out of the way in time. When that happens, you are taking orders instead of selling. It is a thrilling condition that Geoffrey Moore refers to as "in the tornado."[3] An expanding unfair advantage boosted Cisco and Nokia to the tornado stage of growth. Expandable competitive advantages made them into "gorillas" that dominate their market categories.[4] Expandable also means investors and eager employees want to see mountains of unclaimed, fresh market, ready to be converted to sales over half a decade.

Your first product cannot be your best or your last. It must be the beginning of a product family that cascades down the mountain and gathers momentum. Silicon Valley veterans refer to this product family as the *bowling pin model*. Others describe it as product dominoes. Whatever you call it, you need to clearly identify follow-on products for sale to markets related to your first product. The first market must lead you to the second two. Then two must become four so momentum builds and you arrive at the tornado stage.

Experienced entrepreneurs plan a lot of upside to their sales projections, with several additional markets to follow the first. Those cousin markets will supply you with more and more future sales and help your company attain dominance of the new market category. The trick is to pick the first bowling pin and its successors so that they create a selling wave that increases your operational efficiencies faster and faster as you gather momentum and the tornado begins to lift your company toward dominance. That is what scaling is all about. If you pick the wrong bowling pin sequence, your initial success and expended energy will be wasted. You will struggle to hit the next bowling pin. You will lose your momentum. You won't cross the chasm. The gap will remain between your initial market and the next ones you need to reach large sales volumes.

It is dynamic.

With your initial unfair advantage working for you, your company will begin selling its first product, opening a new market, the fresh category you are aiming to dominate. But then your competition will react, the market will shift, and you must make a countermove. Your planned competitive moves are called *dynamic strategy*. It is part of your unfair advantage. It is a strategic plan filled with movements. Movement makes it harder and harder for the competition to figure out how to beat your company. For example, after your first product wave, you introduce the next set of products. Meanwhile, you are working on a second new technology to use to build products for the next wave of sales to another market bowling pin. You are planning to add a new level of higher-quality customer service. And so on. Your unfair advantage is dynamically changing. You make progress and along the way respond to changes in the competitive market. You become a moving target, harder for the competition to get a focus on, making it more difficult to knock you off the leader's throne. When you have unfair advantage, you are ready to respond to provocative questions from the press such as, "We woke up this morning to discover that Microsoft just announced a product virtually the same as yours! Now what?" When you are able to respond on your feet to such tough questions, you are beginning to comprehend what unfair advantage is all about. It is very dynamic.

It changes continually over the years.

Unfair advantage is not about dreaming up the impossibly great idea and riding it to IPO glory. History shows otherwise. Yes, a killer idea is important; it is a starting point on to the road to success. However, you would be naive to expect to win by defending a single innovation over years of subsequent attacks by competitors. It is not a patent that protects you. Nor is it a deal with a giant strategic partner that dominates your customer base. It is not getting your money from a famous venture capital firm. It is much more than that. If your unfair advantage does not change, sooner or later (sooner is better) the competition will find a weakness and break through your defenses. Then you will be history. New enterprise competition is not a one-move game. The long, long march along the start-up trail will expose you to aggressive competitive battles with new rivals and harsh responses by established companies. As you react, you will change your unfair advantage. You will scramble to shore up weaknesses and innovate to increase strengths. In a few years, you will not recognize your latest unfair advantage when compared with your first. That is one reason venture capitalists (VCs) are so eager to find experienced start-up leaders: they look for people who can manage the changes needed to develop an unfair advantage. They know how hard the competitive attacks can be. They expect unthinkable surprises that will pop up along your start-up road. They look to you to keep changing your unfair advantage.

It appeals to lots of potential customers.

To first-time entrepreneurs, it sounds obvious to claim that a large potential market is waiting to be conquered. In their presentations to investors, they essentially say, "Trust us! Millions of people will buy our products. Give us money, and we will prove it to you." But investors in new ventures want to see evidence that your claims are true *before* they invest. They want to know what is compelling to early buyers about your first product. They want you to do market research and generate numbers that count how many potential customers are willing to pay the price you are asking for your product or service. Investors also want you to give them telephone numbers and email addresses of a select list of real people, real customers, with whom they can speak. In other words, you will need to work hard to back up your optimistic claims about the large size of your target market. That is why an engineer cannot get the attention of experienced investors by relying on breakthrough technology. What the customer thinks of your idea is more important to the stakeholders than a technologist might think. That is why experienced entrepreneurs never complete their business plan until they have done exhaustive surveys of potential customers.

UNFAIR ADVANTAGE QUESTIONS

How do you know when you have an unfair advantage? You can easily begin to test your initial idea by asking three simple questions:

1. What else is similar?
2. How easily can it be copied?
3. How hard is it to maneuver around?

Try the questions out on real companies you know a bit about. For example, try a patent-rich company such as Xerox. In its best days, Xerox was said to have had over 700 patents related to plain paper copiers. That sounds impossible to overcome, and yet the competition still figured out a way to get around the patents. The market turned out to be enormous. Competition lusted after it and figured out how to get a piece of it even though Xerox had the finest patent lawyers in the world working to defend its growing portfolio of intellectual property. Unfair advantage is much more than trade secrets protected by patents.

Question 2 is different from Question 3. To copy Xerox means you must produce a nearly identical copy of its products, using nearly the same technology. If Xerox had no patents, you could copy its products. However, in order to compete with a new enterprise that owns patents, you must find a way around its intellectual property barrier. In most developed countries, copying would be considered theft of intellectual property products and is forbidden by law. To get around Xerox's patents legally means you would have to invent a different technology to produce plain paper copies and thus use your proprietary technology to get around the Xerox patents. That is what the competition did.

You can learn to test unfair advantages by making a game with friends. As you read about new companies in magazines, use the three questions to test their unfair advantages. Examine the strength of their unfair advantages and discuss how you think they could build better ones. Practice until you can quickly reach confident conclusions about unfair advantages. That is some of the best training for learning how to create an unfair advantage for your own new enterprise.

EXAMPLES OF UNFAIR ADVANTAGED COMPANIES

Now let's examine some organizations that gained an unfair advantage and have kept on advancing it until they have become world-class brands. You may be surprised to see schools and even countries on the list, yet each organization has an unfair advantage.

Example 1-4   The Unfair Advantaged

- **BMW:** This German corporation produces sportive driving machines aimed at young professionals with rising careers.
- **Mercedes Benz Chrysler:** This German corporation produces luxury sedans for more mature people with established lifestyles.
- **Germany:** This country creates superior-performing products designed with highly respected German mechanical engineering.
- **Japan:** This country produces consumer and industrial products renowned for their superior quality.

- **MIT:** This is a school for people who excel in mathematics and science.
- **Cornell University:** This school is the world's largest Ivy League university and one of the largest research centers in the world.
- **Dolby Laboratories:** Dolby is the dominant choice for superior consumer and industrial electronic listening systems due to the passion, skills, and focus of its founder, Ray Dolby.
- **Microsoft:** The world's largest computer company was founded on Bill Gates's strategic skills that led the company to a virtual monopoly on personal computers' operating systems.
- **Cisco:** This enterprise, backed by substantial funding from the veteran VC firm Sequoia Capital, created a behemoth in the form of a worldwide selling machine led by a sequence of outstanding sales people as CEO.
- **Nokia:** The founders' vision about the changing world of telecommunications transformed the Finnish timber and tire company into the world's largest cell phone provider. The fresh opportunity was triggered by technology invented in Norway and America. The determination and skill of the core Nokia leadership team resulted in brilliant execution of the original vision.

SOURCE: *Nesheim Group.*

DIFFERENTIATION

Differentiation is the title of a vital lesson to be learned by first-time entrepreneurs. Most learn it the hard way. I find nearly all neophytes begin with ideas for me-too businesses. Such new enterprises—"quicker-faster-cheaper"—are especially abundant in developing countries in Asia, and most recently in China. They begin as lower-cost sources of products produced by relatively less expensive labor. At first they succeed. But after a few years of success, their costs inflate, and fresh competition springs up in the form of new me-too companies that offer the same products at prices lower than the prior company. Soon competition arrives from many other newly emerging countries, and the original company seeks trade protection from its government. This kind of start-up thinking even occurs in high tech centers like Silicon Valley where naive engineers are convinced they can get started at lower cost and will later figure out how to make a big business out of the small beginning. Instead, almost all go bankrupt. They did not have enough differentiation and had no superior value added. Each lacked an unfair advantage. I have watched this happen wave after wave for three decades.

Example 1-5   Me-Too Companies Suffer: China Overtakes Leaders

The dramatic stampede of moving manufacturing businesses to China is already forcing a painful lesson on the formerly low-cost manufacturing tigers of Southeast Asia. As the year 2000 passed, China had taken over leadership of the low-cost, light manufacturing market formerly dominated by Hong Kong, Taiwan, Singapore, Korea, and the rest of the herd (Malaysia, Thailand, the Philippine Islands, and Indonesia). India was failing to match their GDP growth rates, falling further behind. The dragon was winning over the tigers, small and large. Economic success inflated labor rates in successful Asian countries. The original unfair advantage (producing goods in Southeast Asia's developing countries instead of in the United States or Europe) was reduced and finally turned into a disadvantage that could not be overcome with technology and productivity improvements. Entire businesses had to be moved to China in order to survive. Unfortunately, the herd moved together in a desperate race to try to attain low-cost manufacturing advantages. Differentiation between companies did not change much after shifting from the home country to China. Few companies emerged with stronger unfair advantages based on crisply differentiated products and services.

To overcome this kind of competitive disadvantage, companies operating in the now-expensive Southeast Asia tigers have been forced to try to innovate to add enough value to create differentiated products. Formerly they produced lower-cost commodities such as shirts and computer boards made under contract. Now they have to add more value to justify their higher production costs. The transformation to more value added would occur if the companies could understand how a shirt can be converted to a fashion item aimed at specific consumer markets and emerge as a brand that can compete with the best worldwide. The key to such a transformation lies in understanding how to create an unfair advantage—one that is distinctly unique.

Special forms of unfair advantages in countries can come to an abrupt end, leaving entrepreneurs in deep trouble. This is especially vivid when governments modernize and start enforcing intellectual property protection laws. A company caught in such a dilemma is India's Dr. Reddy's Laboratories. As reported in the *Far Eastern Economic Review*, in 2002 this copycat drug manufacturer was facing an end to its circumvention of patents of global pharmaceutical firms.[5] It could see the tightening of India's commitment to start respecting product patents by 2005. The reporter asked the CEO, G. V. Prasad, what the company would do, and he replied that the fastest route to becoming a global player is through innovation, by investing in drug discovery. A patent on a new proprietary drug can be the beginning of an unfair advantage. From that, an entrepreneur can build more differentiation and develop it into an unfair advantage.

SEARCHING FOR UNFAIR ADVANTAGE

Searching is an unavoidable struggle that is part of building an unfair advantage. It is hard work. Luck is not part of it. There are unknowns in the process. It is neither obvious where to begin nor clear how to proceed with an initial idea. An unfair advantage has to be found. Like a miner looking for diamonds, entrepreneurs are searching daily for the new, new, new thing that might be the beginning of a great idea and powerful unfair advantage. Anyone keen on investing in new enterprises is constantly looking for it. Serial entrepreneurs are digging for it. Wannabe start-up employees are lifting up rocks searching for it. Reporters are snooping about for it. They all seek it while they sleep, while they eat, exercise, vacation, and work. It is their passion. It is a part of them. It is a struggle to find it, like buried treasure, and it is worth the struggle. This is the "hidden-riches-I-know-it-is-there-I'll-find-it-I-just-know-I-will" part of unfair advantage. It is buried deep in the mine. It is hard to find. It is even harder to extract and convert into wealth. But after you have found it, you can become rich, very rich (in more ways than just wealth), as I discovered observing a meeting of the leaders of Nokia Venture Partners.

Example 1-6   Venture Capitalist on Unfair Advantage:
                BlueRun Ventures

After a presentation by a start-up team, John Malloy, one of the founders of BlueRun Ventures, explained how the day had gone for the firm: "During the morning's all-partners meeting, we spent our time discussing a list of new venture deals we are very interested in. We examined in detail what we saw in each start-up. We talked about what made up the unfair advantage in the people, their ideas, and plans for their business."

YOUR PRIMARY OBJECTIVE AND UNFAIR ADVANTAGE

Now let's connect unfair advantage to three important business tools: the objective, task, and goal of the new enterprise.

* The number one *objective* of the new enterprise is *to become the leader of a new market category.*

* The number one *task* of the new enterprise is *to create and exploit an unfair advantage so that the company dominates the targeted new market category.*

* The number one *goal* is *to accomplish the primary objective and complete the number one task within five years.*

The following example, based on my studies of a very successful company, Research in Motion (RIM) applies the terms *objective, task,* and *goal* and explains how they relate to unfair advantage. Note especially the method the company used to create a fresh unfair advantage. After a wave of success as a new enterprise, the company had found itself without an unfair advantage and in a difficult business situation.

Example 1-7   Initial Idea: RIM Email for Mobile Professionals

A Canadian company, Research in Motion (RIM) was founded in 1984 to design, manufacture, and sell pager products and services. Over the next ten years, RIM watched pagers become cheap commodities and pager services become noted for cutthroat pricing. The RIM pager business had become difficult to grow, intensely competitive, and especially awkward to differentiate. Cell phones added more value, and their sales grew, while sales of pagers declined. RIM searched for a way out of the quagmire. Employees were challenged to respond, and they did. Innovative minds came up with a novel idea: create a business based on a specialized handheld wireless communications device that would use RIM's pager technology to receive and send email. That was the beginning of what became the wildly successful BlackBerry business. But until a lot more was added to the initial idea, there was no unfair advantage for RIM.

The number one objective of the new enterprise is to become the leader of a new market category. At this moment in the story, the category for RIM's idea did not yet exist.

Example 1-8   Primary Objective: RIM Plans to Lead a New Market Category

RIM proceeded with the initial idea and soon developed a prototype. It proved to be economically possible to use pager technology to send and receive emails on a specialized handheld device. Its black color and lumpy-looking keyboard led to the name *Black-Berry*. It was sold as part of a service to customers who paid by the month. Soon it became very popular, especially in large corporations. "You gotta have it!" became the mantra of eager employees. By 2002, RIM's BlackBerry had become the leader of wireless email, a fresh market category.

In the early days of this market, several companies were trying to deliver mobile email services using different technologies, but none had yet dominated any of the related customer segments by the time RIM entered the competition. RIM was not first, but it was first to get it right. It assembled a carefully selected set of elements into a unique mixture that became its recipe for an unfair advantage. It got it very right. It won the gold medal. It achieved its primary objective.

The number one task of the new enterprise is to create and exploit an unfair advantage so that it dominates the targeted new market category. RIM next set out to execute their exciting idea.

Example 1-9   Executing the Plan: RIM Constructs and Exploits an Unfair Advantage

RIM was convinced it could create a great unfair advantage. It was a pager telecommunications provider with an extensive paging infrastructure already installed and operating in North America. Its engineers had created a technology that could (1) move email from corporate personal computer servers and networks (2) onto RIM's pager network, and then (3) onto to a special, proprietary personal digital appliance that would enable users to read, display, and send emails. Mobile professionals would be able to communicate via email messages without a tethered personal computer. They could send and receive emails in airports, hotels, rental cars, hallways, and meeting rooms.

The new market was open, with no leader yet established. Pager technology was lower cost to install and operate than cell phone technology. RIM already had contracts for paging services with large corporations that would be ideal customers for RIM's mobile email service. RIM had manufacturing capabilities that were producing pagers. Its engineers were eager to design a cool BlackBerry device. Management was well connected with the leaders of the personal computer industry, including Intel and Microsoft.

Those were some of the elements that RIM used to build its unfair advantage. It kept the plan secret until the day it announced the BlackBerry service. The press release surprised the world, and RIM was off and running. The competition was left standing at the starting line.

Your goal is to accomplish the primary objective and complete the number one task within five years. RIM shot out of the gate and kept running to IPO.

Example 1-10   Achieving the Goal: RIM Dominates Within Five Years

RIM announced the BlackBerry mobile email service in 1998. Within two years, it rose to king of the hill of the new market. Competing services wilted. RIM focused on delivering just email; attachments would have to be read back in the office. RIM did not get sidetracked adding bells and whistles—those many new features that complicate a new product (referred to as creeping elegance). It stayed focused, working very hard to capture the largest share of the new market as quickly as possible. It succeeded. By 2002, the BlackBerry service had become the undisputed king of the wireless email hill. Its strategic partners included the finest names in computing and networking. The corporate customer base was blue chip. The BlackBerry became so popular that meeting managers opened by announcing that, "This is a Black-Berry meeting." That meant it was permissible to do emails during the meeting (on your Blackberry). The BlackBerry device had become a status symbol and measure of coolness, as well as a productivity booster. In five years, RIM had achieved its primary goal.

Now that you have a better understanding of what unfair advantage is about, let's shift gears and discuss how to communicate your unfair advantage to some of the key stakeholders: an investor or prospective employee or the media.

THE ELEVATOR PITCH: QUICKLY COMMUNICATING UNFAIR ADVANTAGE

An elevator pitch is a very short, very exciting explanation of your unfair advantage. It is a message so compelling that your audience demands to hear more immediately. When you have your elevator pitch figured out, you will discover your unfair advantage is deceptively simple. It can be explained in just a few sentences. The hard part is to get a long story shortened without losing its appeal. Writing a short story is much harder than writing a long one.

When you have a carefully crafted unfair advantage, you can present it to an investor very quickly. It does not take an hour to deliver it. You do not require thirty PowerPoint presentation slides and complex technological explanations. No especially dramatic performances are necessary. It takes just a few words. In fact, you can state it in less than 30 seconds. That is the time you have before the person you happen to meet on the elevator gets out on his or her floor in the hotel.

Here is an example based on real-world episodes described to me by an icon VC and some of the participants.

Example 1-11 Elevator Pitch: Kim and DT on the Elevator

As he left the Korean restaurant, Kim stopped, turned, and decided to head for the Grand Hotel. It had been a day of disappointments: no responses from countless emails and not a single call back from many telephone calls to venture capitalists. Kim knew his personal savings would hold out for only a few more months. "Then back to becoming a wage slave!" he exclaimed to himself.

"Maybe a walk through the lobby of the Grand Hotel will boost my spirits," Kim thought. "After all, this is the place where venture capitalists and investment bankers meet to talk about IPOs and hot start-up deals."

As he emerged from the revolving door, he thought, "I belong here! Now is my time. Oh, money, where are you?"

The lobby was imposing. The tall marble columns dwarfed the uniformed hotel bellman who greeted him with an enthusiastic,

"Welcome to the Grand Hotel, sir!" That brought a smile to Kim's face. "I feel better already!" he thought.

As he slowly wandered through the vast lobby filled with businesspeople in dark suits, he found himself walking past the elevator bank. Suddenly he recognized a familiar face! Was it, could it be, yes, it was. It was DT, the revered venture capitalist of Silicon Valley, founder of Plitheron Ventures with a legacy of start-ups second to none! This was too good to be true.

"Man, what luck! This could be my day!" Kim rejoiced. He sensed the surge of adrenaline and felt his courage rise. "Do I dare approach DT? Will he brush me off? I heard on a bad day he eats entrepreneurs for breakfast!"

DT did not seem to notice Kim standing now an arm's length away. DT reached to push a button to go up. The doors to the elevator opened. Two passengers stepped out, and DT stepped in. Kim hesitated a split second, gathered his courage, and followed DT into the elevator, knees shaking. No one else got in. The doors closed with a soft thud.

DT did not seem to notice Kim and pushed a button for the fifteenth floor. Kim felt the elevator lift gently upward. The short ride had begun. *Now is the time!* said a tiny voice inside Kim. As the elevator passed the second floor, Kim took in a deep breath and began: "DT, my name is Kim Lee. I am a Cornell biotech engineer with six years' experience, most recently managing a product team for NutroCellonics Corporation. We introduced the OPTI-3000X, the world's first optically alterable genetically engineered immune protein synthesizer that the media have been writing about lately. You may have heard about it—it can cut time to market by half for a new pharmaceutical drug. Two coworkers and I have come up with a fresh idea that could make a great start-up. We call it Nice2Kids. I thought it would be attractive to a venture capitalist like you. I would like to tell you about it. Could I have a moment of your time?"

DT slowly turned his head, looked Kim in the eyes, and—in an almost soft voice—said, "Sure, why not? You have until I get out on my floor. Fire away. The time is all yours."

Kim knew his time was very short. Before the elevator got to DT's floor, he would have to present everything that was great about his idea for the new enterprise. He wondered if the elevator was accelerating.

It was the fastest presentation Kim had ever given. No slides. No preparation. No coaching. Just pure Kim and his idea. Everything he could think of packing into the short seconds before the rocketing elevator arrived on DT's floor. Kim blurted it all out faster than he could think, nearly faster than he could talk. He tried to control his pace, but it was of no use. It all spewed out like water from a fire hose.

DT did not say a word.

The elevator perceptively slowed and came to a halt. The doors slowly opened, and Kim stopped talking.

DT quietly stepped off, turned to look at Kim still standing in the elevator, and after what seemed to Kim to be the longest pause in his life, said, "Young man, step out of the elevator and tell me more. What is your name?"

Kim could hardly believe his ears! Incredible!!

Suddenly he recalled what he had to do next: get off the elevator! As the doors began to shut, he lunged through them and came to a halt in front of the venture capitalist.

Looking at DT, Kim thought he perceived a slight smile. *Did he see me madly stumbling or is he amused by people making fools of themselves?* he thought. His heart was beating so hard he was certain DT could hear it. That's when he recalled his buddy Bryan. The start-up veteran had met Kim last week at his favorite restaurant and said, "Kim, never forget: after an elevator pitch, if the VC says, 'Tell me more,' that is code for, 'You have my attention, so start all over. You have 3 minutes this time.' It means you have him nibbling at the bait, so go for it!"

And that is what Kim did. This time he paused between points and proceeded in a more deliberate manner. The words came out more relaxed, more confident. He could sense he was telling his story the way he wanted to. It came from his soul. He was slower, yet still excited. He liked what he said. He thought it was good— very good.

In about 3 minutes, Kim had finished. He stopped talking and waited for a response.

DT did not move. His eyes pierced Kim's. Kim sensed he was being scanned. Obviously DT relished this moment.

Time seemed to stand still. Kim thought he needed to find the men's room very soon.

Then DT calmly said, "Why don't you present your idea to me at my office? Can you make next Tuesday at nine o'clock in the morning?"

Kim thought his heart had stopped beating! He knew this sought-after venture capitalist was booked solid for the next two years. No one ever bypassed his administrative assistant. Kim envisioned DT's parking lot filled with the skeletons of entrepreneurs who tried to get an appointment.

Incredible! Kim shouted inside himself. *He just invited me to a meeting next week!* With a heart beating so fast it seemed to jump out of his chest, Kim responded, "Sure."

He had won! At last—the big break. He had gotten through the impossible door. He had done something tougher than getting beyond the expert level of a computer game. *The great DT wants to hear more! Wow!*

Gathering his composure and trying to lower the tone of his voice, Kim said, "I'll call your office this afternoon. Thank you."

Kim shook DT's hand and both turned to go their separate ways without another word spoken.

Kim pushed the down button. The elevator quickly arrived. As he stepped in, he turned and looked. DT was out of sight. Then the doors closed. The elevator silently descended to the lobby floor.

Kim had no idea how he got home—perhaps by transporter beam.

He closed the door to his apartment and slumped onto the sofa. As he came out of his euphoria, he realized he was thirsty and walked to the refrigerator to grab a soda. Then he remembered what else Bryan had said: "When the VC makes the appointment for you after the elevator pitch, it means he is thinking, 'Maybe this is the next Google!'"

Kim felt great. "Amazing what a few words can do," he said to himself.

Short Is Power

That is how it is done in the real world of start-ups: short and with power. Elevator pitches are the ultimate test of a good idea. They require you to throw out all but the essential ingredients, presenting only the parts that are essential to the power of a very short story. Then the essence can be presented in 30 seconds. The idea will be emotionally exciting without the need for Hollywood acting. The story will attract the essential resources: eager funding, talented employees, and excited reporters.

Kim and DT represent real characters from real elevator pitches (disguised here). Fortunately for Kim, it went well. It took courage, and it took prior preparation. Kim had a deep understanding of the ideas he had worked on for years. Yes, I said *years*. He had done a large amount of preparation prior to running into DT.

A first-time runner does not expect to win an Olympic gold medal by showing up for the big race based solely on a spontaneous emotional urging. It takes hard work, sacrifice, and years of preparation. Yet the Olympic race is measured in seconds. So is an elevator pitch.

Short is harder than long. The American humorist author Mark Twain is said to have written this introductory sentence in a letter to a friend: "I didn't have time to write you a short letter, so I wrote you a long one." If you want a professional speaker to talk for an hour, he will think of something to say as he enters the parking lot. If you ask him to speak for 6 minutes, he will need six weeks to prepare. Short is hardest. Serial entrepreneurs respect that.

What Goes into an Elevator Pitch

So what goes into an elevator pitch? What does one look like? Following is a good example of a 3-minute pitch I prepared based on a real business plan. It is a bit too long for the desired goal of 30 seconds, but is much better than the more common 10-minute version that loses the attention of the listener. Kim used this elevator pitch with good success. With some practice, he could have cut it to the more desirable 30 seconds. After reading it, try your hand at revising Kim's pitch so that you can present it in no more than 30 seconds.

Example 1-12   Elevator Pitch: Nice2Kids

Nice2Kids was founded to develop vaccines that can be administered to children under the age of ten by a new noninvasive method. No more needles. The vaccine is grown in edible plants. Kids eat the special food made from the plants and are thus vaccinated. Grow, eat, vaccinated, done!

It is our goal to claim a substantial share of this new and rapidly expanding billion-dollar market segment. No one else has anything on the market like this for kids. Our vision is to market and produce affordable edible vaccines aimed at preventing currently debilitating diseases, while offering a new level of comfort to the patient. Products will be very low cost and thus expand the addressable worldwide market.

The technology is proven and ready for commercial applications. Our core team of scientists has worked with it for three years in the laboratory of Dr. Peter Jones, research professor at one of the great universities of the world. First trials will begin in three years. We will start the FDA approval process two years later.

Nice2Kids seeks to raise $4 million in its seed round of venture capital financing to complete proof of concept. It will be followed by a $10 million B round to complete the research and develop our first product, a chickenpox vaccine.

In addition, we will design new processing methods that will further our unfair competitive advantage in the marketplace. Our intellectual property will include a substantial library of patents.

We are looking for a world-class venture capitalist with outstanding life science resources to help us build a great company based on our plan. In exchange, we plan to offer initial investors an ROI of 133 percent per annum, or twelve times their investment. We will be ready for an IPO in six years.[6]

WORKING YOUR WAY TO THE INVESTMENT DECISION

Excitement

You have to get the investor excited. Unfair advantage is what gets them excited. To a venture capitalist, discovering an unfair advantage is as thrilling as discovering the largest diamond in the mine. It is what they lust after. If you do not get investors excited, they will not reach for their checkbook. Top talented people will not want to become your employees. The media will not write about your new company.

If you do not excite their emotions, investors will not reach for their money. Investors in new enterprises—whether they are corporations, governments, private venture firms, or angels—all end up making a decision on the basis of how they *feel* about the plan of the new enterprise. After reviewing an exhaustive collection of facts and forecasts and numbers and presentations and checking of the facts, the decision to invest, or not, is an emotional one. Investors are humans. Entrepreneurs have to stir their emotions. They do not invest because a certain number was 1.6092 instead of 1.6091. They invest because they become enthusiastic about what might become of the company. "There is a substantial amount of emotional content in decision-making," said Flip Gianos, partner at Interwest Partners in Menlo Park, California.[7]

But beware: the investment decision is based on facts. It is not just an emotional whim. Each experienced investor follows a special process that he believes has guided his investment decisions (see Table 1-2 for an example). Numbers, facts, and figures are analyzed, as well as nonquantitative factors such as management and perceived risks. Facts are reviewed and re-reviewed. Calls are made to potential customers and possible strategic partners. A list of basic issues is produced. And then the investor digs into even more before reaching a conclusion. It can take many months before the investment decision is final. Knowing the basics of the investing process can prepare the entrepreneur for what founders will be going through before they get their money.

The top-tier venture firms work very hard on improving their proprietary decision-making processes. They are a special form of the vast world of people-intensive, technology-savvy, financial service firms. None wants to ignore or miss the next great start-up with an unfair advantage. Each small group of VC partners spends considerable time reviewing and altering how they reach their decisions. They do it in their Monday meetings and at semiannual off-site sessions. Each venture firm is different from its competitors. Entrepreneurs are well advised to research those differences before contacting investors.

Unfair advantages are not easy to see when they are crafted poorly in the beginning. Investors understand that and expect to see ideas that mostly do not yet have an obvious unfair advantage. Experienced VCs are very eager to find the few ideas that have been crafted by experienced entrepreneurs into a powerful unfair advantage. But most of the time, investors see ideas that need a lot of improvement— ones that can be used to create an unfair advantage only after applying the resources of an experienced venture firm and its network of allies. Although they expect incomplete ideas, VCs are willing to look at many because they do not want to miss the next Cisco. Their radar is constantly scanning for signs of an idea that can be shaped into an unfair advantage. Leading investors feel strongly about what they look for in a start-up. Details about the more important things that they look for are included in later chapters of this book.

Here is a fly-on-the-wall glimpse of an investment decision session from inside the walls of a top-tier venture firm. It is typical of what I have observed in the offices of venture investors. We begin with the partners gathered around the conference room table for their Monday morning meeting.

Table 1-2 Investor's Decision Process

Investor's Decision Process	First Contact	First Meeting	Decision to Invest	Due Diligence	Term Sheet of the Deal	Investor Syndicate	Closing the Deal
Partner 1	1. Day one: CEO does elevator pitch	2. CEO presents for 1 hour	2.1. Decides on presentation to next partner	5. Leads detailed checking on start-up's claims	6. Leads negotiations	7. Leads attraction of additional investors	8. Signs legal papers
Partner 2		3. CEO and team present for 1 hour	3.1. With partner 1, decides on yes or no for presentation to all partners				
All Partners	4. CEO and team present for multiple hours		4.1. Vote on yes or no to invest				

Associates

5.1. Do grunt work checking of company claims

Lawyers

6.1. Convert term sheet into final deal agreement

8.1. Prepare final closing papers

SOURCE: *Nesheim Group*

Example 1-13   Investment Decision: DT and Nice2Kids

"Good morning, fellow Rough Riders. Today is the day we decide on Nice2Kids. It is time to write a check or say goodbye. You may not like the company name, but that will probably change, regardless of who invests."

The partners chuckled at DT's remarks. He had brought the Nice2Kids deal to Plitheron Ventures.

"This one has been pretty well dissected during the past six weeks. And as usual, you worked me over pretty hard. Each of you did your worst to me along the way, as usual." The partners laughed.

A few weeks ago, DT had invited Kim to present his idea at the Plitheron office. The team included Rachel, the company's chief technologist, and Peter Jones, the head of the laboratory. They presented their slides in about half an hour with few interruptions by DT. He used the rest of the hour to ask penetrating questions. Each presenter had responded to DT's questions without being intimidated or defensive.

DT had made some suggestions for improving the company's strategy, particularly possibly altering the choices of large corporate partners and patent lawyer. Kim and his core team thought the suggestions were excellent. They were impressed by DT's openness about his track record as lead investor of several well-known life science start-ups. He had told them about some fiascos as well as winners and had suggested Kim contact the CEOs to learn more about how Plitheron Ventures works with start-ups. Kim thought it would be awesome to get DT to be on their board of directors.

After the presentation at the Plitheron office, DT had casually asked if the Nice2Kids team could present their idea the following Tuesday at eleven in the morning to Jean-Claude.

Unknown to Kim, Jean-Claude was the partner who was notorious for giving DT the hardest time about investing. So when Kim and his people finished that presentation, they knew what it felt like to try to catch spears thrown at you. Jean-Claude had been curt, loud, and opinionated, interrupting, asking stinging questions, and challenging the presenters. It had hurt, but as DT escorted them to the door, he grinned and said to Kim, "Nice work. I'll call you." Kim and his team gave out a loud sigh of relief in the parking lot.

A few minutes later, he was driving home with Rachel and Peter

Jones when his cell phone rang. It was DT. "Hi, Kim, I wanted to tell you that we talked it over and would like you to present Nice2Kids to our all-partners meeting this coming Monday afternoon at two. Can you make it?"

"Of course," Kim said. "This is exciting!"

"Yes, it is," said DT. "We are all looking forward to seeing you and your people. We have a few ideas about how we can accelerate your time to FDA tests. Come ready to start at 10:00 a.m. See you then."

Like many other venture capital firms, Plitheron's partners met Mondays behind closed doors and would later emerge to listen to one start-up presentation in anticipation of making an investment decision.

The Nice2Kids team had presented very well and had responded to negative criticism without becoming rattled. After they left the Plitheron office, Kim felt the partners of Plitheron were very likely to be investing as the lead venture firm funding Nice2Kids.

DT said goodbye to Kim and the presenters and closed the door. He turned to face the partners.

"I think we should do this deal. What do you think?" DT said. Susan responded, "I really like Kim; he's a good guy. He might survive beyond the B round."

"Right," grunted Jean-Claude. "And his technology person—she is an ace. She needs a lot more understanding about how a business is run, but I know a coach who can help with that."

"And the technology is awesome!" exclaimed Bill. "Their strategy is focused and clearly hard to duplicate. One of our big pharmaceutical partners in Europe would be keen to take a look at them. I think this business could take the lead and dominate their market. So shall we invest in this one?"

"Well, it sure is better than the mediocre leadership and competitive mess of GeneZTech," sighed Susan. "What a great idea they have! But what a confusing marketing plan! They are going to need a lot of help finding the right marketing vice president. That won't be easy for a core team with such inexperience."

"Do I hear a go for Nice2Kids and a no for GeneZTech?" inquired DT.

"Feels good to me," Susan exclaimed. "How about you Jean-Claude?"

"*D'accord*," responded Jean-Claude.

"Ditto, should be a great one," said Bill.

"Guess that settles it then," said DT. "I'll call the law firm and get Mario started on the term sheet today."

The decision was a go, a yes. The partners got excited. They saw an unfair advantage. Nice2Kids was funded. That is how investing decisions are done in the real world. After the time-consuming, detailed fact finding, the moment comes for a go or no go decision. That is where emotions come into play. Emotions complete the deliberate investigation process. The investor's decision is made rationally, looking at issues and facts and then deciding in the face of great risks and unknowns and dreams of huge financial returns and waves of fame. Yes, the final decision is made with powerful emotions racing through the soul of the investor. Investors talk about adrenaline rushes, fear and wild enthusiasm running through them at that moment. It never ceases to amaze me how emotional the final decision is.

Storytelling

People enjoy listening to stories. So do investors, employees, and the media. "A long time ago, in a land far away" begins a classic epic that stirs the imagination of readers as the tale unfolds. Stories enthrall listeners as a visionary hero sets off on a great adventure, vowing to do good, expecting to encounter difficulties and dangers on the way to the goal. The leader of a small band of loyal followers begins the long trek in spite of many unknowns, large risks, and evil forces. Along the way, the leader and his trusted companions have fun in spite of what they encounter. In the end, the band finds a hidden treasure. They end up sticking together and forging deep relations that last forever. The reader is treated to a delightful epic, a true adventure.

The story of a great new enterprise has the same ingredients. It is filled with exciting chapters that are stirring to listen to. Presented chapter by chapter, it draws in the audience, inspiring them with a vision for a new enterprise. You want them to believe as you believe. You have an idea that could do a lot of good for many. Your trusty band of entrepreneurs has the abilities and courage to overcome unexpected surprises, including attacks by stomping giants and small, crafty start-up competitors. Everyone gets to share in the buried treasure.

"In the end, I have to admit that the best storytellers get the money," said one of the icons of Silicon Valley. "You have to get investors' attention in the first 30 seconds," said a veteran employee of several new enterprises. "If you see glassy eyes in the first 5 minutes, you might as well just stop and walk out. You have lost them."

Your response might be: "What do the great investors mean by the importance of telling exciting stories? What is new enterprise storytelling all about? Isn't a new enterprise about high technology, the laws of physics and biology, and patents, and the honest facts about how things work? What about truth and integrity? And where do management and leadership and execution of plans fit in? Surely this is not about making up a fictional story, is it?"

In response to those good questions, consider two different groups of people. They disagree about storytelling for new enterprises. Both groups acknowledge an effective story triggers emotional responses that lead to a decision by the listeners. The first group says entrepreneurs should never tell a story because a story is something fictitious, made up by a dreamer. Stay away from storytelling. Instead, stick to hard facts and present your company accurately using proven numbers and researched data. The second group says a start-up is all about the future and unknowns. Your job is to paint a picture of how you think it will turn out. Describe the future using all the storytelling tools available: colored slides, graphics, human drama, lights, sound, videos, even put on uniforms or costumes and dance if you think that will work.

So who is right?

I like to imagine a story about a new enterprise as a story told by excited parents hoping for the healthy birth of an eagerly expected child. Theirs is a story about dreams for a healthy birth and robust growth of the child, the new enterprise. Like a real child, the future of the new enterprise is described in glowing terms. The founding team speculates about the best outcome. They believe good will come from the new venture. They believe in their plan with a personal passion. They eagerly answer questions about the soon-to-arrive fledgling. They are pregnant with ideas and dreams of a first child. They are doting parents-to-be.

Risk

Storytellers also describe associated uncertainties and risks. That triggers sharp emotional responses in listeners. Adrenaline starts to flow. Hearts start pumping. People get excited. Once the story grabs the attention of the audience, they want to hear more.

You must carefully include the risks of your new enterprise in your presentation because the experienced audience expects them. After the

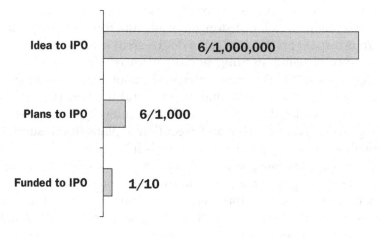

Source: *John L. Nesheim,* High Tech Start Up
(New York: Free Press, 2000), figure 1.1.

Figure 1-1 Chances of an Idea Getting to IPO

Internet era bubble popped, investors, employees, and the media were burned. The venture community became the world's most skeptical listeners. They became major doubters. They were shocked by many bankruptcies of what they thought were great ideas. The results of all the hard work and spirited innovation disappointed first-time entrepreneurs and their backers. Now they view the future of a new enterprise with deep skepticism. Battle-scarred veterans see the world of new enterprises much like extreme sports: only a few succeed in a very special world of ultimate risk that produces amazing results only after years of hard, painful work. The rest of the herd crashes and burns. As a result, the risks in new enterprise stories are carefully scrutinized and examined before stakeholders commit to support a new enterprise.

Due Diligence

When stakeholders spend time scrutinizing the facts behind your story, they go through a process referred to as due diligence checking. It is not a time of fun for entrepreneurs. The presentation and submitted business plan are challenged, dug into, day after day and week after week, until the core team is weary. Questions follow questions. Requests for more information seem endless. People get intense, in your face, rough with their questions and demands for instantaneous answers. Everything is expected immediately, as if you had nothing else to do. Emotions run high. You get poked to see how high you can jump. You are deliberately insulted to see how you deal with difficult people. Your fellow managers are jabbed and kicked verbally to see how they think on their feet in moments of stress. Due diligence checking is one of the facts of life for leaders of new enterprises. Expect it, and just get it done as quickly as you can.

When telling your story, beware not to leave out risks of technology, competitors, and other dangers. That sets the stage for rejection. During due diligence checking, if underlying support for important parts of your story is discovered missing—elements that your audience believes are critical—the investors will quickly cool. They will no longer answer emails. They forget you and become captivated by the next alluring story told by others.

Technology

Technology is an important part of your story, but there have been many engineers who were surprised that investors do not rely on a technology breakthrough to make a company successful. First-time engineers are confident that their new technology will be *the* thing, the big breakthrough that will excite investors who will shower them with money. Then their company can become the next giant killer. But when the engineers presented their technology in all its powerful glory to investors, they were surprised to be asked for responses to questions such as, "What would the competitive advantage of the company be without counting on technological dominance?" Even worse, people wanted to know details about how the first products would be marketed and sold. And they asked to talk to real customers. And the questions went on and on, as if the technology was a minor part of the story. It seems common sense to many first-time entrepreneurs that the first company with the great new technology would win big. But experienced investors see matters differently.

Ask yourself what you remember about the history of technology breakthroughs. What happened to the best technology each time the pioneer brought it to market? History is filled with examples that end the same way: the first company with the new technology loses. The first to exploit it wins.

Veterans around the world agree: The next best mouse trap is not what gets the money. More is required—a lot more. It all adds up to unfair advantage.

To make it clearer, let's listen in on a real telephone conversation

---

Table 1-3 First Technology Loses

- **Univac** introduced the first electronic computer. **IBM** followed later and went on to dominate that new market.
- **Altair** produced the 8800, the first personal computer. **Apple** became the leader of that new category with its Apple II.
- **Valid Logic** transformed inventions of its founders into the first computer-aided engineering systems. **Mentor Graphics** became the giant.
- **Xerox** invented the Star, a new graphically designed computer system. **Apple**'s Macintosh made it ancient history.
- **Motorola** introduced the technically superior 68000 micro-processor. **Intel** counterattacked with Operation Orange Crush, leaving Motorola as an also-ran.
- **Netscape** produced the first commercial browser. **Microsoft** wiped it off the radar screen.
- **AltaVista** was created in 1995. It created the world's first full-length Internet database and quickly became the early leader of Internet search engines. But by 2001 it was being chased by more than eight others. **Google** started in business in 1998. It used its proprietary technology and creative company culture to emerge in 2004 as the gorilla that went public in an IPO worth billions of dollars.

SOURCE: *Nesheim Group.*

(only the names are disguised) between a veteran start-up coach, Mike, and Woody, a respected venture capitalist. They know each other well. Mike has decided to give Woody a call because Mike has been asked to advise the founders of a new enterprise called Zargan.

Example 1-14   Failure to Excite the Investor: Mike, Woody, and Zargan

Mike: Hi, Woody, how is your golf game?

Woody: Pretty good. I'm still finding I can hit that little ball. How is your game?

Mike: I'm still swinging, but I seem to be digging holes more than hitting the little ball. Woody, I need more than help with my golf game. I would appreciate your advice about a start-up I have been asked to coach. I think it has something great that can solve a big problem for a large new market. It could be a big winner for the right investor. Your thoughts on the opportunity would help me make a decision, lead me in the right direction. It might be a good investment for you. Is this a good time to talk?

Woody: What is on your mind, Mike?

Mike: I'll get right to the point, Woody. This company—it's called Zargan—has a tiger by the tail. Since 9/11, customers have been all over it for product. It has a wireless security solution that authenticates that you and only you are using your cell phone or PDA when you try to buy some stock, access your company's sales data, or look up private information stored on your handheld device. It expects to be shipping its first product in about two or three months. Zargan is looking for a world-class venture partner to lead the B round. It needs a lead investor who knows the wireless markets in Japan, Europe, and the United States."

The CEO is a good guy from Intel who did a pre-Internet start-up that an Asian company bought. He seems to have learned his lessons. He will need to find people for the first sales ramp-up, but the references I checked say he picks the right people.

I think this is a good acquisition candidate as well as early IPO possibility. It uses proprietary technology that is patentable. The competition is weak and focused on other platforms. How interesting does Zargan sound to you? [silence]

Woody: This is a field that has had people trying to make money in it for decades. There is not much to look back on to brag about. The security sector is not red hot, at least not based on the ROI to investors over the past decade. Mike, how do you know people will want this thing? I mean the end users? How do you know the dog will eat the new dog food?

Mike: Well, there are four Japanese cell phone manufacturers waiting for parts from Zargan for their 2.5G phones. And one of the top U.S. shippers of PDAs wants product for a corporate data access version to be released this year. My contacts in Scandinavia and the U.K. tell me wireless security is a top concern to almost every IT person over there and that mobile commerce is being held up until someone comes up with a better security solution than PINs. Zargan thinks it has the solution. It looks to me like there is a big potential market out there, Woody.

Woody: So what do you want from me, Mike?

Mike: I want a top-tier VC to look at this deal and see what can be made of it. I need an investor who knows the emerging wireless markets around the world, who has a desire to work with the founders to build a great company, and who can lead the B round that the company needs like yesterday to fuel its growth. This is a tiger by the tail, Woody. [There was a very pregnant pause on the phone. Time seemed to tick away forever. Mike wondered if their cell phones had disconnected. Finally after what seemed to be a century of waiting, Woody responded.]

Woody: Well, Mike, I don't know anyone around here who knows enough to respond to this one. I'll have to pass on it.

Mike: I understand, Woody, and appreciate your time. I think I'll call that new VC firm in Atlanta and see what they think about it. They say they only do wireless. I'll keep you plugged in as things develop.

Woody: Do that—and keep working on hitting the little ball!

Mike's client did get funded about six months later. But the episode with Woody shows how an investor did not get excited about a deal, even with some pretty attractive progress on the part of Zargan and some enthusiasm from a trusted person. Woody did not get turned on because he did not think the business could be built into a great new company. Some of the key pieces that Woody was looking for were there, but not the combination that he thought constituted an unfair advantage.

UNFAIR ADVANTAGE DRIVES AMAZON TO SUCCESS

In the famous start-up called Amazon.com, there is a fascinating tale of an initial unfair advantage that went through dynamic change. I have enjoyed studying the company from its earliest days and have learned a great deal. The following is my version of how Amazon's original idea grew and grew, becoming a living, more powerful unfair advantage, day by day. Especially note how the company added fresh elements over time to boost the strength of the initial advantage.

Example 1-15   Advancing Unfair Advantage: Amazon.com

Amazon.com has an amazing competitive history. It includes an outstanding set of successive strategic movements that reveal how dynamic change can continue to keep the leader's competitive advantage unfair.

When Jeff Bezos founded the business we know today as Amazon, a web search revealed more than a dozen companies selling books online over the Internet. That sounds like a huge disadvantage: starting late, well after others were way ahead of Amazon. After all, isn't first-mover advantage everything?

Amazon launched its e-commerce business with a flanking move. Bezos identified an overlooked segment of the book business: buyers wanting to avoid disappointment when looking for a book. He adopted the theme, "One million books online" for the first public relations and advertising campaign. Amazon got headlines and customers. Book buyers reacted by first clicking on Amazon.com instead of smaller, established competitors. Word-of-mouth spread by email. Amazon began to grow very rapidly. *Battle 1:* Won by Amazon.

The following year, the world's largest bookstore chain, Barnes & Noble, reacted. Its advertisements went something like this: "3 Million Books! = Us. 1 Million Books = Them." It implied that Amazon had a 3:1 disadvantage. What happened then? Amazon moved the bar higher by using its outstanding engineering talent. The company had hired world-class technologists bursting out of Silicon Valley who were looking for the next challenging technology. They were eager to do something "way cool." The innovative engineers delivered a way for readers to do online book reviews at no cost to Amazon. Customers reacted with delight and spread the news to more buyers: "Amazon has the most books and most book reviews." Barnes & Noble fell further behind. *Battle 2:* Won by Amazon.

How did the competition react? Several smaller start-ups also tried to become online bookstores by trying to copy Amazon's every move in cities and countries and languages around the world. But sales at Amazon kept getting larger by the hour. Amazon announced sales in

Europe. Barnes & Noble soon added reader-driven reviews and then reviews by professional reviewers, but it could not catch up. It was too late. Amazon was gaining momentum and market share. *Battle 3:* Won by Amazon.

Meanwhile, Amazon had surveyed its customers and found an opportunity to make online shopping even easier: it invented and patented its 1-Click™ ordering feature. When you spotted the item you wish to purchase and clicked, it immediately went into your shopping basket, ready for checkout. Today that sounds rather simple, but in 1999 it was revolutionary. Pollsters ranked Amazon number one. Reporters clamored to write about the new enterprise. Résumés flooded Amazon. Barnes & Noble reacted by doing a me-too: they copied the single-click order feature. Amazon sued to enforce its patent. The court agreed with Amazon. Barnes & Noble withdrew the one-click order feature. *Battle 4:* Won by Amazon.

By now the score was: share of market for Amazon 30 percent, with Barnes & Noble at 16 percent and falling. Then Amazon made another move: into CDs and DVDs. That added more momentum to Amazon at the expense of competitors. The second and third bowling pins (CDs and DVDs) turned out to be close cousins (similar customers) to the first: books. It was risky because dangerous product line extension moves seldom work out well. But in less than a year, Amazon became the largest e-commerce seller of CDs and DVDs. *Battle 5:* Won by Amazon.

The Amazon unfair advantage story is far from over and will continue to be exciting to follow. You can debate with your core team how well Amazon makes its next moves. Will it become the Wal-Mart Stores of online retailing? After your debate, try to sketch your own story about how you plan to advance the unfair advantage of your new enterprise. How will you change and dynamically respond to shifting markets and attacks and counterattacks by competitors? Answers to those questions will help you plan your unfair advantage moves over the next five years.

Amazon learned how to turn its rough stone into a shining diamond. Now it is your turn to try it. To help you get started, the following chapter discusses individual parts you can use to construct an unfair advantage.

2

WHAT ARE THE PARTS OF AN UNFAIR ADVANTAGE?

*L*et's get started by thinking about food. Unfair advantage is like Grandma's secret sauce. Do you remember her favorite dish? It was the one she made for you each time you visited her. It was made up of many ingredients, most of which were a mystery to you.

Unfair advantage is like Grandma's recipe. It is not just one thing. It is a combination of things that together produce an exceptional dish. People talk about it with excitement. The dish called unfair advantage contains ingredients to make a world-renowned dish. Each ingredient has its own taste; when brought together, they become collectively something much better, much more appealing. It also works that way in business. History has not been kind to businesses that relied on a single element to succeed. It takes a lot more. Your grandmother knows that.

INGREDIENTS FOR BUILDING UNFAIR ADVANTAGE

So where do these ingredients come from? Just what are the elements that can be used for building an unfair advantage? How do you find them? Where do you get them?

I suggest you start by selecting elements from ones that go into a plan for a new business. Each element of your plan should contribute at least one element to your unfair advantage. Each person in your dream start-up team should also contribute one or more elements. You can weave them together to create the recipe that becomes your unfair advantage.

Table 2-1 Examples of Elements for Building Unfair Advantage

- **Customers:** What enables you to say, "We know them and their needs," and thus gain a competitive advantage?
- **Competition:** What are the behavior patterns of their leaders, companies' strengths, numbers, chinks in armor, patents, and more?
- **Capitalization and investors:** Which are the world-class best for your start-up?
- **Strategic partners:** Which are the corporations that add power to your new enterprise?
- **Strategy:** What are the clever things you will do to outmaneuver the competition?
- **Progress:** What is your head-start, early-mover advantage, all about?
- **Culture:** What makes your company a great place to work in the eyes of your employees?
- **Compensation of workers:** What besides cash and options will attract and retain the best employees?
- **You + core team + key contributors:** What is the unfair advantage of each person?
- **Big breaks:** Experience and skill in reacting: What is your demonstrated ability to make good out of the best and the worst surprises?

SOURCE: *Nesheim Group.*

Some of the more popular elements used by veterans of great Silicon Valley start-ups are listed in Table 2-1.

Let's drill down to get a richer appreciation for each element. I will start with customers and proceed through the list. As you read, create your own list by picking the elements you could use to build your own unfair advantage. When you finish, you should be well on your way toward the construction of a world-class unfair advantage.

Customers: We know them and their needs.

Special knowledge about your targeted customers is a powerful part of an unfair advantage. Competitors typically do a superficial job getting to know customers, failing to attain an intimate, personal relationship with them. That is an opening for you. It clarifies direction. It leads your employees to more quickly discover and anticipate what your customers want in the first product and in the following one. Following is a classic example of a new enterprise I did some work for. Its core team had many talents, including an outstanding ability to use customer knowledge to become very successful.

Example 2-1   Know Your Customer: Cirrus Logic

Cirrus Logic is a start-up that focused on making a new generation of microchips that control disk drives. That microchip market was already an intensely competitive business. Cirrus looked for a way to become outstanding.

The CEO formed a world-class team of veteran chip engineers and product marketing managers. They chose to emphasize doing a superior job assisting their customers, the disk drive manufacturers. The industry was composed of fiercely competitive people who sought to build better and better disk drives in a hot growth market.

Soon Cirrus chip designers became able to anticipate and design the next generation of disk drives with skills equal to those of leading disk drive designers. They earned the respect and trust of the customers' engineers. Cirrus people became virtual members of the customer's product design teams.

As the engineers continued to work together more closely, the result was a series of superior disk drive controllers that brought greater and greater value to the customers of disk drive companies: the computer giants. The mutually created successes were remarkable: Cirrus Logic's share of the disk drive microchip controllers market climbed to over 60 percent. (Thirty percent is generally considered to be the sign of a dominant competitor.)

By committing to gain superior knowledge about their customers and their needs, Cirrus Logic built a powerful unfair advantage.

Competition: Know their managements, strengths, numbers, weaknesses, patents, and more.

It is tricky to convert competitive knowledge into an unfair advantage, especially for first-time entrepreneurs. Certainly, start-ups have to know their competition well if they are going to compete. But that means much more than knowing the companies' names, addresses, a few product features, and a weakness or two.

Veteran entrepreneurs study their competitors in depth by starting with the CEO. You don't know how Microsoft will compete until you know how Bill Gates behaves. Or Larry Ellison at Oracle. Or Michael Dell at Dell Computer. Start-up veterans do a behavioral analysis of the CEOs of their main competitors. Their goal is to figure out how competing CEOs will behave under competitive duress. Without competitive CEO knowledge, it is hard to make a wise selection of the type of strategy that has a chance to outmaneuver the competitor in the new market. Technical people are typically not very good at analyzing people, and that weakness shows up in this part of building unfair advantages. Learn how to do CEO behavioral analysis, and you will add a powerful element to your unfair advantage.

Serial entrepreneurs study their competitors with the same intensity that professional sports coaches study competing teams. This becomes a lifestyle. It is what they talk about over lunch. They are constantly looking for weaknesses and openings. They are figuring out their competitors' most likely next moves. It becomes a game of strategic business warfare. It is a form of high tech three-dimensional chess. The goal is to gain superior competitive know-how. It is one reason VCs put industry-experienced people at the top of their list of must-haves. The veterans already know the CEOs they are going to have to fight.

Stealth start-ups are nasty competitors. Known competitors are easy to identify. Gathering information about secretive, private, venture capital–backed start-up competitors comes with a special problem: there always exist the inevitable stealth start-ups. They are the dangerous organizations that are hidden, cloaked like science-fiction enemy starships. They are those pesky new companies that you, the founder CEO, know are out there, but no one can find a trace of them. So what do you do to find stealth start-ups? Serial entrepreneurs say, "Keep your eyes and ears wide open, and listen to rumors. Meanwhile, get your business started, and always remember the battle-scarred veterans' adage: 'Experienced entrepreneurs always run scared!'" That is one reason that gossip and rumor networking are important skills for start-up leaders to master. They help reduce the chances of a shocking or even lethal surprise. They help you craft a powerful plan to outmaneuver your competition. They add to your unfair advantage.

The next example comes from delightful experiences I have had at a special home in the heart of high tech country.

Example 2-2   Competitive Intelligence: Ben and Jessie of Casa Bidwell

The house in the heart of Silicon Valley was quickly filling with guests. Ben greeted each at the door with his refreshing smile. Jessie, his wife, was showing their first child, Rudyard, to friends as they entered.

Ben had tables in the back yard prepared for board games. Like many other serial entrepreneurs, he found rest and recovery in a departure from herds of start-up engineers trying to do the seemingly impossible as quickly as possible.

"Hi, Ben! Hi, Jessie! Hello, Rudyard. Good to see all three of you again!" said Kanji. "Hey, Ben, has Jessie finally told you it's time to make up your mind and either do your own start-up or get a job?" Kanji grinned. He could always be counted on to pep up a party.

"Not yet, but if things keep going the way they have recently, I'll be a wage slave soon enough," answered Ben.

Ben pointed to the second table and said, "Kanji, that new game from Deutschland is waiting for you." Kanji joined the engineers who had already begun translating the German directions.

"I heard the Malp core team is going to make a move soon," said the bearded Chas at the end of the table. Silence followed. Playing pieces were now being placed in front of the four contestants seated at the outdoor table.

Chas rolled his die and, without looking at Kanji, he said, "Could be a spin-off." A few heads nodded in silence. Putting her bottle of juice down, tiny KK with her usual confidence added that just yesterday she had a lunch with Ginger, her friend at Palm, and their chat substantiated what Chas had just alluded to.

Similar give and take continued during the afternoon, as quiet talks took place over the latest technologies, companies, and managements. As the sun began to set, food and drinks came out to replace the mostly finished bags of munchies. Games went on hold as players stood to stretch. Some headed for the barbecue that was emitting enticing smells of dinner cooking.

As she took a bite of the Texan-style chicken, KK turned to another engineer, Ben, and said, "So tell me about this wireless security idea you hinted at in your cryptic email. Are you are think-

ing about doing something serious with it? I was just talking to
Zebra. She had a consulting job at IdentaTe a while back. It seems
they also might be going in that direction."

At the game tables, similar discussions were well underway.
Some began debating the merits of the latest generations of technology. Religious levels of intensity emerged about the advantages
of Bluetooth over 802.11 while others swapped news about the latest hacker breakthroughs in digital set-top boxes.

"Microsoft is going after the networking gang. Looks rough for
Sun and Oracle." "Yeah, I heard from the Real gang that Uncle Bill
has the attack plan code-named RedNet." "Bet Novell is history."
"Was, you mean!" "Ellison has got to make a move soon." "Don't
count on it; they are an aging sales machine." "No way, Cisco has
become *the* selling machine. Get that straight, man!" "They just
want to buy technology companies and sell their stuff worldwide,
fast. Money is no problem." "Did you hear that Nokia might buy
Rastitude, that optical start-up?" "No way. Joran has way better
technology, dude—at least an order of magnitude better. And a
super core team. Strong unfair advantage."

"Did you catch the postings last night on slashdot.org? Wild!
Joran looks like they could be on to something. But Kraulikboy still
thinks the code coming from Linux will level them in the long run!
Did anyone check on what George Gilder has posted?"

The buzz rose to a din. The chicken rapidly began to disappear.

Tomorrow emails would fly. Inventions would be stimulated.
Start-up ideas might be born. Decisions would be made. Unfair
advantages formed. The Casa Bidwell guests know what other
technical people have learned: by networking the right stuff, you
can add powerful competitor and strategic insight to elements that
contribute to unfair advantages.

Capitalization: Select investors wisely.

"Who are your investors?" is one of the first questions curious media,
customer candidates, and potential employees ask. Name-brand
angels and venture firms can add instant credibility to a new enterprise. A start-up gets attention with financial backers like Jim Clark,
Kleiner Perkins, and New Enterprise Associates. Add Intel and Nokia,
and you get headlines.

New enterprises get favorable press attention after receiving
financing from famous venture capital firms. Reporters consistently

write stories about deals done by top-tier VCs who back start-ups.[1] It becomes a circle: the start-up announces funding from a blue-chip venture firm; that makes the start-up hot; the venture firm brags about the hot start-up and attracts more hot start-ups. It becomes a seemingly self-fulfilling prophecy.

How do you find the best investors for your new enterprise? Table 2-2 is a checklist I compiled based on tips from experienced entrepreneurs.

Pick your investors wisely. Your company will have to work with them for over half a decade. Good choices add to your unfair advantage. Your stakeholders will be much more comfortable knowing that your new business has been thoroughly checked by an experienced partner (not an associate) of a top venture firm. Employees-to-be and the press rely on the credentials of your financial backers as capable and wise investors. Customers also want assurances evidenced by the quality of your investors. That is another reason that experienced start-up founding teams eagerly seek blue-chip, top-tier investors. New enterprises need to quickly establish credibility for their many claims. Investors with pedigree can speed the process. Great investors are very valuable.

And don't forget to mention the amount of total capital you have raised. The larger the number, the more awe your enterprise will get. But what if you do not have tens of millions of dollars of pedigree financial backing? Then try making the glass half full. One serial entrepreneur told me that when he is in that situation, he tells his employees, "We do not have the gut-wrenching troubles and con-

---

Table 2-2 Finding Investors: Tips from Experienced Entrepreneurs

- Ask experienced entrepreneurs.
- Use your lawyer and accountant.
- Ask angels and other investors for suggestions.
- Scan the list of members of your local venture capital trade association.
- Research web sites of venture firms that appear attractive.
- Attend events where investors speak.
- Interview individual partners of venture firms.

SOURCE: *Nesheim Group.*

straints put on our creativity because we do not have a flock of vulture capitalists sitting on our board of directors, telling us how to run our business. Instead, we have used our own money and that of experienced friends and angels. Backing us are industry veterans who represent smart money. They are patient investors—people who became successful using their innovative creativity." That is one way of making a half-empty glass into one that is half full. With some innovative thinking, you can make your capitalization and investors add to your unfair advantage, regardless of who they are.

Strategic Partners: Select for power.

Giants can be part of your unfair advantage. Large, blue-chip, world-class corporations that have contractual working arrangements with your fledgling business will add to its competitive strength. After all, they picked you, not your competitor, didn't they?

Marquee value is one thing you are looking for, but remember that the reason for picking them includes more than size and name recognition. The partnering corporation is valuable because it is world-class at doing something better than any other corporation. That skill adds to your bragging rights.

The strategic partners do not have to be the largest corporations. Smaller ones with key technologies or selling skills can also boost your unfair advantage. Whatever their size, have a very good reason to boast about them as strategic partners. That adds a special power to your story.

Strategy: Clever things you will do.

Clever strategy is a powerful element of your unfair advantage. Great start-up leaders are strategic from day 1. They plot and plan, change and modify, simulate and emulate. Their minds work that way. They eagerly think about what the competition is most likely to do in response to the launch of the start-up's first product. They are eager to create plans to respond to possible moves of competitors.

Like military thinkers, they know what type of strategy works best in competition with which type of competitor. They also know what to do with each strategic move. They are confident they know how to execute their planned maneuvers and outdo the rivals. (I dig into more detail about strategy in a later section.) Great start-up CEOs are great strategists. They make that part of their unfair advantage.

Progress: Head-start, early-mover advantage.

Being first in anything can kill a start-up. Yes, a head start is valuable, but it is not the "everything" that it seems to be. In fact, it can be the source of what brings a new enterprise to ruin. Veterans have painfully learned that first is not the powerful killer advantage that most first-time entrepreneurs think it is. I mentioned earlier that the first technology loses. It is also true about other firsts.

Most start-up veterans know they will be trying to enter a new market before competitors see that the market exists. That is one reason so many experienced entrepreneurs are so secretive. It is why we have a stealth start-up named South San Francisco Fork Lift when it is actually starting an advanced high tech business.

The experienced leaders know the old Silicon Valley adage: "Pioneers get a lot of arrows in their backs." It is based on painful tales told by former high tech pioneers. A long time ago during the American Wild West days, people learned from the stories of the trials and tribulations of pioneers seeking new lives in new lands. It became clear that it was easier to follow the wagon wheel ruts to Oregon after the first settlers found the way. They followed the skeletons along the trail. "First loses" is one of the most painful lessons learned by eager novices. In sports races, being first off the starting line is no guarantee of winning. Many times the first to start loses the race. In high tech start-ups, first is almost assuredly a guarantee of losing. It is wiser to say that early-mover advantage is better than first-mover advantage. Or try, "First to get it right wins most often." Those are much better than first to die.

A later, well-prepared entry into a new market is better than a poorly prepared one that is rushed. Yes, a head start is valuable, but try to not be too early. And don't be too late: the closing window will smash your fingers. For instance, the first personal digital assistants were introduced by giant Japanese electronic firms. But until Palm arrived, the market did not take off. The pioneering PDAs are now in the junk heap. Palm rules. Microsoft entered the PDA market very late and struggles to get products using its CE software into high volume sales.

Be first to get it right. Early is better than first. Timing is a strong part of an unfair advantage. The following example is from my research into Dell, including observing it in action from its first days. I especially recommend you study the early moves by Dell Computer.

Example 2-3   Early-Mover Advantage: Dell Computer Corporation

Dell took advantage of the shakeout of the pioneers of personal computer distribution and sales.

Computer giants like IBM sold PCs to corporations through established sales forces. Others sold to consumers through new, untested retail stores (Compaq). Both IBM and Compaq established unfair advantages that way.

As the shakeout of the first phase of the personal computer revolution took place, Michael Dell found himself selling surplus PC inventories (from distressed retailers) direct to consumers (fellow students). He saw an overlooked market segment and focused on serving it best. By 2001, Dell had become the world's largest PC supplier.

Dell was not the first to sell PCs or the first to sell direct to consumers. It was the first to become the market leader of directly selling PCs, to any person or organization.

Dell figured out how to take advantage of the pioneers' painful experimentation with sales channels. Perhaps that is what you can do with your new enterprise. In doing so, you could bolster its unfair advantage.

Culture: Great place to work.

Knowing how to attract and retain top talented people is a powerful part of an unfair advantage. Your first core team is perhaps your most important ingredient of your unfair advantage. Its values form the initial culture of your company—what it stands for and how it treats employees day to day.

Being able to brag about your people is a powerful part of your unfair advantage. Their skills set the standard for what excellent means in your new enterprise. Your core leadership team will be expected to be able to spot great people and hire them. That is a very difficult job. It seems as if every company is trying to recruit the great people you need. So how do you attract top talent? And how do you retain them? The following tips are from my interviews with leaders of new enterprises and their favorite professional recruiters.

Start building a dream team years in advance, beginning with your core team.

Building a world-class team takes a lot of time and effort. Jeff Hawkins, designer of the Palm Pilot, waited eleven years before doing his first start-up. By then he knew exactly whom he would team up with to lead his new enterprise. A core founding team with pedigree is worth taking time to assemble. If your group has a track record of working well and making good decisions together, it will stand out. Remember what is at the top of the list of things investors are looking for: "management that can get the job done." In today's competitive world, you cannot expect to start out alone as founder and CEO, get funded, and then hire an outsider to recruit a great core team. Life in start-ups does not work that way.

Plan on doing most of the recruiting yourself.

Great start-up managements are not formed by paying a recruiting firm to hire a group of strangers. You have to find the first wave of talent on your own. Venture firms can help, but the heavy lifting will be up to the leaders of the new enterprise. It is true that recruiters play an important role later when the company is growing very fast and has to hire a lot of people quickly. Some companies use in-house recruiters—people who only do recruiting. Others look for venture capital firms that have recruiters on staff. Examples are Austin Ventures in Texas and Symphony Technology Group in Palo Alto, California. Planning the timing and role for recruiters can add to your unfair advantage. But if you go to talk with investors, be expected to arrive with your entire core team ready to go to work as soon as you are funded.

Use company culture to attract talent.

Company culture will attract or reject employees more than money. It is the flower that entices the bees that make the honey. It is the collection of predominating attitudes and behavior that characterizes the functioning of the new enterprise. It is about how people treat each other on the job, working and having fun. Your employees can be great recruiters.

Company culture is one of the first things experienced founders go to work building. They quickly create the DOF, the Department of Fun, led by a couple of socially gregarious employees. This is not a frivolous activity done spontaneously. Veterans quickly institutionalize all-employee communication gatherings, sales meetings, and weekly social events. They motivate employees to talk about each other, how they work, what kinds of people chemistry get the most done with the least irritation, and what kind of people the company should hire next. They decide on how to spend the budgets for food and social celebrations. The people's values collectively become the company's culture. And they can tell potential employees and other outsiders precisely the characteristics of the culture. The company practices reciting descriptions of the culture. Its description is put on the walls, in the halls, and on the company web site.

Fitting into a company culture is very important to excellent people. They are not easy to attract. The best have many good choices for employment at any time. When they are looking for a new thing to do, a new challenge, they are looking for something more rewarding in material, physical, and spiritual ways. They expect more than a job, free food, and an espresso machine. They look for more than stock options and an impressive title. They expect to find a company culture they can be proud of joining and contributing to.

Today, start-up people in all parts of the world are very mobile. Peter Drucker noted that knowledge workers are the most mobile workforce in modern history.[2] "Have passport, will travel!" is the mantra of youth today. They have no qualms thinking about joining a hot start-up in Shanghai or San Jose or Seville. The workplace thus rises in importance for a new enterprise. A start-up culture must be more than a nice building, health benefits, and a casual dress code. A magnetic company culture becomes mandatory in the intense competition for world-class people. Like a garden, it must be built and then cared for if it is to stay attractive. Serial entrepreneurs work hard on doing exactly that, beginning on the day the company is founded. When you can do that, you will add one of the most important elements to your unfair advantage.

Compensation of Workers: More than money.

How you compensate workers will stand out in your unfair advantage. People work for a lot of reasons. Picking the right ones can add strength to your unfair advantage. Incentive compensation is complex and filled with many psychological rewards. That presents opportunities to attract the best of the best talent. It demands people who understand people.

Countless studies show people work for much more than cash and stock options. Creative minds have found many fresh ways to motivate employees—ways that are not cash expensive or overly complex. You can pick from many and create your own set of "compensation" packages for employees as part of your company culture. Bob Nelson noted in his helpful book, *1001 Ways to Reward Employees* that few management concepts are as solidly founded as the idea that positive reinforcement of people works best.[3] It works because employees find personal recognition more motivational than money. Ken Blanchard, coauthor of the classic *The One Minute Manager,* says that everyone, both managers and the managed, wants to be appreciated. Humans need others to help feel valued.[4]

Use forethought to create a plan to share the wealth.

Prepare your equity distributions with care. Have a plan. Document it in detail, for five years. Lay out stock option shares by the job. I find most start-ups fail to do that. In my experience, the equity-sharing plan is typically the worst part of an otherwise outstanding plan for a new enterprise. Salary plans are prepared in great detail, but stock option plans are not of comparable quality. Take the time and make the effort so that instead of a liability, your equity plan becomes part of your unfair advantage.

Nonmonetary compensation is key to hiring knowledge workers.

How the start-up management compensates people in other than monetary ways is filled with opportunities. Experienced managers know that today's knowledge workers are mobile and self-confident. By understanding their values, you can be more creative than your competition when building your company compensation program. There are many possibilities according to Peter Drucker and other gurus.[5] Today's young, mobile knowledge workers have to be treated and managed as volunteers. Treating them as employees to be hired and fired at will misses the mark. People want to know what the company is trying to do and where it is going. They are interested in personal achievement and personal responsibility, which means they have to be put into the right job. And today's knowledge workers expect continuous learning and continuous training. Above all, they want respect, especially for their area of knowledge. They have moved beyond traditional workers who used to expect to be told what to do. Knowledge workers, by contrast, expect to make the decisions in their own area on the job. When you can creatively compensate that kind of worker, then you can significantly strengthen your unfair advantage.

You + the Core Team + Key Competitors: What is the unfair advantage of each?

People are the most unique element of your unfair advantage. How you communicate about yourselves will have a lot to do with attracting the stakeholders you desire. Your message about your leadership will have an impact on how you get the money, recruit top talent, and entice reporters.

Can you describe what is special about the people who are leading your new enterprise? What does each contribute to the company's unfair advantage? What is the personal unfair advantage of each person on your core team? Why should an investor risk millions of dollars investing in a business you and they will lead? What about you would make a skeptical world-class engineer eager to follow you? What makes you interesting to a reporter? The stakeholders in your business will expect you to roll out satisfying answers, and quickly.

"People are what I invest in!" exclaims Dick Kramlich, the icon venture capitalist from New Enterprise Associates. When all goes wrong (and it will), it is the core management team that is looked to; they must find ways to get out of the mess and back onto the path of growth and success.

You must learn to get good at telling strangers about yourself and your core team. This skill is especially important if you are seeking to turn a mediocre idea into a world-class unfair advantage. Talking about the unfair advantages of the core team members is a very important part of your story—some say the most important part.

Big Breaks: Reacting with skill.

Responsive skill in reacting to the unexpected is especially important for new enterprises. How you will cope with surprises, the bad breaks of the game, is part of your unfair advantage. New ventures do have good surprises, but the veterans of high tech start-ups tell me over and over that the good news arrives much less often than the bad news.

Adventurers expect many surprises along the trail as they venture out seeking their fortunes. So do start-up leaders. But in the military, an old saying is that even "the best war plans don't survive the first test of battle." Some VCs think that the only thing that counts for a start-up is how management reacts to surprises. They believe it because they have seen so many unknowns pop up and surprise a fledgling business. Managing surprises is an important part of the execution of the business plan. Because experienced investors and businesspeople know that, if you pick wise investors, you will not dread board of directors' meetings. Instead, you will find creative support from the board while your company goes through the inevitable growing pains. Board members with new enterprise experience are worth their weight in gold.

Failure: Talk and learn.

Serial entrepreneurs, investors, and reporters are often more interested in how you cope with the bad news than how well you do with the good. They are eager for you to tell them how you have dealt in the past with fiascoes and disasters, especially ones you caused. They especially want to know how you are going to deal with the most likely surprise in a new enterprise: trouble. Remember that history reveals most start-ups get into deep trouble and go out of business.

Are you ready to tell your war stories, your experiences, about how you worked through your disasters? Even the greatest of businesses got into some big trouble along the start-up road. (Be prepared to address the topics in Chapter 30, and check your work using the lists in Appendixes B and C.) Reporters in America are trained to ask hard questions that can be very embarrassing. VCs also love to do that. Telling them what you learned about helping a start-up go bankrupt is one part of the game, according to many of the serial entrepreneurs I know. They are good at talking about their fiascoes. It adds color to the story.

For some of us, talking about our failures is hard to do. The social values of Asians, for example, make it embarrassing to talk publicly about personal troubles. But the experiences you gained through failure are especially what the veterans of Silicon Valley want to talk about.

I well remember listening to a young entrepreneur after his first presentation to a venture investor. The grizzled venture capitalist had asked him about failures. The young man finally asked the gray-haired VC how he felt about people from bankrupt companies who came to him looking for money for a new start-up. The VC exclaimed, "I love those guys! Do you know why? Because they learned on someone else's money, not mine! And now they are really excited. This time they are going to get it right—with my money!"

When you can respond constructively to questions about how you manage bad news, you are well on your way to constructing an unfair advantage.

Summary of Ingredients

I have provided examples of some of the ingredients for a recipe that together could become your unfair advantage. There are many other elements you can add. All the parts need to fit together well, so that your advantage is very strong.

Now you can also see better why it is important that your unfair advantage be alive, organic, and able to grow. And you can appreciate why you must continually work on your unfair advantage, improving and strengthening it, every day.

Note carefully that unfair advantage is not your mission, strategy, objective, goal, or plan. You will need them, but they are other things than unfair advantage. Try your best to not get them mixed up.

Next let's shift to another view of unfair advantage. Let's examine different levels of advantage.

LEVELS OF UNFAIR ADVANTAGE

Investors have learned that you can create unfair advantages at different levels. VC icons like Don Valentine have tracked new enterprises from their first days to gorilla status and can recite how unfair advantages started, grew, and changed to get the start-up to emerge as giants on the top of the hill. The levels of unfair advantage can range widely, from a product to a company to a country and even to yourself. When you get good at spotting unfair advantages, you can detect them (weak or strong) in everyday news that you read, see, and hear. Table 2-3 sets out some examples.

Now you can see that unfair advantage is like a diamond: it can be viewed from many different angles. Each angle adds something to your appreciation and admiration of its brilliance. You can also see that there are many elements to use to construct an unfair advantage. The elements are chosen as part of a creative process. People choose them carefully because they are passionate about building a competitive advantage so strong that even the largest competitor cannot overtake their new enterprise. Knowing that, you are ready to examine in detail how to build an unfair advantage. That is covered in Part II.

Table 2-3 Levels of Unfair Advantage

- **Product: Apple Macintosh versus Microsoft Windows**
  The Macintosh is very easy to use. Windows is everywhere. Two world-class products, each with a strong unfair advantage

- **Company: BMW versus Mercedes Benz**
  BMW is a company that makes sportive cars for youth-minded people—"the Ultimate Driving Machine." Mercedes Benz makes luxury cars for luxury-minded people. Two world-class companies, each with a strong unfair advantage.

- **Country: Germany versus Japan**
  When people think of Germany, they often think of precision products made by German engineers living in the land of Beethoven, bratwurst, and beer. When they think of Japan, they think of quality products made by committed Japanese engineers living in the land of sumo, sushi, and sake. Two countries, each with a strong unfair advantage.

- **School: Cornell versus Harvard**
  Cornell University is the largest Ivy League university with one of the world's largest technology research centers, perched over beautiful Lake Cayuga in the pristine college town of Ithaca, New York. Harvard University in metropolitan Cambridge, Massachusetts, has a revered business school and a global reputation as a place for the elite to send their children. Two world-class schools, each with an unfair advantage.

- **New Enterprise: YourCo versus CompetitorCo**
  What is the unfair advantage of your company? Your competitors? Can you summarize it in a short sentence or two? Try it right now. For most of us, that is hard to do the first time. But when you can say it in a short paragraph, you are well on your way to building a stronger unfair advantage. Two competing companies, each with a unique unfair advantage.

- **Personal: You versus Another Person Competing for the Same Job**
  Finally, how about you? Can you recite your own personal unfair advantage? Can you do so relative to the competition, telling what value you bring, how it will benefit a prospective venture investor, and how you plan on strengthening it in the future? You are important. After all, management—people—is at the top

of the list of important things investors are looking for. So get going! Start creating your own unfair advantage, and practice telling your story

SOURCE: *Nesheim Group.*

PART II

CREATING UNFAIR ADVANTAGE

3

BUILDING BUSINESS PLANS WITH UNFAIR ADVANTAGES

The business plan is the storybook of your unfair advantage. How do you communicate your unfair advantage? Simple: by speaking or writing. In either case, your message depends on what you document in your business plan. The business plan is the core of your story and is what you will refer to each time you communicate about your unfair advantage.

The initial purpose of your business plan is to attract investors. The eventual purpose is to help you become the leader of a new market category. A different plan is used to run the business day to day; it is called the *operating plan*. You will use the business plan as the reference guide to your positioning wording, proprietary names, description of competition, strategic plan, and so on.

Other stakeholders besides investors also want to understand your company and its plans for growth. They include potential customers and suppliers, employees and their families, the press and local community, and strategic partners. How do you find one story that works for all of them? Tell them your unfair advantage story. That will get them excited and eager to hear more.

EXCITEMENT

Your stakeholders want to get excited about working closely with you. The investors will hold on to their cash until they get excited. Employees will not ask for job offers until their emotions rise. Key suppliers, outsourcers, and strategic partners will wait until they get stimulated about doing deals with your company.

If your business plan does not stir the emotions of investors, they will respond with those dreaded words: "We have decided to pass on this round of your funding." That is venture-capital-speak for, "No, we will not invest." Once they have said that, it is time to depart politely. They do not change their minds. If you are later successful, they may regret not investing in this round, and they may decide to join your next round. But for this round, you have lost them. They did not get excited enough about your deal.

Similarly, the employee candidate also needs to get excited about joining your company. The top talent has a lot of choices. Your company needs to stand out in a stimulating way. That is also true for potential strategic partners and suppliers. You have to capture their attention and hold it until they sign on the dotted line.

WHAT INVESTORS AND OTHER STAKEHOLDERS ARE LOOKING FOR

Like radar sweeping the horizon for approaching aircraft, venture investors are constantly looking for unfair advantages, 24 hours a day, seven days a week. They eat and sleep scanning for unfair advantages. Silicon Valley techies send out email probes by the hour, attentive to fresh rumors and gossip, eager to spot the next great thing before the other person does. Reporters call and call and email and email and talk and talk, trying to get a handle on a new story line, to get the scoop on the other reporters before the day's deadline. All of the stakeholders hunt relentlessly for unfair advantage. They lust after it. It excites them, as the following example illustrates. I distinctly remember how shocked the audience was after KT finished his first sentence.

Example 3-1   Unique Ideas or Unfair Advantages: KT Speaks to
               Singapore Technologists and Entrepreneurs

"There are no unique ideas, only unique unfair advantages." KT was opening his talk to young techies from Singapore. They were listening intently to his tales of trial and tribulation, victories and vanquished foes. "What I mean is this," he continued. "When a person's idea becomes a real product that sells well—that is what counts for engineers in Silicon Valley. That's what I can put on my track record."

KT was a serial entrepreneur, with the scars to prove it. His quest began years ago in Texas and took him through wave after wave of attempts to build cool new products based on break-through technologies. The decades had brought him closer and closer to his dream: joining the founding team of a start-up that does something really great with cool technology, becomes world-class, and goes IPO.

Two start-ups ago, he had cashed in big on the sale of the start-up. He had joined the company as an early employee. But the most recent one had gone under with no cash reward for him or his fellow core team members.

"In spite of not yet hitting the IPO, I see a gain in each of my steps," he went on. "I have learned a lot about important new technologies and how to use new product development methods to accelerate time to market. That helps me create products that sell better and add to a company's unfair advantage."

KT went on, "Keep in mind the importance of differentiation and emotions. At this very moment, I believe there are dozens of individuals around the planet thinking about the same idea for a new technology, new product, and new business. None of them is unique. To succeed, what they must do is start with that idea and craft a unique competitive advantage that stands out from the crowd. It must be something that investors and employees and customers will get thrilled about. When you can do that, then you know how to craft an unfair advantage from your idea."

I could see that the audience for KT was eager to hear more. That is how you want your stakeholders to react. When they think they have spotted an unfair advantage in your story, they want more. While you are presenting, the stakeholders are thinking about what they could do to boost, improve, and strengthen your idea and arrive at last with an unfair advantage. They listen and probe and test and simulate what-if situations while listening to you. They interrupt with questions to test what you have said. They question and talk about more than what you came to present. They are looking for additional things that might be added or altered to boost your competitive power significantly.

In the presentation of your story, the audience expects you to deliver several of the key ingredients of your unfair advantage. They are especially eager to hear about a few secret elements that contribute zest and power to your recipe. After you finish, they begin doing their own research. As they dig up more information, they make notes about how each ingredient contributes to your unfair advantage and what could be changed to improve its strength. Then they reassemble your story into their own version of your story. They will express their version to other venture partners and close business friends. Finally, they will come back to you and tell you their version in order to get your reaction to their interpretation and ideas for improvement.

Stakeholders insist on being confident about your story before they join you. They have to become believers themselves. Once they are believers, they will be very confident that you can attract follow-on funding, hire and retain the next wave of top-notch employees, and go on to impress the media, customers, and strategic partners and suppliers. They become evangelists for your business. The buzz starts. It grows. And grows and grows. You are launched! It all starts with unfair advantage.

WHAT INVESTORS FOCUS ON

Among your community of stakeholders, investors are the hardest to please. You can learn a lot about good and bad unfair advantages by examining what they are seeking. Remember that venture investors invest in fewer than six in a thousand business plans that they receive.

Investors are picky and tough with their questions. To prepare you, some evaluation sheets for presentations and written business plans have been presented in the later sections (see Chapter 30, Appendix B, and Appendix C). Here are some examples of questions to expect:

- "What is the big problem you are trying to solve?"

- "What is the compelling value your idea presents to the ideal customer?"

- "What is the technological brilliance of this idea, and how large a barrier is it to the competition?"

- "How large is the value of the potential growth and profitability of the new enterprise?"

- "Tell us what and how you know the domain, particularly the customers and their problems and the solutions for them."

Let's open up the big picture and then dig into more detail. Your audience will want to discover more about what those reluctant

---

Table 3-1 What Investors Look For (in rank order from most important)

1. Management that can get the job done
2. Large, open, rapidly expanding market
3. Brilliant technology or idea that can be commercialized
4. Attractive exit strategy for investors
5. Strong (unfair) advantage that ties together all of the above

SOURCE: *Nesheim Group.*

---

investing people are looking for in the new enterprises they invest their millions in. Just exactly what do they want? I will start with the list in Table 3-1 compiled from interviews with some of the best people from high-tech start-ups in Silicon Valley and from experienced investors and successful entrepreneurs in other cities of the world. The list ranks the important things they said to look for in new enterprises.

1. Management That Can Get the Job Done

The phrase "that can get the job done" may sound a bit overwhelming at first. But people are not expecting you to be the next Bill Gates or Scott McNealy or one of the rare CEOs who founded a start-up, took it to IPO, and still run it as a multibillon-dollar world-class corporation. Instead, the phrase means that you can get the job done for the foreseeable future. You will be expected to be able to raise the next round of funding and deliver the key accomplishments required in the next stage of the growth of your new enterprise.

So what if you are not very experienced managing a business of any size? Can you get the investors to put their money into your start-up? Maybe.

I have watched first-time founders get very uncomfortable during presentations to venture capitalists when one of them asks, "Just how do you feel about being CEO?" Serial entrepreneurs know that is code for, "When the board of directors reaches the conclusion that the business has grown beyond your ability to be the leader, are you going to give us trouble when we announce to you that we are ready to find a great person to step into your place and take over as CEO of the company?"

The founder's first response might be, "You can't do that to me! That isn't fair! It's my company . . . isn't it?" But experience will show that as soon as you have one employee and one investor, the company is no longer yours. This will be more understandable if you review the stages of growth that a start-up typically goes through.

Start-up Phases of Growth and Management Succession

Since 1990, a pattern of waves of start-up management succession has emerged. No longer are the founders expected to be the superhumans who take the new enterprise from day 1 to the day of IPO. The most likely start-up management growth pattern I have observed shows new groups of top managers arrive to guide the new enterprise through successive stages of growth. Each new management team specializes in something—a skill especially important for managing the unique work needed to go through the next stage. When the stage is finished and their work is done, management will then step aside and usher in a new team. The new team prepares to take on the challenges of the next stage of the company's growth with the support of the prior team.

This happens so frequently that it is becoming a universal expectation. The most likely life expectancy of a founder CEO is now measured in months, at best a year or so. The following stages find CEOs in the president's chair only a few years. These changes in leadership are not so much a case of professional failure or incompetence as they are an attempt to increase the chances of success by adding specialists for each stage of growth.

Part of the cause for this pattern of waves of management succession is that most founders are woefully inexperienced business managers. Investors on the board of directors have to manage that lack of inexperience. Technologists know how to invent breakthroughs but understand little about how to make a profit. Some managers have managed people in a department such as marketing but have never run a business. They can be founders, but founders are people with an idea and not necessarily lots of experience running businesses with $50 million of sales that are growing 50 percent a year in eleven countries around the world.

I have found there are a few classic phases of a new enterprise, and each phase calls for a special set of skills in its managers. Table 3-2 sets out the phases that I see most often in new enterprises. They reflect the original research done for *High Tech Start Up* and work done during the Internet era. Others have documented their versions of start-up

---

Table 3-2 Pattern of Management Changes in a Start-up

1. **Team 1 = Seed to B Round** → The founders plus a handful of others—typically buddies—form the **Core Team.** It creates the first business plan and finds seed round investors and the second round of capital. (The seed round consists of selling shares of Series A preferred stock. The second round is often dubbed the B round.) Typically the first product or service is created, tested, and launched by this team. Management is intent on getting the company to become the leader of the new, targeted market segment. Team 1 management becomes respected for their clever new idea. The company aims to become known as a "cool" new enterprise that is a good place to work at.

2. **Team 2 = Growth to 50 Employees** → The second top management group—the **50s Team**—develops the company to about fifty employees who launch second and third products or services. The company crosses the chasm and gains sales momentum. Team 2 management becomes respected for raising the C round and building the infrastructure that supports accelerating sales at an exciting new enterprise. The company becomes known as a venture-backed start-up that people should start watching seriously.

3. **Team 3 = 50 Employees to 300 and IPO** → The third top management group is the **IPO Team.** It develops the company to IPO size as the business enters the order-taking phase of growth. Team 3 manages to finance and control the rapidly expanding size of the business and huge number of new employees. Indeed, the company now seems to be nearly exploding as it rockets toward the next fueling station: the IPO. Team 3 is often hired as the people "who decorate the prospectus." They are respected by institutional investors and the venture community. The company becomes known as *the* leader of a hot, new growth market. Résumés from eager prospective employees flood in via email. Investment bankers send champagne.

SOURCE: *Nesheim Group.*

---

phases, which may also be helpful to you. Geoffrey Moore names four phases: "Early Market," "Bowling Alley," "Tornado" and "Main Street."[1] Robert X. Cringely wrote in *Accidental Empires* that there were three phases, beginning with commandos leading the first phase.[2] Whatever concept of phases of new enterprises works for you, be respectful of how demanding each phase is and that investors are very likely to change managements for each phase.

Management Failure: What Really Happens

If the founder is replaced, is he or she a failure? Not to experienced entrepreneurs. They expect waves of managements to come and go. They have seen it before. The rapidly expanding fledgling enterprise goes through successive stages of demanding growth. Each stage calls for and then hastens the need for experts who can better manage the next phase. Personalities find one phase exciting but other phases of little interest. For instance, founders of Team 1 typically find managing large numbers of people in a well-controlled corporation to be boring. Serial entrepreneurs understand that and do not automatically label parting management as failures.

The 50s Team leaders are excellent working with fast-changing organizations. They excel at reacting decisively to surprises in competitive selling but loathe day-to-day administrative duties.

IPO Team people are delighted at getting the wild company under some semblance of control and focused on dominating its favorite market. They are less able at managing the chaos and ultra high risk of the prior raw stages of the new enterprise and much better at getting the wild horse saddled and ready for the IPO show.

So what happens to the people in the prior management teams? That depends on how the management succession is managed. Experienced boards of directors prefer to have the original founders remain. The faithful few of the Team 1 keep alive the originating flame—the flame that gave birth to the new enterprise. Remaining core team people can be inspirational to new employees and help hire missing talent. They are often good communicators to the outside world. Unless they are incompetent, bungling fools, the wise founders step aside and support the new CEO and the team that he or she chooses. Fights about power and turf drain scarce resources, distract management, and demoralize employees, customers, suppliers, and strategic partners, as well as investors. Serial founders avoid such errors and become famous, even wealthy, and have a chance to enjoy life in a special way. According to Sequoia Capital, the transition of management at Yahoo is a classic case of how to do it right.

Example 3-2   Successor Management: Jerry Yang and Yahoo

Jerry Yang, cofounder of Yahoo, said he came to see the moment when experienced management was needed to take over the next phase of growth of the company he cofounded.

When venture capitalist Michael Moritz of Sequoia Capital called for a meeting to talk about the next CEO, Jerry did not throw him out or put up a big fight and call a lawyer to start attacking the company's board of directors. Instead he cooperated with the management transition, helping the new leader get started and then continued on in a responsible role as a spirited, knowledgeable spokesperson for Yahoo to the outside world.

He was also instrumental at working on keeping Yahoo an attractive place for top talented employees. The result was a company that became respected as a leader in its hot new market, staffed with a management team and employees able and ready to build Yahoo into a dominant market leader.

Yahoo is not alone. Take a look at the history of Cisco, and you will find that there were also successive top management leaders in place before the company's IPO. Greatness does not depend on the first management team's being the only team the company ever has. In fact, the opposite is far more likely to be true. A wise management successor plan is an important component of your unfair advantage.

2. Large, Open, Rapidly Expanding Market

Investors want to see a field of competition that is not crowded. They do not wish to find the market filled with many venture-backed companies fighting for differentiation. Nor do they desire to encounter the land occupied by giants who enjoy stomping the life out of pesky little start-ups.

The market must be growing. That implies it already exists. It suggests investors do not want your company to be the first to try to show that a new market does exist. "First always loses" is a rule to respect. First to get it right wins.

A growing market is also one that does not demand your company must educate customers to buy the first product. Instead, customers must be eager to purchase your first offering. If you have to educate potential customers about the benefits of using your product, then you are in the education business. Experienced investors do not like to put money into such companies.

3. Brilliant Technology or Idea That Can Be Commercialized

Brilliance implies your technology or idea is novel and fresh. The eyes of investors pop open when they first hear about it. That is one reason "cheaper, faster, better" are not good reasons for you to go into business. Your idea needs to be distinctly different so that it stands out and sparkles. That attracts top talented new employees and gets the media excited.

You should not be working on science. Only a few life science start-ups have the luxury of working out the details of a new science before starting on building the first product. With information sciences, there is no time to work on science because the competition is already running fast, building their first product prototypes. Your company must have engineers with a technology ready to be used to build the first product. Investors do not want to invest in an unproven science.

Your business model should not be an experiment. How you make money can be clever and creative, but the more you deviate from the business model that is common in your industry, the more risk you add to your deal. That makes it harder to get your money. The Internet dot-coms experimented with a new business model, and most failed. David MacMillan of BlueRun Ventures puts it this way: "The only deviations from established business models should be where they gain a confirmed unfair advantage."

4. Attractive Exit Strategy for Investors

Your investors will want alternative exit ramps—different ways to convert their cash investment into valuable cash returns. One exit is not safe. They insist on multiple avenues for cashing in, including ones to be used in case of extreme emergency.

The IPO is the golden goal, the big win. Its large return on investment reflects the high risk: fewer than one in ten funded start-ups reach IPO according to my research. Investors want to put money into companies that have a good IPO chance based on an unfair advantage. However, the sale of a new enterprise (at a good valuation) to an established company is much more likely—about three times as likely according to my findings. In some cases, the sale of a new company will generate a handsome return on investment for the investors in less than five years.

But there is a less attractive situation that results in the sale of most new enterprises. The assets, mostly the technology, will be offered to some other company for a fraction of the cash invested in the business. That is because things did not go well enough, and the company is put on the auction block. It is sold in pieces for a small or zero return on investment, or even at a substantial loss. Statistically, that is the most likely outcome for any new enterprise. I find that happens to about 75 percent of the high-tech start-ups.

"Should we plan on being purchased instead of going IPO?" is a question first-time entrepreneurs frequently ask. After all, many stories have been written by start-ups getting snapped up by giant public companies such as Intel, Microsoft, and Cisco. So why not your start-up? The answer is this: if you do not try for the gold medal, you are unlikely to get even the silver or bronze. You are most likely to undershoot your target. Thus, your fallback position from missing a sale of the company to a wealthy giant is not a good one: it is most likely bankruptcy.

Another reason to aim for IPO is that investors want to put a lot of cash into great big start-ups. They are not interested in small businesses that have a cautious ten-year plan of eventually, possibly, being bought by a large public corporation. If you do not plan on IPO, do not look for venture capital funding for your idea. There are many good-sounding deals for investing in start-ups that are planning on IPO. Investors will typically turn down anything less.

The only exception to this is during the hot, near-insanity phase of boom-to-bust waves, such as during the Internet glory years. So prepare a plan that can get you to IPO with an unfair advantage, and include alternative exits that will be satisfying to investors.

Following is an example of what happens when an ambitious start-up is sidetracked on the road to IPO.

Example 3-3   Alternative Exit: Alchemy Semiconductor Acquired by AMD

A press release flew over the Internet in February 2002 announcing another acquisition by a public high-tech giant. AMD, the famous chip company in Silicon Valley, announced it would acquire

Alchemy Semiconductor of Austin, Texas. Alchemy was a MIPS-based microprocessor developer for personal connectivity devices. Its people and products complemented those of AMD that were focused on integrated circuits for the personal and networked computer and communications markets. Alchemy had received $15 million in its first round of funding from Austin Ventures, Cadence Design, Telos Ventures, and U.S. Venture Partners. The price of the acquisition by AMD was not disclosed. Such press releases are much more common than ones about IPOs.[3]

The press release did not reveal why the business was sold instead of trying for IPO, but it is safe to assume the future for Alchemy as seen by the board of directors was better to join a giant like AMD. And you can be sure the venture investors of the high quality who backed Alchemy did so in the first place by knowing that if the IPO did not work out, a favorable sale of the business could.

5. Clever, Strategic, Unfair Advantage: the Unifier, Glue

The thing that holds investors' attention is your unfair advantage. Unfair advantage is what investors and the other stakeholders are looking for at the end of the day. When you finish your presentation, when the business plan is finally read, investors and the other stakeholders expect to be able to refer to it, in simple terms, with enthusiasm and clarity, in as few words as possible. If you succeed, some will say they "get it" because they think you have revealed to them a new "killer app." As one VC put it, "It's what I say 'Aha!' to when I see it." It may remind them about Grandma's secret sauce. It is what unfair advantage is all about.

Now that you have studied its pieces, let's go on and show how to assemble an unfair advantage.

4

HOW TO ASSEMBLE AN UNFAIR ADVANTAGE

By now, you know your prime objective: become the dominant leader of a new market category. You achieve that using an unfair advantage.

You have an idea for a new enterprise. You want to create a plan to become a world-class success. The next step is to assemble selected elements to become your recipe for an unfair advantage. You are the cook who has to deliver the alluring dish. That is what this chapter is about.

BUSINESS PLANS ARE STORIES BUILT WITH ELEMENTS OF AN UNFAIR ADVANTAGE

You get stakeholders excited when you can tell them an exciting story about how you plan on converting your idea into a world-class business. That means you have to be a good storyteller.

Telling your story is more than slick delivery, smooth oratory, or Hollywood skills. Yes, practicing a presentation is important. But great delivery of a poor story is still a poor story. You need a great business plan built on a great unfair advantage. Winners of the coveted Oscar movie awards all know the adage: "Great screenplays make great stars make great movies." The corollary is: "Great unfair advantages make great business plan stories make great entrepreneurs."

There is a trick to this. Stakeholders want more than emotionally stirring story telling. Chefs say, "After the sizzle, diners want the steak." Yes, they do want a presentation that gets the audience standing on their feet, so practice your delivery skills. But your stakeholders will also insist on seeing evidence supporting your exciting story. They will ask you for facts based on research and later will want to read a thorough, well-written plan—one you have worked hard to produce.

I advise the start-ups that I coach to expect to take at least nine months to finish a world-class business plan. It will contain many sections, many chapters, charts and exhibits, and a lot of numbers. Yes, the media reports and email rumors contain stories about sensational start-ups that got money in a matter of seconds. But that happens so seldom that it is not real. It takes a long time to prepare a great story.

A great business plan reflects a great unfair advantage. Its elements are written into every page of your plan. The plan is written in chapters that are woven together into a tapestry that depicts an exciting competition that ends in victory. It is constructed using frank, tough thinking. Its construction puts intense demands on personal creativity. It is hard work. It takes a long time to finish.

TIME, THE EVER-PRESENT ENEMY

"We don't have time to do all the research and write all this stuff down! By the time we do, someone else will have thought up our idea and take over the market!" I hear that lament often from first-time entrepreneurs. It shows they have a good sense of urgency, like start-up veterans. But the veterans know there is much more to success than being first to get started. In fact, they believe what our research has shown: first to get it right wins, while first to try is death. Rushing can take you over the cliff to the rocks of ruin. The value of patience is shown in the next example about a founder and his company I have gotten to know over the past decade.

Example 4-1   Take Time to Plan: Jeff Hawkins and Palm

Jeff Hawkins waited eleven years before doing the start-up that produced the Palm personal digital assistant. Jeff and his core leadership teammates, Donna Dubinsky and Ed Colligan, began by picturing in their minds various possibilities for a new generation of computers. As chief product designer, Jeff followed his intuition. It was grounded on his real-world business and technology work experience. Others in the core team contributed their insights from experiences in general management, marketing, and technical disciplines. Their combined insights told them that there was a good market for smaller computer devices. Meanwhile, time kept marching on.

As the core team continued to debate the latest version of their cool new idea, they began to address concrete, practical issues—physical size of the hardware, user preferences for features, which sales channels to use, pricing, value proposition to the ideal customer, the ideal assembly of strategic partners, and so on. Those kitchen table discussions led to conclusions that began to be documented. Their story began to take on a firmer shape. Meetings outside working hours continued to put more concrete shape into their plans. The more they worked on the idea, the more they realized they would like to start a business to introduce a new generation of practical, useful devices for mobile professionals. After some nearly disastrous false starts, they decided they would produce a handheld device that would fit into a shirt pocket.

That took time. It was not easy to be patient. Secret start-ups were believed to also be working on similar ideas. Large companies were debating in public forums about the merits of small devices for computing. Yet the Palm team, like others I have observed, kept working out answers to issues, resolving problems likely to be encountered, and kept on adding shape to their story while keeping it top secret.

As the plan became clearer, it also became more compelling. It eventually attracted funding from the finest of venture firms. The first Palm product got top awards at a trade show. Outstanding talent lined up to work for Palm. Reporters demanded interviews. The company fundamentally changed the way people work by solving a big problem.

That success was not founded on a sudden revelation in the shower and a quick drive up the road to get funded. Success was not instantaneous. Instead, it took hard work by smart people working quietly for a long time to shape their first idea into a strong unfair advantage.

Taking time to get it right is not unique to the core team of Palm. Great new enterprises around the world follow that pattern. I highly recommend it.

During the mania phase of a boom, it is emotionally draining to wait, to take time to figure out how to get it right. Tempted by stories of kids who obtained funding in twenty minutes or less, first-time entrepreneurs feel desperately out of it, left behind, if they don't rush to get going "like everybody else." That is how the herd effect gains momentum. It is what is described as lemmings rushing over the cliff to their deaths.

History is not kind to start-ups that skipped taking time to construct

Table 4-1 Internet Era: Funded Start-ups, 1995–2000

Went IPO	978	7%
Acquired	1,529	11%
Out of business	1,180	8%
Remaining	10,776	75%
Number of start-ups receiving venture funding	14,463	100%

SOURCE: *Kleiner Perkins Caufield & Buyers, Nesheim Group.*

a plan about how to get it right (racing on "Internet time"). In the five years 1995 to 2000, one study by a venture capitalist from Kleiner Perkins, Vinod Khosla, revealed that less than 7 percent of funded start-ups went IPO (see Table 4-1).[1] That is far below the one in ten that venture capitalists like to talk about. Substandard returns on investment will not be high enough to attract new money to the venture partners who need fresh funds to continue in existence. It is what happens when there is a rush to funding without taking time to craft thorough business plans that reflect a strong unfair advantage. I believe that is the primary reason the Internet era rose so high and fell with such a loud bang.

GETTING STARTED AND OTHER TIPS FROM START-UP VETERANS

How do you get started creating the elements and assembling them into a great unfair advantage story? How do you document it in the form of a great business plan? Let's examine how the serial entrepreneurs do it. Later you can modify the process to fit your special needs. This process also works well for new products created inside large corporations and for nonprofit organizations. Let's begin with some practical starting tips from the veterans.

Get started EARLY!

You need time to discover the important issues and creatively resolve them. "I don't know" is not a good response to a tough question during a presentation to a world-class investor.

Think of building your unfair advantage like an artist shaping a statue. First it is a lump of soft clay. As you begin to work on it, little by little it begins to take on a form. As you progress, you make changes. In some cases, you start over with a fresh lump of clay. In the end, it becomes a beautiful statue. It will not be exactly what you had in mind when you began. Instead, it will become much more than you dreamed of at the beginning. It will be a more beautiful statue, a wonderful creation that you are proud of. Think of that as you get started.

Use looping to shape the clay statue.

"Where should I begin?" The best results come from a looping, sequential process. During the first drafting process, you will find a lot of holes in each chapter. Your unfair advantage will seem more like a very weak idea. Finding the holes makes your job easier: they tell you where to go to work next. The best sequential steps are these:

1. Write a first draft, the Executive Summary, about three to four pages.
2. Try a first draft of each of the chapters of the business plan.
3. Complete the first estimates of the financial forecast for five years.
4. Go back to step 1, and start shaping your statue, working toward completion.

As you continue to loop through the four steps, you will find a fresh unfair advantage beginning to emerge. You will grow more encouraged. Your statue will begin to take more and more shape. Try to complete the first draft of each of the four steps before going on to the next one. The process will give you a sense of accomplishment and completion. That will help you during those bleak days of discouragement that are inevitable.

Begin your business plan by writing your presentation!

Now that you know the process, how should you gather your thoughts as you begin writing a good business plan? Here is a tip from the pros with all the scars: begin documenting your thinking by drafting your first presentation.

Begin by putting Microsoft PowerPoint into outline format and start typing. Just type. Hold the graphics until later. Tell your story by simply typing what you speak as you tell your story. Ignore the page breaks. Ignore what does not fit onto a page. Just tell your story as you type.

A word of caution: You are not done with your business plan after you have finished your presentation. Investors want to read the plan. It should be about forty pages long, with color graphics and a five-year financial statement forecast with supporting charts, and bound. That takes time, so plan on it. Many are the unfortunate founders who tried the impossible: to finish a world-class business plan in two weeks after they had made a presentation that excited an investor (who asked to read the business plan). Unfortunately, few of them get their money.

When documenting your presentation and business plan, try to write as if you are speaking while telling a story. That is how serial entrepreneurs do it. The story grabs and holds the attention of the audience. It provokes and entices. It is enchanting. It is even entertaining.

Write a business plan, not an operating plan.

Be sure to avoid a common error of first-time entrepreneurs: do not write your business plan as if you are going to use it to operate your business. For running the start-up day-to-day, you will need a detailed annual operating plan approved by the board of directors. It is not a business plan. You do need a section in the business plan about how you will conduct operations of the new enterprise. (That is discussed in the Operations section.) But those comments are not an operating plan (The operating plan contains deep amounts of details for running the business by the week, by the month, for one year.). The two plans are cousins but have different structures and purposes. Pick the one you are going to create, and finish it. Do not use one plan for both purposes. (Table 4-2 compares the plans.)

Table 4-2 Comparison of Business and Operating Plans

	Business Plan	Operating Plan
Purpose	Get the money	Run the business
Emphasis	Strategic	Tactical
Time	3 to 5 years	1 to 2 years
Detail	Annual numbers	Monthly numbers
Creation	Top down	Bottom up

SOURCE: *Nesheim Group.*

Use the classic business plan outline.

"What is a good outline for a great business plan?" Stories have structure, and so do business plans. They begin by grabbing the attention of the audience and flow toward an exciting conclusion. My research shows that your best chances of success will come from using a classical business plan outline (in Table 4-3) that has emerged after decades of presentations to the venture capitalists on Sand Hill Road in Silicon Valley. (Appendix A provides a detailed version of the outline.)

Table 4-3 Classic Business Plan Outline

1. Executive Summary (Chapter 5)

2. Customer Need and Business Opportunity (Chapter 6)

3. Strategy (Chapters 7, 8, and 9)

4. Marketing (Chapter 10)

5. Sales (Chapter 11)

6. Business Development (Chapter 12)

7. Strategic Partners (Chapter 13)

8. Customer Support (Chapter 14)

9. Operations (Chapters 15-22)

10. Engineering and Technology (Chapter 15)

11. Legal and Intellectual Property (Chapter 16)

12. Manufacturing, Outsourcing, and Internet Operations (Chapter 17)

13. Information Services (Chapter 18)

14. Management and Key Personnel (Chapter 19)

15. Facilities and Administration (Chapter 20)

16. Financial Plan (Chapter 21)

17. Valuation and Ownership (Chapter 22)

18. Appendixes

SOURCE: *Nesheim Group.*

The outline of a business plan is useful as a mechanism to help provoke your ingenuity and define your uniqueness. Building an unfair advantage stimulates ingenious minds. Your challenge is to advance a simple but clever idea. You are to move on with it, shape it into a robust plan—one that emerges as a strong unfair advantage. Your unfair advantage cannot be obvious (or else it will be easily copied and thus is not an unfair advantage). You have to be a clever thinker to create a clever unfair advantage. Originality is demanded.

Expect to get a bit discouraged; your first draft will leave you feeling very exposed.

As you begin to try to fill in the details of each chapter of your business plan, you will quickly find you have to do a lot more of everything: more research, more counting, more strategic thinking, and so on.

You will be challenged as you type every word. Intense pressure will be put on your presuppositions, assumptions, and favorite rules of thumb. Many will have to be abandoned. Surviving ones will have to be bolstered by support and evidence from the real world. Think of this process of trying to complete your business plan as one of telling your initial idea to a friend (someone you trust to challenge you, expose weaknesses, and make constructive suggestions).

As you get provoked, focus on finding ways to strengthen your unfair advantage. As you type, think less about getting the money and hitting the headlines and more about what you can do to prevent me-too copycats from leaping over you.

Do your own writing, and write clearly.

Do not hire someone to tell your story for you. Storytellers do not find others to tell their stories for them. Serial entrepreneurs know that does not work well; they prepare and tell their own stories. Take a lesson from their pages of experience. Investors want you to create and articulate your plan personally. It is you they are investing in, not the hired help. Employees want you as their leader, not contractors who wrote a business plan. Reporters want to write about you, not about hired guns.

If you need assistance writing well or help improving your grammar or enhancing your story, you can get help from friends who know you. Ask people you trust in companies in your industry. Ask them to read and make suggestions for improvement. Be sure to run the spell checker and to turn on the grammar suggestion software. Basic errors in spelling and poor grammar are signs of laziness and lack of care with details. Investors who turn over millions of dollars to an entrepreneur want to see signs of professional competence in the details of your work. Employees do not want to work for sloppy bosses. Reporters have been quick to pick out writing errors and use them to add some color to a story about you. Basic errors and poor writing will quickly turn off the excitement of your stakeholders. They will move on and begin looking at other business plans while they shred yours.

Now let's start the assembly process. The next chapters address the components of your unfair advantage. The devil lies in the details, so you need to dig into very specific elements that are used to build your story about your unfair advantage.

5

THE BEGINNING: THE EXECUTIVE SUMMARY

Venture capitalists begin looking for unfair advantage by examining the executive summary of a business plan. That section gets the reader intrigued, leading to excitement about reading further.

The next section VCs read closely is on management. Remember that people are on the top of the list of what investors are looking for. Other stakeholders agree.

After looking for special abilities of management, the VCs return to the beginning of the business plan and read the entire document through, cover to cover. They want to read the whole story in one sitting. They want to understand how you are going to grow and become profitable, what resources you will need, how you will move strategically, and how you will get a return back to investors.

It all starts with the executive summary. If it is not good, all end there. The executive summary is hard to write because it is so short— four pages maximum. It is worth spending a lot of time writing very well. Now let's look at some tips from serial entrepreneurs who know what goes into an enticing executive summary.

The executive summary is an exciting short story representing 100 percent of your business plan and its inherent unfair advantage. It is a collection of short paragraphs, each one is a summary of such chapters as customer need, marketing, management, and financials. Each paragraph is a complete story in itself. Each contains a strong element of your unfair advantage. Together they tell your entire story. They get the investor excited.

"Why are you here?" should be answered in the first paragraph. Since you are raising money, jump right in telling the reader how much cash, what round, and for what. Why waste time telling a story if you need seed money for a biotech start-up but the reader invests only in later stages of information science companies? Wasting time is foolish. Get your order for money declared up front. Your story is not trying to change a tiger's stripes—that would be like trying to move a venture capitalist from being a later-stage biotech investor to a seed round semiconductor investor. It will not work. Avoid disappointment and wasted time. Address your response to, "Why are you here?" in the first paragraph of your executive summary: "We are raising $750,000 for the seed round of Newco Inc., a new kind of wireless services security company."

Next, follow the classical business plan outline to an exciting conclusion. Write your executive summary in the same sequence as you write the detailed sections of your complete business plan. Why the same sequence? Experienced venture investors will be expecting it. They preach the same things as I am telling you. They make the same suggestions for writing a good business plan. Serial entrepreneurs agree. Use the experiences of others. Experience is much cheaper second-hand (than having to make all the mistakes yourself the first time).

Who are you? That is a vital paragraph and will determine if the investor will read further. Battle-scarred start-up veterans will tell you that you cannot do enough to describe your core team of leadership in a special way. You have to do that in a superb manner, and in just a few sentences. You are portraying your people and their competencies, their experiences and camaraderie, why you have assembled them, and why they can do the job needed to make your new enterprise an astounding success. This is perhaps the hardest paragraph to write in the entire business plan. Each person's unfair advantage must blend with those of the others to become an entirety that the investor sees as a team that is able and eager to try to make a great company out of the business idea.

Be sure to include a compelling graphic. The old adage is true: a picture is worth a thousand words. Pictures appeal to the right side of our brain. That half sees a lot of information in a picture. Males and engineers are most likely to process with the left half of their brains, but all of us use both. Graphics appeal to all people. Graphics also provoke emotions, which is one thing you are trying to accomplish with your plan. Pictures are also easy for people to recall. They convey concepts in a form that helps clarify a novel idea difficult to describe in words the first time. It might be an economic chart, or a technological comparison table, or a photo of a customer needing your product in a special situation. Whatever it is, your compelling graphic should be so effective that if you had only one PowerPoint slide to tell your story, you could use the compelling graphic slide. It

Table 5-1 Financial Table for the Executive Summary

	Year 1	Year 2	Year 3	Year 4	Year 5
$ in thousands					
Sales	$450	$3,000	$11,700	$24,000	$44,000
Gross margin	2%	45%	64%	66%	67%
Operating profit	($2,129)	($2,477)	($364)	$3,432	$8,985
Percent	-473%	-83%	-3%	14%	20%
Total head count	12	32	60	106	170
Equity capital	$2,750	$5,750	$5,750	$5,750	$5,750

SOURCE: *Nesheim Group.*

would guide the investor to understand your story and be interested in learning much more.

The financial summary should conclude your Executive Summary simply and clearly. It should include an exhibit with the key numbers potential investors need. A few words should explain the key financial milestones. Table 5-1 is a good example.

The financial summary should answer these questions:

- How large will sales be in Years 3 and 5?
- When will the operating profit be at break-even?
- How profitable will the business be in Year 5?
- How many people will be required?
- When will the company turn cash flow positive?
- How much cash will the business need over five years?

The financial summary table, placed at the end of the executive summary, concludes with an exciting summary of your complete story. Though simple in design, the executive summary is complete. It is short. It is very important to write it well. It gets the reader eager to read your entire plan.

6

CUSTOMER NEED AND BUSINESS OPPORTUNITY

Start this section of the business plan by telling the reader why a potential customer would want your product or service. Then go on to explain how that customer need opens the door for an exciting business opportunity. This is where the inspiration for your idea can be described. It is the section about "the crying need that no one is filling." It should stimulate the desire to learn more. It is about seeing an opportunity that no one else has yet, and you are about to let the reader in on a very valuable secret. A simple example will make customer need and opportunity clearer.

Example 6-1   Need and Opportunity: Singing Machine

During business trips in Asia, a businessman named Edward Steele realized he should get his struggling business (making karaoke machines) out of an intensely competitive, established market and move into an overlooked new segment that did not yet have a market leader. He finally spotted that missing opportunity: the home karaoke machine market. The industrial karaoke machines were priced at $2,000 while the home market called for $200. That opened the door for a creative plan that converted Singing Machine from a struggling company into a winner. Sales took off, and soon Singing Machine was king of the home-karaoke hill—and was soon suffering from its success as it took orders faster than it was prepared for.[1]

Such an inspiration is a good beginning. The guru of entrepreneurial inspiration, Guy Kawasaki, agrees when he says, "Use your knowledge, love, and determination to create something great without getting bogged down in theory and unnecessary details."[2] But remember: although your vision must inspire the stakeholders, do not dwell on it too long. The investor wants to immediately hear more about customers, not concepts. Move on and answer the following key questions (the favorites of David BenDaniel, professor of entrepreneurship at Cornell University):

- What is all of your excitement about?

- Why would anyone want your device or service?

- Why is no one else doing it?

You might describe your idea, need, and opportunity by putting your ideal customer into a situation where she is using your product in a real setting. That can get the investor emotionally involved and it helps explain more precisely what you propose to create for sale. Another method is to cite surprising statistics that grab the attention of the reader. "Did you know that 63 percent of cell phone time is used for short messaging services by teenagers in Europe but less than 16 percent in America?" People like to discover new things. Then go on to explain how your idea exploits the opportunity suggested by the numbers. The following is an example I spotted in a location that surprised me and a lot of reporters.

Example 6-2   Need and Opportunity: CelPay in Africa

How about starting your technology-intensive business in Africa? Some entrepreneurs did and opened the door to an overlooked market segment with an unfulfilled demand for their wireless service.

In the fall of 2002, MSI Cellular Holdings of Amsterdam boldly announced its launch of a wireless phone service starting in Zambia aimed at people who need a convenient and secure bill payment service. It was much earlier than its rivals in Europe.

The service enables merchants, corporations, and mobile phone users to make and receive payments using a wireless handset. That is attractive in a part of the world that uses mostly cash, can be dangerous, and has a poor postal system that makes collections a big problem. Payment by cell phone is much more convenient.[3]

Those entrepreneurs focused on a special need of a special customer segment and innovated a clever way to fill the need. The customer determines the opportunity. Seeing it before the competition does is part of your unfair advantage.

CUSTOMER NEED

Your idea may be very clear to you, but it rarely is to the first-time listener, especially skeptical investors.

This example of customer need comes from a good business plan created by some of my entrepreneurial students. They spotted an opportunity to combine their knowledge of medical services and information technology systems. The customer need section contains the kind of detailed information that helps clarify what the cool idea is all about from the point of view of the end user. They worked hard to make the complex idea for DataMed very clear.

Example 6-3   Customer Need: DataMed

Based on a report from the Institute of Medicine of the National Academies (1999), medical errors kill some 44,000 people in U.S. hospitals each year. Another study has a much higher estimate of 98,000. Even using the lower estimate, more people die from medical mistakes each year than from highway accidents, breast cancer, or AIDS. This stunningly high rate of medical errors is alarming and unacceptable. Creating an electronic database is an effective way to minimize medical errors because it eliminates a large proportion of human involvement in the handling of patients' data.

Current IT systems in many hospitals are remarkably inefficient. Findings from EpicCare Corporation show that while science and medical technology continue to make significant breakthrough progress in dealing with human disease and injury, the management and clinical processes have made little progress in the past twenty years. Major clinical workflow still depends on manual, paper-based medical record systems augmented by spotty automation. This causes hospital operations to be economically inefficient and produces significant amounts of medical errors. In the January 2001 issue of the *Family Practice Management Magazine,* it is estimated that each hospital can save up to $3 million U.S. dollars and 36 lives annually with an upgraded IT system.

According to the Health Insurance Portability and Accountability Act (1996), hospitals must provide access for patients to their records. Right now, the procedure for patients to retrieve their records is inconvenient and time consuming. Therefore, there is an urgent need for hospitals to computerize the patients' records for easy retrieval.

Apart from these, there is a need for a centralized medical database that links the patients' data from all hospitals. The current procedures for patient referrals involve complicated faxes and phone calls that by their very nature are very error prone. Also, as people become more mobile in the future years, there is a need for hospitals in different regions to have access to patients' records created elsewhere. An inter-linked medical database will allow faster retrieval of patients' medical records when they are referred or when they have moved or traveled to another area.

Also, a collaborated database can improve the efficiency of data collection in medical research. Pharmaceutical companies take years to research a new drug because it takes a very long time to collect all the data needed for the drug development. A lot of the data needed is scattered and inaccurate, thus taking a long time to develop a clean set of research data. Hence, pharmaceutical companies need easy access to accurate medical data.[4]

When finished with the Customer Need section of the business plan, you have significantly advanced your unfair advantage. You have seen something that (hopefully) is very new, unique, that others have not yet seen. Your reader will be interested in reading further. Let's go on and examine the role for customer surveys.

CUSTOMER SURVEY

The Customer Need section is a good place to display what you found by talking to real people who represent your potential paying customers. Remember that you have to convince stakeholders that "the dog will eat your dog food." You cannot expect to tell investors, "Trust us. Give us $2 million, and we will go out there and see if anyone wants to buy our product." Future employees are not likely to blindly trust your hopeful ideas. The press will not write about your unsupported dreams. That happens only in the most extreme mania phases of a boom era.

So go talk to people. Get on the phone. Send some emails. Find out how eager your ideal customers are about what you will try to sell them. It is better to find out that your product is boring before your potential investors do.

Yes, you will have to figure out a way to disclose some sensitive information yet keep some secrets. That is a bit tricky, but serial entrepreneurs have learned how. So can you. Think about how to ask good questions of potential customers without giving away all your secrets. Describe some (not all) portions of your product. Ask what the person would pay for it. Find out what they like best and least about your product. Keep on asking questions. Then return to your product plan and make modifications. Keep shaping the clay statue.

Use a table summarizing your findings, comparing alternative products and competitors. It is a powerful way to get an investor or employee excited.

THE VALUE PROPOSITION: THE COMPELLING REASON TO BUY

You must discover what gets your ideal customer excited about what you will sell him. Your offering must compel your ideal customer. The end user must be eager to purchase your product or service. You have to prove that will happen. It is not acceptable to assume it will.

Do not rely on your intuition and say, "I believe end users will flock to purchase our first product." Venture investors will not invest based on your hopes.

The value proposition discovery often fools the entrepreneur.

Even serial veterans are often surprised at responses by end users. Question: "Why is a refrigerator compelling to an Eskimo living in the bitter cold at the North Pole?" Answer: "Eskimos need refrigerators to keep things from freezing." That is not at first obvious to most of us. It may even surprise you.

Similarly, it was not at first obvious why the first CAE (computer-aided engineering) design system businesses were successful. The first systems were created by impatient, frustrated engineers who had to do a lot of boring work to finish exciting product designs. They had visions of revolutionizing the engineering world. They expected a lot of bored engineers to flock eagerly to use the new revolutionary design systems. The CAE inventors expected to be rewarded because their systems would save huge amounts of time and effort on behalf of frustrated engineering staffs. They were surprised by what happened in the real world: the CAE customers found their marketing staffs more interested in using the new CAE systems for speeding new products to market instead of benefiting the engineering departments. Saving months by getting sales started sooner was much more valuable than improving the productivity of bored engineers.

Discovering what gets the customer excited can surprise your entire founding team as well as everyone else trying to figure out the new space, the new market. You want to be the first to figure out that secret. It is part of grandma's secret sauce. It is what turns on the users of your products. It is what excites your targeted customers. You have to talk to real people to figure it out.

The value proposition must be compelling.

The proposition must provoke powerful emotions. Hunger triggers a strong desire to eat. You want strong emotions to go into action. A mild poke will not be attractive to your potential customers or your other key stakeholders: investors, employees, and reporters. Work hard to discover what makes the dog bark excitedly, not just yawn.

Value propositions also need numbers.

Just words will not do. You can boil down most ideas and their benefits to fit two buckets: they save either (1) time or (2) money. Both can be quantified. Most products do only one or the other, but a few do some combination of both. Entertainment and fashion may at first appear to be difficult to quantify, but businesspeople know how to quantify them. Investors will be looking for your value proposition numbers (and how you got to those numbers). Here are a few examples:

- "Our new brokerage service will increase your profit margin by 8 percent."

- "Our new add-on hardware augments your existing telecommunications equipment, forestalling by one to two years the date you must scrap your equipment and upgrade the entire system."

- "Our new medical device will cut by at least 40 percent the time to perform bypass heart surgery."

Let's examine a first draft of a real value proposition and then strengthen it. The next example is the first value proposition from the DataMed management.

Example 6-4   DataMed: Draft 1 of a Value Proposition

DataMed will create that DataMed Medical Network Architecture to satisfy the needs for hospitals, doctors, nurses, patients, as well as pharmaceutical companies. Our product will be released in stages and thus we will tackle this diverse group of customrs at different times.

After surveying customers, DataMed found this first proposition was too mild to provoke a compelling desire to purchase. Notice the absence of numbers and lack of supporting details.

That was a good start but not too compelling. Later, the core team of DataMed created a more attractive value proposition. (It will be shown later.) They learned that this is very hard work and that weak value propositions are typical of the first plan of first-time entrepreneurs. DataMed leaders grew respectful of the importance of doing at least one customer survey. In the end they got very good at supporting their claim that their product compelled their targeted customers to be eager to purchase their first product.

Next, let's go on to the section that tells the reader in detail what is offered to customers.

YOUR SOLUTION

After describing the need, go on to describe your solution that fills the needs of the customer. The solution is not just a single wonderful product or service. It is the genesis for many products or services that will become families of things that will add to the growth of your new enterprise. The solution will be a combination of elements that make up a whole. Let's look at one example of a solution.

Example 6-5   Solution: DataMed Value Proposition

Note how DataMed's value proposition has strengthened since the first attempt.

Product—DataMed Medical Network Architecture (DMNA)

DataMed will create a DataMed Medical Network Architecture designed to satisfy the needs of hospitals, doctors, nurses, patients, and pharmaceutical companies. Our product will be released in stages and thus, we will tackle this diverse group of customers at different times.

DataMed Medical Network Architecture

- stores medical data in local hospital database, with easy input and retrieval
- automates workflow and clinical process within hospitals
- links hospital local databases into a central database
- allows patients to retrieve their own medical records online
- educates patients with health information and drug knowledge
- provides aggregate patient data for drug research in pharmaceutical companies.

Initially, we will set up the DataMed Local Data Repository (DLDR) together with the DataMed Chart (DC) in our client hospital. DLDR and DataMed Chart are the core features of our Architecture. All of our clients must have these systems installed. In addition, there will be a mobile version of the DataMed Chart for mobile input of patients' data.

The rest of the solution from DataMed is in Appendix F. It is several pages long because the core team took care to make the solution both clear to the reader and compelling.

A note of caution here: there is a strong tendency to emphasize "first" or at least "early" in each Customer Need and Business Opportunity section. And there is a lot of technology in it. However, this is not just a first-mover advantage or "superior-technology" section. Those are issues to be addressed in the Marketing section of the business plan.

This section began by getting the reader involved in the role of a customer. It proceeded to describe a significant customer need and an exciting solution from you that will fill that need. Now you will have the reader beginning to ask follow-on questions (most of which you will answer in the sections that follow). The most immediate question is: "How are you going to stay ahead of the competition (after they see you enter the market)?" So let's go on to the next part of your story: how you plan on outmaneuvering those ever-present competitors.

7

THE NEW ENTERPRISE STRATEGIC MIND

Clever strategic thinking can significantly boost your competitive power. Unfortunately, I find in most start-ups the strategic plan is among the weakest parts of an unfair advantage.

STRATEGIC WEAKNESSES

There are many types of strategic weaknesses. Here are a few examples.

Time Perspective Too Short

The core team spends most of its time thinking about months instead of also looking years ahead. It does everything as fast as it can. "Hurry Up" is the motto of the culture of the company. But a start-up is a marathon, not a sprint. Trying to run a marathon as a sprint will be fatal. Your business will run out of energy and resources. You will end up burned out.

Wrong Thinking

Strategic thinking is misinterpreted as business plan thinking. A business plan is how to get from here to there. A strategic plan is how to outmaneuver your competition.

One-Time Event Planning

Competitive thinking is limited to one-time events rather than a series of moving actions and reactions. Static strategic planning is based on one-time events, but the competitive world is dynamic. It reacts to events. Then you must react to their reaction. For instance, let's assume you will surprise the world when you launch your first product. Then how will your competition react? And after that, how do you plan on reacting to their reaction? That is dynamic strategic planning.

First-Move Obsession

This is a situation where the company's leaders are focused on how to launch the first product as soon as possible. They believe the follow-on products and plans can be figured out in the future rather than now. However, that leaves an opening for competitors to leapfrog the company. The result is a weak unfair advantage, one especially lacking on how to secure a leadership position in a new market and then defend it.

Tactics First

Tactical plans, not strategic plans, dominate a new enterprise. Day-to-day and month-to-month actions consume most of the time of the company's leaders. After the launch of its first product propels it to the position as leader, follow-on competitors strategically leapfrog and outflank the tactical-dominated company. Over the next two to three years, the initial leader finds itself outpositioned and outgunned, with its initial advantage getting weaker by the day. Both tactics and strategy are required to create a sustainable, strong unfair advantage. Do a great strategic plan. Weak strategic thinking is a primary reason that so many start-ups get a "no thank you" from investors and other stakeholders.

START-UP STRATEGY

Now I will turn to more positive thoughts and spend a moment examining what real start-up veterans mean by strategy. Then I will show how to use strategy to build your unfair advantage.

My thanks go especially to Al Ries, Laura Ries, and Jack Trout for sharing in their books the experiences of a lifetime of creating competitive strategies for struggling enterprises, large and small. Their marketing books make great reading for entrepreneurs. Especially useful is the seminal work, *Marketing Warfare*, which has become a classic belonging on the shelf of every entrepreneur.[1] The more recent,

The Fall of Advertising and the Rise of PR explains how communicating start-up strategy and market positioning can be very confusing and lead to fatal errors.[2]

How to Outmaneuver the Competition

Start-up strategy is all about how to outmove (from the French military word *maneuver*) your competition in the battle for the new market you are entering. Recall that Amazon's application of strategic moves and countermoves enabled it to become number one in its category.

The key word is *move*. Strategy is not static. It is dynamic. It is about a sequence of planned moves designed to achieve a singular goal: to end up far ahead of your weaker and tiring competitors. You want to become *the* acknowledged leader of a new market segment, far ahead of the number two competitor.

Think of strategy as a sequence of responsive moves by you and your competitors as you fight to capture the chair of king of the new hill. Strategy is not just a single brilliant move that you make after which all is won. It is not a knock-out punch. Instead, it is a sequence: (1) action (by your company) leads to (2) a reaction (by a competitor) that leads to (3) a re-reaction (by your company).

Here is a generic example. You launch your first product and win the applause of the critics and gurus writing about the new market segment. Shortly after, a giant established corporation announces it will soon introduce a better version of your product. And then a stealth start-up pops up and announces that a me-too version at lower cost and with more features will be on the market in a matter of weeks. You respond by declaring your product as the branded leader and send out a press release about your next version of your first product with even more features, benefits, and services. It is even more compelling to the first targeted customers according to the customers' testimonies cited in the press release. You also announce a clever second product for a new set of customers related to the first targeted group. In doing so, you have followed a sequence of successive strategic moves. That made your company a moving target, harder for competitors to leapfrog. It also increased your competitive lead. Your modified unfair advantage enabled you to retain your position as the leader and make it much harder for the competitors that chose to enter your market. This will become clearer after you look at some pointers from graduates of the school of hard knocks.

Minds of Entrepreneurial Strategic Thinkers

New enterprise people like to talk about strategy. I find they think in special ways, noticeably different from large company strategic minds. They have special characteristics. Some of the important ones are discussed next based on findings from people I have interviewed and observed at work in new enterprises.

Strategy minds are tricky.

Veterans of the wild world of new enterprises like to think of strategy as a combination of sneaky tricks that surprise their competition, advance their leadership, and strengthen their unfair advantages. They make their moves without warning; they are not obvious. Their moves are creatively designed to surprise the competition, keeping it off balance and stumbling to respond to each move. Tricky moves created by innovative minds are an important characteristic of the winning core team's unfair advantage.

Serial entrepreneurs are clandestine about their strategic moves.

They are serious about keeping the competition guessing, especially the me-too start-ups that are expected to try to copy them after the first product is announced. Secrecy is a requirement for a new enterprise. Veterans prepare secretly so they can exploit the best time to announce and spread the word with public relations.

Veterans are mostly concerned with bad surprises from stealth start-ups.

Their concern borders on paranoia. New enterprise leaders seem to see and hear shadows and spooks in the dark. They know serial entrepreneurs are very secretive people, and stealth start-ups operate in cloaked secrecy until they launch their first product. The clever ones use disguised names for their high tech consumer electronics companies. "Rearden Steel Technologies" sounds like modern iron until they launch their product (Moxi) and issue the press release that announces who they really are (www.digeo.com). It is very hard to find them and prepare for their surprise emergence. That is why techies listen so intently to rumors.

*First-time entrepreneurs rarely understand the responsive
nature of strategy.*

They typically tell their strategic story in the form of how superior the
first product will be when compared with existing products. They
assume the first move will be sufficient to win against competition.
But single-move strategies are weak because they are not part of a
greater plan that thinks about and prepares for how competitors will
react. Nor do one-time strategies prepare a new business for the day
two years from now when several companies are expected to also
arrive as new enterprises to compete for the same market segment.

*Investors want to know what will be the most likely sequence of
strategic moves.*

Investors want to see the chess game played out before it begins. VCs
wisely seek to understand how your start-up will cope after competitors react to your surprise entry into the new market. Investors have
learned that established organizations and other fresh enterprises
have grown more adept at reacting quickly and leapfrogging so-called
first-mover start-ups. It is the second and third moves that experienced venture investors want to hear about. Be prepared: have your
strategic moves documented.

Second-mover advantage is seen as stronger than first-mover advantage.

Sequential thinking helps you plan your second move. When you
anticipate the reaction of your competition to your first move, you can
plan how to stay ahead. This form of strategic thinking is called reactive strategic planning or dynamic strategic planning. That is the way
veterans of new enterprises think. They build dynamic strategic plans
into their story and use them to strengthen their unfair advantages.

Strategy leads to action.

New enterprise leaders use strategy to get ready to go into action.
They know their number one competitor and have chosen how they
will position themselves against that competitor. They have prepared
for a tough fight. They have lined up specific resources ready to use:
they have a map telling them the path to get to the goal, where along

the way they expect to fight marketing battles, and a calendar of their planned actions. They do not blindly run out to fight and see what will happen, figuring out what to do after competitors make their countermoves.

Experienced start-up strategic planners are deliberate.

Founder CEOs take the time necessary to think deeply about their business and what actions will move competitors in what directions. They do not invent strategy casually or lightly or with just a few minutes of preparatory thinking. They maintain balance between a high sense of urgency and taking time to make deliberate choices for a strategic plan.

Start-up leaders are proactive.

Although start-up leaders are both reactive and proactive, the veterans of new enterprises are prepared leaders. Preparation makes them highly effective, reactive responders, especially in reaction to the inevitable surprises. They have learned it is much better to be as proactive as possible, thinking in advance about competitive moves, and prepared to react as needed. They are eager to lead, not follow, the crowd.

They prepare an emergency backup plan.

"If all the planned moves do not work well, then we will do XYZ." Start-up veterans are realistic. They know surprises, good and bad, are going to happen. They know they will have serious trouble with both bad and good news. Bad news can be an order for 1 million pieces that was just canceled (even worse, your competition got it). Good news can also bring problems. Veterans know they will have immense problems from a surprise "bluebird" (an unexpected and good) order for 1 million pieces from a giant customer. Veterans have a backup plan that covers both bad and good news possibilities. They know how to avoid going bankrupt from surprises.

Firsthand experience from start-up veteran David MacMillan led him to make this observation: "I've seen a lot of start-ups that snatch defeat from the jaws of victory by building into their plans restrictions that make it impossible to seize upside luck. For instance, they pick a supplier that cannot scale, or they insist on doing things in-house, which limits their ramp rate, instead of outsourcing it to an established player that can easily add volume fast. If your competitor can seize upside luck and you can't, then the competitor exploits the break, and you'll be left in his dust."

Veterans of start-ups work hard to avoid thinking like gods.

Strategic thinking can make you feel invincible as you charge into battle, leading a new market segment, awed by a vast, increasingly admiring audience. Leading new enterprises leads to adrenaline highs. Pride and arrogance begin to creep into the soul. It is not easy to be humble in start-ups. Doing a new enterprise triggers a lot of internal chemistry, lifting you higher and higher, day after day. Adrenaline addiction begins. It is an ego boost to have reporters start writing stories about your company's incredible products, its brilliant people, its ingenious products, and so on. Senior VCs know it is dangerous when the core team begins to believe their own press releases. Veteran founders have painfully experienced firsthand how quickly a high dissipates and depression sets in. They know how pride rose and arrogance followed, got in the way of clear, reasoned decisions, and led to at least a drop in leadership abilities—and often worse. If you do strategic thinking, it can confront you with the reality of the competitive battle before your ego takes you blindly over the cliff to business and personal ruin.

Founders know that unrealistic dreaming kills start-ups.

New enterprise minds are very optimistic, but the veterans are also realistic. First-timers march into the face of impossible odds, too often blindly believing they are sure to win. Most end up as bloody carnage in a business obituary. Experienced entrepreneurs know how to balance optimism and realism. They know when to yield to a victor, cut the burn rate, and head in a more promising direction. An orderly retreat allows a company to fight another day. An unrealistic fight to the death runs cash to zero, and the business ends up in the graveyard of new enterprises. Always remember the first commandment of finance: Thou shall not run out of cash! Realistic plans keep start-ups alive and cash flow flowing. Blind hope leads the company to obituary headlines. Realistic optimism is part of the character of the experienced leaders of new enterprises.

Strategy for a large organization appears to be mostly dull, boring, and feeble to entrepreneurs.

Big companies focus mainly on how to defend positions of hard-won leadership in huge, slow-growing market segments. The competing companies are well entrenched. They survived decades of battles and emerged with the few survivors. The giants spend a lot of effort thinking strategically about how to outdo each other. They innovate to try to stimulate mature markets whose growth rates are slowing each year. They spend billions in fiercely fought battles aimed at taking away a small percentage of the slow-moving market from competitors. A half percent in one year is considered a big victory. They are not stupid. On the contrary, they are very wise about the battles they now fight. However, new enterprise strategic minds do not think that way because they are fighting to determine who will eventually emerge as the gorilla of a new market. That calls for a different kind of strategic thinking.

Strategy for start-ups is exciting and very creative.

Small, quick-moving, very flexible new enterprises have many more strategic choices than established corporations do. Their leaders' minds dart about, examining where and how to quickly maneuver. That lets clever people in your new enterprise be very innovative. That is good news because innovative strategic planning can add much to your unfair advantage.

The bad news is that from among the many fascinating strategic alternatives, entrepreneurs must choose. They have to pick the right strategic alternative from those available. That is not easy. It is also dangerous: picking poorly can kill a tiny start-up. The strategic planning road for new enterprises is lined with skeletons of CEOs who picked the wrong strategy to fight the battle. Your job is to learn what the strategic choices are, pick the right one, and apply it to your company. Pick right or die.

Now you know more about the mind of a strategic entrepreneur. Next we dig into the details of how to use strategy to boost the unfair advantage of your fledgling new business. I will introduce the basic strategic alternatives for new enterprises, discuss their special characteristics, and then show how the real companies used them.

8

FOCUS: CONCENTRATION OF RESOURCES

Start-ups are like newborn infants: their parents are hopeful about their future but know the babies are fragile and will need a lot of support as they grow. New enterprises will have to struggle to stay alive, let alone thrive. If they run out of resources, they wither and die. They have very limited resources—cash, people, and technology—that must be used wisely. Focusing the limited resources concentrates them. That increases chances of success. It is one of the best ways to increase unfair advantage. Let's examine how veterans of start-ups have learned to focus resources so the new company boosts its competitiveness and sustainability.

FOCUS IS A WORD THE SERIAL ENTREPRENEURS AND THEIR VENTURE INVESTORS LIVE BY.

Focus becomes part of their souls. They have learned the hard way that a start-up must concentrate on doing one thing very well: pick a target and focus all their resources on hitting the center of the target to be the leader of an exciting new market segment. That big win is the focus of the entire company. Focus becomes a way of life in well-run new enterprises. Start-ups do not diversify; they commit all to a single purpose.

FOCUS IS NOT MADE OF WORDS LIKE "SHOTGUN," "ALL," AND "EVERYWHERE."

Applied to a start-up, words like *all* mean the company will take any order from any customer, build any customized version in order to get a sale, go to any city in the world to present a product. That is like shooting at a target with a shotgun: the pellets quickly spread out, dissipating energy with the result that only a few are likely to hit the target, and even then will do so with weakened force. It is also difficult to tell a sales team, or product development staff that their market is everywhere: they do not know where to focus their limited time and talent. That dissipation of scarce resources typically bleeds the fledging enterprise to death. The people get spread too thin, doing too many tasks not very well. At best, they end up as tiny businesses that do a little bit of everything and never amount to much of anything.

These collections of many tiny businesses are often found in developing countries where first-time entrepreneurs operate reactively and opportunistically. They behave like corks in the ocean, reacting to the push of each new wave. They start any new business they think might become a big one and never give up on the last one they failed to make big. They start small, and the survivors typically end up as a collection of tiny businesses desperately struggling to stay alive.

FIRST-TIME ENTREPRENEURS AT FIRST BECOME WEARY OF BEING REMINDED, "YOU HAVE TO FOCUS MORE!"

Yes, an unfair advantage is a collection of several elements. But if too many things are attempted to be done with an idea for a new business, it will run out of control and crash. That is why focus is talked about so frequently at board meetings around the world, in new enterprises in all sorts of industries. There is a message implied by the frequency of that urgent focus message. It seems that entrepreneurs never get focused enough, no matter how focused they think they are. "They are not focused enough!" is the prime complaint of the icons of venture investing with whom I have worked over decades. I am quick to remind my start-ups that when they are focused enough, they will be able to give many examples of opportunities to which they have said no.

THE OVERRIDING PRINCIPLE IS "CONCENTRATION OF FORCE."

The most firepower on the smallest target wins. A tiny laser burns through thick steel walls. It is scary to drop all else and do a single thing very well the first time. That requires confidence and commitment. It also goes against the traditional MBA style of training of managers in large, established corporations. Their leaders have been browbeaten into passionate pursuit of risk reduction. For even the most revered of the existing gorillas, business history has shown that diversified risk reduction wins more battles in the long run than does focusing on a single thing. Therefore, we have become expectant that all companies will use diversification, and their leaders are wise to analyze the risk of doing something risky until success seems certain. Entrepreneurs disdainfully dub that behavior *analysis paralysis*. After months or even years, the giant corporation finishes its risk analysis and launches the $100 million campaign for the new product. Risk reduction is what keeps giants going, even growing, over decades. That is the stuff of traditional business school education. It works for them but is death for a new enterprise. That is one reason executives doing their first start-up typically experience intense pain and high chances of early failure.

START-UP FOUNDERS HAVE FOUND RISK-REDUCTION THINKING BRINGS START-UPS TO RUIN.

Instead of planning diversification and seeking safety, venture firms and serial entrepreneurs have discovered that new enterprise winners are built by people who take the ultimate business risk: focus the entire company on delivering one thing better than any competitor. Do what it takes to dominate a single new market segment. Winner takes all. If that fails, the company fails. One bullet to be fired. Risk maximization. Focus on one thing.

This does not mean that experienced entrepreneurs blindly charge headlong into competitive battle. Never. Instead, they prepare carefully before they act. Yes, they do look for ways to reduce risk. Their minds are always spinning, doing their homework before they launch the charge into the new market. They do not act impulsively or foolishly. They plan and focus. But they do not diversify. Instead, they spend a lot of time talking to potential customers. They find out in advance what is most likely to work best for their start-up. They count and measure and calculate before finishing their business plan. They mix the findings together and add learned intuition and emerge with a strategic plan that is powerful and compelling. How did they do it? They focused, found out, and refocused, and kept at it until they were satisfied.

Now that I have you focused, let's examine the basic strategies you can choose from.

9

TYPES OF STRATEGIES

*I*have found a pattern in the strategies chosen by leaders of new enterprises: they pick strategies from a distinct list. The list I found them using closely fits lists of strategies observed in consumer goods and the military. Consulting firms have applied similar basic strategies to their large corporate industrial and nonprofit clients. Even large universities use similar lists.

The basic list of entrepreneurial business strategies is founded on real military thinking. I find such strategies can be simplified into a short list. A study of the classifications and principles of each strategy can be a very practical and powerful way to strengthen a good idea that lacks an unfair advantage.

Start-up strategies fall into distinctive categories. The best categorical thinking on start-up strategies mirrors the original thinking of the Prussian general Carl von Clausewitz (1780–1831) in his classic work *On War*.[1] There are many books, web sites and organizations that study and apply his principles, including, *Marketing Warfare*[2] by Ries and Trout. It has become a classic, and I base much of my discussion of strategy on it. The principles of Clausewitz fall into four clear, simple, basic strategies, according to Ries and Trout. I have found entrepreneurs delighted after they pick from one of those four choices of strategy. That leads to a crisp, clear path out of the dreary swamp of jumbled and overintellectualized strategic thinking. It helps avoid wasting time contemplating how to modify and make big company strategic thinking work in a small new enterprise.

Some contemporary strategic thinkers have also made effective contributions to strategic thinking for new enterprises. Recently the guru thinkers, the big kahunas of the business schools and expensive consulting firms, have found elements of giant company strategies applicable to smaller organizations. Respected examples include works by Clayton Christensen,[3] Peter Drucker,[4] Michael Porter, and C. K. Prahalad:

- Christensen explained how and why giant companies struggle with disruptive technologies and why they are so ineffective when they try to respond to innovative entrepreneurs.

- Drucker discerned several primary strategic methods employed by entrepreneurs and offered reasoning on why they work for new enterprises.

- Porter saw basic forces at work on competing companies and showed the value of using the forces to focus corporate resources on the goals of the business.

- Prahalad found large companies succeeded more by concentrating on core competencies, a small number of competitive advantages that were discovered to be fundamental to the expertise of an entire organization.

As we entered the 2000s, retrospective looks at the Internet boom-to-bust era resulted in the thinkers and gurus of strategy returning to Clausewitz and his strategies. Large consulting firms rediscovered the value of the general's basic strategic thinking.[5] For the serious student of business strategy, I find these strategic thinkers are all worth studying. I have found their different views helpful to new enterprises. The trick is to know what to use and what to discard. Reading strategic materials about big corporations can also help leaders of tiny start-ups: they are going to have several of the giants as strategic partners.

In the following section, I borrow and apply some of the thinking of the contemporaries but mainly emphasize Clausewitz and creative ideas from Ries and Trout. I have found companies that creatively apply Clausewitz's principles of strategic thinking end up with unfair advantages.

IDENTIFYING YOUR COMPETITORS

Where do you start to pick your strategy? Begin by identifying your number one competitor. Then you can focus on that company. Focused, you can set goals and objectives, pick strategies, and make plans. To outmaneuver a competitor, you need to pick a competitor to outmaneuver. You need a target to overcome, outflank, or avoid. If you do not pick a competitor, you will run into it when you least expect it and are most vulnerable. Do not begin by creating your strategic plan and then pick the top competitor. It will be a waste of effort. Start with the competitor.

Pick the existing market leader.

The market leader is the company you will be competing against when you launch your first product or service. It may be simply the (old-fashioned) existing way of doing things. Before cell phones, the only mobile devices were clunky portable radio phones. Or it may be an existing giant corporation in Asia already selling a related product. The first Palm PDA competed with various organizer gadgets from Japanese consumer electronic companies. Or it may be a product that you expect an existing start-up in Taiwan to introduce fourteen months from now (a few months before your first product will be ready). Or it may be a start-up in Austin, Texas, that you have only heard rumors about—one that is said to exist (but you cannot find) and one that respected venture people say is very likely to become your head-on competitor shortly after you launch your first product. You have to pick your market leader before you can pick the right strategy.

Focus on the market leader.

Pick apart and analyze the market leading organization from top to bottom. Get to be an expert on everything about it. Start with the CEO's name and personality type. Analyze his or her business behavior and competitive track record. Then examine the company's management style, its culture, financial condition, strategic skills, products, technology, and so on. Get to know everything you can about it. Why did it get so far, and why is it so successful? Gert Kindgren, a Swedish serial entrepreneur suggests, "Another good way of finding out more about the market leader is to call up some of their customers, which might be your customers in the future. They should know why they are buying, what they like and dislike." Customers will tell you what is missing from products and services of the market leader. That can guide you to your strategy. Do more than figure out how to build better products than it does. Especially figure out how the CEO typically operates strategically under periods of extreme competitive duress. Does he or she immediately start a price war? Or

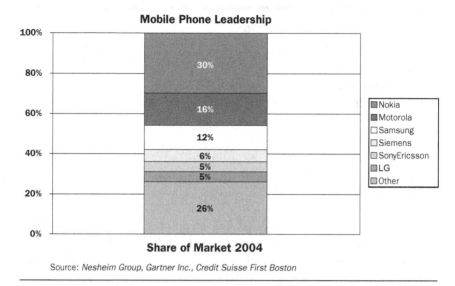

Figure 9-1 Share of Market: Gorilla 30 Percent

begin an advertising barrage? Or call up the press and start telling distorted stories? Or call in help from giant strategic partners? Or double the commissions of the sales force? Figure out the person who is the leader of the market leading competitor. You cannot understand Microsoft, for example, without understanding Bill Gates.

How do you know who the market leader is? One tip: the leader in an established industry typically has about 30 percent market share. In 2004, Nokia owned about 30 percent of the cell phone market, Motorola 16 percent, Samsung 12 percent, and a dozen others single-digit shares of the market (Figure 9.1). One gorilla, two chimpanzees, and many starving monkeys.[6]

CHOOSE ONE BASIC STRATEGY

After you have named your market leader, it is time to pick the right strategy for your company. The wrong choice will result in lots of lost blood. The father of modern warfare, Carl von Clausewitz, invented methods that were successful in winning wars with less loss and greater victory. His fundamental message was that you must learn how to outwit the enemy or else you will suffer carnage, blood all over the battlefield. Clausewitz preferred brains at work to the more common pattern now known as "blood and guts" (named after the battle methods of the American World War II general George Patton).

Table 9-1 The Four Types of Strategies

1. Defensive
2. Offensive
3. Flanking
4. Guerrilla

SOURCE: *Al Ries and Jack Trout,* Marketing Warfare *(New York: McGraw-Hill, 1986).*

Businesspeople have applied the strategies of Clausewitz with good success. So let's take a look at each of Clausewitz's strategies, beginning with the four basic classifications that Ries and Trout created in *Marketing Warfare* (Table 9-1).

Defensive

Is the defensive strategy the best for your start-up to begin with? Note the defensive marketing warfare principles in Table 9-2. Then rethink your consideration of acting like the defender: How wise would you be if you used that strategy and its principles for your company?

I find first-time entrepreneurs pick defensive most often. We all like to be the leader. The defensive strategy seems to be the most desirable one to start with. It is common sense to try to emulate a leader. That is why defensive is the first to be chosen by the well-intended but inexperienced entrepreneur who thinks his new enterprise is going to become the leader of a lucrative new market.

However, the defensive strategy succeeds only when it is applied by *the* market leader. There can only be *one* market leader. History has

Table 9-2 Defensive Principles

1. Only the market leader should consider playing defense.
2. The best defensive strategy is the courage to attack yourself.
3. Strong competitive moves should always be blocked.

SOURCE: *Ries and Trout,* Marketing Warfare.

shown that when other competitors try to act like the market leader, they die trying. Only one can play the defender and win. That is a common error in both consumer and industrial businesses around the world. It is almost always fatal. Cisco dominates routers. Amazon is king of online books. Nokia is the citadel of cell phones. Many companies tried to copy them and made the mistake of behaving like a market leader. They are now forgotten names. There is room for only one market leader of each new market category. The rest must follow and use different strategies. The market leader will be applying the defensive strategy. You should not—until you are the leader of your target market category.

Offensive

The second big strategic mistake is for a start-up to act like an aggressive attacker, charging the market leader head-on, with flags flying, filled with bravado and dreams of glory about the little company that will topple the giant. This David and Goliath mind-set results in a consistent outcome: Goliath wins; David is crushed. The dragon eats the brave knight for dinner. The first-time entrepreneur commonly plans to compete against the gorilla market leader by counting on start-up gusto and energy to win, coming out guns blazing, attacking on all fronts. Instead, the start-up launches, the gorilla counterpunches, and the start-up is squashed like a bug. Reporters write, "How brave, too bad." Employees skip the funeral and look for smarter people to lead their next new enterprise.

If you insist on attacking the giant head on, pay special attention to the principles of the offensive strategy in Table 9-3. Notice how the rules require (1) finding a significant weakness in the defender that

---

Table 9-3 Offensive Principles

1. The main consideration is the strength of the leader's position.
2. Find a weakness in the leader's strength, and attack at that point.
3. Launch the attack on as narrow a front as possible.

SOURCE: *Ries and Trout*, Marketing Warfare.

you can attack (focus), (2) staying committed to pouring all the resources into attacking that single weakness (focus), and (3) pouring your limited start-up resources into as narrow a competitive front as possible (focus). That is how the Soviet armies fought their wars during the twentieth century. The regular troops were sent head-long into battle, probing until a weakness in the enemy was found. Then all of the elite troops were rushed into that single weakness, cracking open the defense, causing a rout. Focus wins, big-time.

Offensive start-ups do not have enough resources to attack several weaknesses. The offensive strategy wins by concentrating on exploiting a single weakness. But I see many first-time CEOs try to attack the market leader on several fronts at the same time. They attempt to deliver twice as many features, double the quality of customer support, provide six different versions of each product, and so on. That is not focus.

A significant danger in using the offensive strategy is that the defensive leader quickly fixes the weakness and plugs the hole. Creative technologists often spot weaknesses in the technology of a defending market champion. That is one reason so many high tech start-ups are created with so much emphasis on technology. But not long after the technology weakness is attacked (after the offensive company launches its first product), the defender typically reacts with a similar product or announces a "fix" will be delivered a few months later. That reactionary move blocks the attack of the offensive company. Suddenly its attempt to take the lead is ended. Relying on technology (the better mousetrap) is a common trap for new enterprises using the offensive strategy. When the defender closes the door with a me-too move, the offensive company loses its advantage. Its mousetrap becomes a me-too product. The defender wins.

Another danger of the offensive strategy is getting drawn into features battles: "Our product is faster than yours" or "Ours uses less power than yours" for example. Feature advantages seldom last long. In the microprocessor wars that began in the 1990s between Intel and Advanced Micro Devices, each claimed to have products with more and better features. Soon the claims to fame settled on one feature: how fast the clock on the chip ran. By 2000 the fiercely competing companies' engineers had gotten so close in technical abilities that every six months, one claimed that its chips ran faster than the other's. Feature battles also open the door for a quick leapfrog by a new competitor. That is especially true for start-ups that are exposed to me-too start-ups that quickly jump into competitive action. Over the three decades, the battlefield for faster graphics computer chips is covered with skeletons of companies that were leapfrogged by others with faster chips. The media often see product wars as good food for tabloid-style stories about hot races between heated competitors. Reporters love to write about the latest shift in leaders as one leapfrogs the other. That is why the wily venture investor and his serial entrepreneur spend so much time carefully crafting press releases. You want the news to be about how your company is leading a new market segment, not getting leapfrogged again. The following is an example of a new enterprise that chose the offensive strategy against an entrenched defender.[7] After the first press release by the offensive attacker, I found it fascinating to follow the flurry of press releases, counter moves, and rebuttals.

Example 9-1   Offensive and Defensive Moves: Research in Motion versus Good Technology

A crisp example of the use of the offensive strategy occurred when start-up Good Technology announced its innovative email service. Research in Motion had become the leader in wireless email services delivered via its proprietary BlackBerry handheld device. It had no serious threat until the new enterprise arrived.

Good focused on one weakness of the BlackBerry service: the lack of synchronization of emails on the handheld device with the user's desktop personal computer. Good's service synchronized directly with the corporation's email servers. A deleted email was immediately reflected on the user's personal computer back in the office. With a BlackBerry, the user had to return to home base, place the handheld device in a cradle connected to the personal computer, and synchronize the devices. Good's customers have email information on the handheld device always the same as what is on the desktop, and they don't have to spend time matching up the data. Corporate users save time and money because email needs to be managed only on servers instead of each desktop. The Good service works with a variety of hardware, including BlackBerry devices. Its first customers gave glowing testimonials. Microsoft and IBM supported the Good service. No consumer could sign up for the Good service, only corporations; Good stayed focused on corporations only. Good was well financed by respected venture capital firms such as Kleiner Perkins Caufield & Byers and Benchmark Capital.

Time will tell how the battle between Good Technology and RIM turns out. The email synchronization feature is a critical part of the unfair advantage of Good, but note carefully that it has more than just a single feature benefit in the unfair advantage.

Flanking

I find flanking to be the most successful start-up strategy. It is used most often by experienced new enterprise leaders. It is similar to running around a strong wall or a surprise attack on the enemy's flank. Let's examine how it might work for your company.

To win by flanking, note carefully its three very special principles (Table 9-4): (1) it must be a move into a competitive territory that does not yet have a leader (no other company yet dominates), (2) you must surprise the world (that is why so many serial entrepreneurs are so secretive), and (3) once started, you have to pour all your resources into pursuing your goal (to become the market leader).

If there is an entrenched leader of the market you are planning on dominating, you are too late and have nothing to flank into. Nor is there any surprise left for you to use because the world knows all about the market segment the leader owns. There is no need to rush to attack because several competitors already occupy the market. The only thing left to try is a better, faster, cheaper product for the existing market. But that has virtually no chance of winning.

Instead, you must find a different market segment, one that has been overlooked. It must not yet be dominated by any company of any size. You must look for new customers with fresh needs that others have not yet seen. That is one reason entrepreneurs are so secretive—why they are in stealth mode, until their first products are

---

Table 9-4 Flanking Principles

1. A good flanking move must be made into an uncontested area.
2. Tactical surprise ought to be an important element of the plan.
3. The pursuit is as critical as the attack itself.

SOURCE: *Ries and Trout,* Marketing Warfare.

announced. And it is also why, once they have launched their first products, they are so aggressive. They want to rush to the top of the overlooked hill and become king of it as fast as possible.

Following is an example of flanking used with success by Singing Machine's creative CEO.

Example 9-2   Flanking Move: Singing Machine

In Example 6-1, I noted how Edward Steele, chief executive of Singing Machine Co. came up with an idea for a new business. The strategy he chose fits the flanking category.

Fierce competition had pushed his business to the brink of disaster when, on a business trip, he spotted an overlooked market: karaoke machines for home use. At the time, karaoke machines were sold to nightclubs and restaurants for use by patrons after a few beers. Steele felt his company could produce an effective consumer model with attractive features and would sell for $200, a fraction of the boxes sold by the industrial karaoke manufacturers.

To quickly capture the position as leader of the new market, Steele made some shrewd moves. He signed MTV to a marketing tie-in arrangement and added another with Nickelodeon. He brought out more models aimed at young children. The company sold aggressively, and in three years sales rose from $6 million per year to $59 million. Earnings climbed to over $9 million. That earned favorable stories about the company written by reporters who placed it high on their lists of successful companies.[8]

Other classic examples of start-up flanking include these:

- Amazon.com moved into uncontested online retail book sales while Barnes & Noble continued to expand its bricks-and-mortar retail bookstores, ignoring the flanking move by Amazon until it was too late.

- Sun Microsystems began with sales of proprietary UNIX workstations and became the dominant leader of that new sector. The corporate giant Digital Equipment Corporation continued to broaden its line of minicomputers without quickly blocking the move by Sun.

- Lotus introduced its instantly popular spreadsheet 1-2-3 for the new IBM-compatible personal computer market. Market leader Visicalc remained fixed on the market using Apple II computers. Microsoft built a clever spreadsheet for the overlooked Macintosh named Excel (a flanking move) and later used Excel to attack the weaknesses of 1-2-3 (an offensive move).

- Dell computer went into business selling personal computers directly to customers. IBM sold them to corporations via its direct sales force. Compaq sold via the new retail computer stores.

- Solectron spotted an opportunity to do high-quality contract manufacturing for new products of fast-growing computer giants. Competitors remained focused on delivering cheap computer boards to any customer.

The most desirable market is just beginning to form. It is open, not yet filled with defensive competitors. It is a fresh market waiting for a fresh company to become its fresh leader. That could be your company. Have you discovered that opportunity? When you have, you will be a flanker, making a surprise move into an uncontested territory.

Guerrilla

Guerrilla strategy works well if you face a large, crowded market and have to find a tiny market segment to squeeze into. It is how bootstrap companies begin. It is also effective as a fallback strategy if you have begun your business by flanking but are surprised by powerful competitors that quickly jump into your market and take away the lead. Guerrilla is also a fallback strategy if you discover that your flanking move is into a market that is going to be much smaller than you had forecast. In the real world, optimism about a potentially huge market frequently turns into a disappointment: the targeted market will never be very large. If you wish to continue, you need to switch from flanking to guerrilla and find a tiny, overlooked slice of the market to work with—one that is often referred to as a niche. *Niche* is French for a market that is "too small for anybody else to bother with." It is also too small for top-tier venture firms to bother financing. So be careful. Remember that you have to be able to generate at least $30 million in high tech sales within three to five years in order to get the attention of venture capital investors. Guerrilla funding sources are limited to individuals and the funds of the founders, often referred to derisively as friends, family, and fools.

Table 9-5 Guerrilla Principles

1. Find a segment of the market small enough to defend.
2. No matter how successful you become, never act like the leader.
3. Be prepared to bug out at a moment's notice.

SOURCE: *Ries and Trout,* Marketing Warfare.

Guerrilla is a tricky strategy. It feels a bit like being a leader (acting like defender of your tiny niche). And it feels as if it has elements of flanking in it (rushing into an uncontested market). But therein are fatal errors. Defenders are not guerrillas. Yes, guerrillas can defend their market, but they are not invincible giants, even if they feel that way sometimes. Note carefully the principles for guerrilla in Table 9-5, especially the third rule: Be prepared to bug out at a moment's notice. Once a giant gorilla starts to invade the niche successfully, the wise guerrilla does not put up a fight to the death. Instead, the little guy immediately packs up and leaves, looking for a different niche. Rather than fight the Alamo all over again (a futile, stubborn, heroic stand to the death), veterans know it is wiser to lose a battle and retreat to fight another day.

Let's examine a very successful company that is world famous. It is a fine example of how guerrilla strategy can lead an entrepreneur to become a winner. The founder focused on a small market segment, devoted his energy to becoming the best in the world at serving a very special need of his customers, and became so able and famous that not even the giants of industry could destroy the leadership position of his company. As soon as one market segment became saturated, he moved quickly on to the next.

Example 9-3   Guerrilla: Dolby Laboratories

Ray Dolby is the founder with a passion for producing the world's best audio signal processing systems. The Dolby logo label is on millions of consumer and industrial audio products. It has become a premier brand used around the world.

There is a personal intimacy in the words used on the web site of the company that Ray Dolby founded. The message reflects the clear passion of a founder committed to what he loves. That passion was the engine of a new enterprise that became the guerrilla gorilla of audio signal processing systems. Here is what the web site says:

> In 1965 Ray Dolby founded Dolby Laboratories, with the initial goal of developing electronic systems for reducing the background noise, such as hiss, introduced by the tape recording process. With the success of those systems and many analog and digital innovations since, the Dolby name has come to be associated worldwide with quality audio from film soundtracks, home theater systems, audio and video cassettes, DVD, TV audio, and cable and satellite transmissions. Ray Dolby makes his home in San Francisco, California, with his wife Dagmar.
>
> Dolby Laboratories develops audio signal processing systems and manufactures professional equipment to implement these technologies in the motion picture, broadcasting, and music recording industries. Dolby's primary commitment is to provide the best possible audio for any entertainment environment, including music, movies, television and multimedia. The privately held company is headquartered in San Francisco, with offices in New York, Los Angeles, Shanghai, Beijing, Tokyo, and European headquarters in England.[9]

Dolby dominates its sector, its category. It remains small by many standards. Yet it dominates and thrives. That does things which are very difficult to do. It has an unfair advantage.

Ray Dolby spotted a fresh opportunity in a new, over-looked market segment: get rid of the hiss in the wave of new consumer audio cassette players. The technology was very difficult to create and deliver affordably, but he and his people triumphed. Their solution was so outstanding that giant me-too corporations could not match it. The company name became synonymous with the best. "You 'gotta have it!" Consumers paid premiums for boomboxes with Dolby inside. But Ray Dolby did not rest on his laurels. He kept moving on to fresh opportunities, creating a moving target, one difficult to attack by competitors. Today Dolby technology is used from the smallest handheld devices to huge movie theater settings. Ray Dolby understands how to be a successful guerrilla.

Most companies do not act like successful guerrillas. Instead, they get started and end up with a very small commodity business where each product or service is undistinguishable from those of many similar competitors. That is not being a successful guerrilla. Do not confuse just plain small with guerrilla. The guerrilla successes are profitable, growing companies, respected around the world. They are also rare.

APPLYING STRATEGIC THINKING

Now you know the four basic strategies. It is time to pick one for your company. Begin by choosing your market leader; that company will be using the defender strategy. Your job is getting easier: you only have to pick from the remaining three. The following is a sequential process to follow that will lead you to your strategic decision.

1. Pick the market leader carefully.

The current market leader is one of several possible companies. The choice is seldom obvious, especially if you are going to invent a product that does not exist today.

The market leader can be "how things are done today."

The status quo is a tough competitor. You can position your new product against the leader of today's solution: workstations against minicomputers, PCs against workstations, PDAs against PCs, cell phones against PDAs, and so on. If you are inventing a new category, creating a first-of-its-kind device, the large company that currently dominates the status quo would be the market leader that you have to compete against. Nokia leads cell phones, Palm leads PDAs, and so on.

It is hard work to convince people to change.

Humans do not rush to change. They wonder if your gadget is worth buying because if they do, they have to switch from what they are comfortable using. Is your product going to be exciting enough to get them to change? What will its value be to them? How painful will the change be? And so on. All of that is measured as the switching cost. What you offer must be compelling enough to overcome the cost of switching from the old way to your new way. Your competition is the reluctance of your targeted customers to change their way of working. Most people do not change quickly or easily, nor do they take on the added risk of new technologies and new companies without weighing the pros and cons before making the buying decision. Inventing ways to convince people to change is part of the art of marketing. It can add a great deal of power to your unfair advantage.

If you are entering an established, crowded market, it is critical to find an overlooked, underserved portion of the larger market.

The market for personal computers in the 1980s was filled with established giants (Apple, IBM, Compaq) and countless wannabe start-ups (PC clones). To become unique in such an intense competitive condition, you must find an overlooked market segment (such as direct sales to PC buyers) and try to dominate it (Dell did). The danger is to immediately give in to the macho temptation to attack the giants (defenders) head-on. That is typically a poor choice of strategy (offensive) for a new enterprise. Without finding an enduring weakness in the defender, attacking using the offensive strategy usually ends in carnage.

2. After choosing the market leader, look for its weaknesses.

Begin looking for openings by surveying the existing market segments.

To which market segments is the gorilla selling? Talk to real end users. Can you find segments the gorilla has overlooked or has paid little attention to ("underserving the market")? Try ranking the underserved or overlooked segments in order of how well the market leader is serving them. Then pick the one you think will prove to be most beneficial for your new enterprise to focus on.

Next, look for something important to the customers—something the leader has overlooked or is unable to deliver.

For the time being, try to avoid the temptation to say, "We will get started by selling a copy of what they are doing—one that is cheaper, faster, and better." That will only lead you into an endless features war: "XYZ Corp has faster devices than GiantCo—until next month." Feature wars seldom win much more than temporary attention from the press. Instead, search for things customers are looking for that the leader either does not provide or provides poorly. Technology enabled Amazon.com to launch with the theme of 1 million books to choose from. New technologies can give breakthrough opportunities (microprocessor versus transistors). Doing something never done before gets lots of attention (computer-aided engineering versus drafting boards). Especially look for something customers are eager for but which cannot be delivered by the market leader (direct sales to customers versus Compaq contractually locked into selling only through retail stores). Your task is to find something especially valuable to a lot of eager, overlooked customers.

3. Test your strategic choice by how well you can defend your chosen position (second-mover advantage).

How easy will it be for the market leader to hurt your company or even crush it? You need to prepare a plan to respond to the most likely reaction of the market leader after your announcement of the launch of your first product. That is what second-mover advantage is all about. Serial entrepreneurs do it well.

Within a few weeks of the launch of the Good Technology's wireless email service, the new enterprise received a legal notice: it was being sued for infringing patents held by the market leader, Research in Motion. Before the shock waves from the reports by the media calmed down, Good announced it had countersued RIM for infringing the patents of Good Technology. Action, reaction, re-reaction. The lawyers will be busy for years. But their response shows how well Good Technology management prepared their second move and retained an advantage.

The strategic stories are in the news every day. They go on and on. The example from Amazon.com also showed how a lead can be not only defended but also strengthened by preparing to respond to competitors' strategic moves. These are but a few of the examples of early-stage applications of strategic moves that reveal how powerful it is to choose the best strategy and to become an ace on the art of applying the principles of strategic maneuvering. The stories also show why a dynamic or responsive strategic plan should be prepared in advance by a new enterprise. Your second moves must be planned to surprise attacking competitors. Investors and key employees will ask about that. Reporters will try to pull it out of you. You have to be able to defend your position on the marketing battlefield. It must be planned.

SUMMARY

Now pause to review your choice of strategy. Test it against the principles of the one you selected. As you begin look for ways to use your strategy to build your unfair advantage, you can further test your choice by addressing these questions:

- What is the new name of the new market segment you are focused on?

- What is the condition of the competition in your targeted market segment?

- How are you going to capture the largest share of that segment?

- How are you going to defend your position in that segment against any attacker?

- How are you going to move and react to the moves of competitors, from the day you launch your first product until the day you launch your third product?

Graphs and tables of market research data will also help you explain to stakeholders the complexities, realism, and strength of your strategy. I find there are a few practical tools used to construct the better start-up strategic plans. Serial entrepreneurs especially document the following:

- Show a time line of key product development and launch dates in monthly detail over the first two years and annually thereafter.

- Describe the timing and reactions of competitors to product introductions—yours and those of other competitors.

- Display your total head count and key hires for each of five years.

- Show sales growth each year, and compare it to the growth of your targeted market.

- Note the dates for first profitability and positive cash flow.

- State when the company has enough success to be ready to go IPO.

10

MARKETING

Quantum mechanics has something in common with three important start-up functions: marketing, selling, and business development. Quantum mechanics explains why very small things behave differently from bigger ones. Similarly, marketing, selling, and business development behave very differently in small, new enterprises than in large corporations. The differences open doors to a new world, filled with creative opportunities to use them to build your unfair advantage.

There are many famous examples of new enterprises that rose to gorilla levels of success using marketing, selling, and business development. Intel used industrial marketing skills to outmaneuver giant Motorola in a fierce battle over microprocessors. JDS Uniphase, king of optical telecommunications components, used business development skills to bind the optical telecommunications industry to its proprietary products. Cisco's early success as the inventor of the digital router was expanded with outstanding selling skills. It then accelerated its climb with a focused business development program that acquired many small high tech start-ups with hot technologies.

Marketing, selling, and business development are closely related. Marketing and selling are like close cousins. Business development includes a bit of both marketing and sales. The trick is not to get these related functions mixed together. Each has a specialized role to play. Confusing their roles will confuse your employees and customers. In the following chapters and Appendix H I will explain how to use each function as you build your unfair advantage. Let's begin with marketing.

MARKETING

In a new enterprise, the marketing function manages a sophisticated process that creates customers. It is often associated with war strategy.

There is an old saying; "War is too important to be left to the generals." David Packard, cofounder of Hewlett-Packard, and others espoused the marketing corollary: "Marketing is too important to be left to the marketing people." Serial entrepreneurs say, "Everyone in the new enterprise has to do it." "Marketing Is Everything" is the title of a classic article by Regis McKenna, one of Silicon Valley's most experienced and creative minds.[1]

Although some engineers sneer at marketing as "evil," it is central to building the competitive strength of a new enterprise. All other departments have a way of gathering around the marketing department, waiting for its leaders to call the next move. Strong marketing can greatly bolster a soft advantage. Technology is not unimportant to building a strong unfair advantage. It is very important. Technology breakthroughs and better mousetraps are common sources of great competitive advantages for new enterprises. But it is rare that a technology breakthrough alone leads a new enterprise to override all competitors. Instead, history shows that companies that use marketing to leverage and exploit technology become kings very often. When a company becomes a king, its name is associated with the new category. Intel means microprocessors. It has become branded.

BRANDING

We live in the century of branding and buying. No longer is selling king. Today, buyers (at home and in the office and factory) are well informed about products (via the Internet and other electronically driven waves of information). They make informed choices on their own. Branding presells their selection of products and services. Brands shorten the purchasing decision. That is why your new enterprise must become excellent at branding.

Branding is about putting a name on a product or company that earns (over years) a reputation because it stands for something valuable. Once branded, the name has a clear meaning that is easily recalled by the customer. Branding a name is like a red-hot iron pushed on the side of a cow's hide—it does not come off. You and I believe it: Volvo is the safest car in the world (even though its cars often rank well below number one in comparative safety tests).

STANDARD SETTING

For high tech companies, branding is similar to setting the industry standard for high tech industrial products. Branding and standard setting are both similar and different. Beware of mixing the two: picking the wrong tools can be hazardous to your unfair advantage health.

To set the high tech standard (brand your company and one of its industrial products), you have to pick a particular reputation you want associated with the name of the company and the product. You may have to join industrial standards-setting committees (such as IEEE committees). You may have to do a lot of speaking at industrial meetings. Whatever you do, your goal is to link your company's name with a special meaning, a unique reputation. That special reputation is what you want to insert into the minds of the customers and other stakeholders. In the consumer world, Hertz means rental cars. Playstation2 means console game players from Sony. Pentium means the leading microprocessors from Intel. SPARC means UNIX work-stations from Sun Microsystems.

Your ultimate marketing win is to have your company name be syn-onymous with the new category you are competing in. That is the same as setting the standard for a new category of electronic hardware or telecommunications or software. When you win, your company name will stand for the new category. Xerox means copy machines. Cisco means routers. SAP means enterprise systems software.

MARKET FOCUS

Setting a standard (in a new technology-intensive market) and brand-ing your company (in a new e-commerce market) require focusing your efforts on doing one thing: finding a single market category to dominate.

Concentration of force and singularity of purpose are critical for suc-cess with new enterprise marketing, according to world-class CEOs of new enterprises. That means you have to pick only one thing to focus on, not a long list. Like children, start-up founders have to be taught the meaning the first word parents teach their children: "No!" First-time entrepreneurs do not like to say no to anything that sounds exciting. They love the adrenaline rush from trying something new. But a sale to the wrong customer can defocus the entire company. Naive entrepreneurs want to sell to everybody because their feelings tell them that if they do not, they might miss big business opportunities. The trouble with accept-ing any purchase from any customer from any industry and any country is that it dissipates scarce resources. Such wild actions send the business in too many different directions. That prevents the tiny start-up from becoming the leader in one market segment. The goal is not to become big and then get famous. Instead, it is to become the dominant leader of a fast-growing new category and earn the reputation as its king of the hill. It demands focus. That requires saying no. The next example is based on a discussion I had with two founders who were passionate about their new enterprise.

Example 10-1   Just Say No: Nagrom and the Caribbean Offer

Nagrom was cofounder of an eleven-month-old bootstrap business in San Francisco operating out of his apartment. He and the other founder were technologists with no business experience. They were the only employees and unable to pay themselves a salary. They were barely able to pay the rent. Their first product was still in a very shaky stage of development. It was not yet a standard piece of software code. The business was far from taking off. The two college graduates were desperate for some sales and cash flow to buy food and stop the landlord from checking in each day.

Nagrom called a business acquaintance, Nhoj, who was doing his third start-up, for a bit of advice. "Did you decide on which customer segment in San Francisco you will focus on?" asked Nhoj. "No, we haven't had the time," answered Nagrom. "But we met this guy at a party who said he could sell a lot for us in the Caribbean. We liked him and he liked us. So I think we should do a deal with him. It would be really cool."

"I must tell you that I disagree with you," said Nhoj. "How about picking one customer group in San Francisco and aiming your first product at them?"

"Well, this guy says he knows lots of different customers on the islands who could use our software once it is modified a bit for each of them. That would bring us tons of sales," said Nagrom. "So I think we will try to do a deal with him. I just wanted to hear what you had to say. But now I have to run, Nhoj. Time is short, as usual. Thanks for your advice. Bye."

Sadly, Nhoj was confident of what would happen to a bootstrap desperate for sale from anyone, anywhere. The future looked dark for Nagrom without a focus on a specific customer segment.

Here is a tip from Gert Kindgren: "One way of thinking focus is to imagine a keyhole. When you look at it from a distance, it's very small. But the closer you get, the more you see inside the room behind the door. Once you put your eye to the keyhole, you might find a whole new world in there: your target market segment!"

Until a core management team learns to say no, its new enterprise cannot focus. Until it focuses, the fledgling business cannot attempt to dominate a part of the market. Without domination, standard setting and branding are not possible. Customers do not know what to think about widespread companies selling their products to anybody. Reporters are confused. So are potential employees. Investors doubt the marketing abilities of the CEO. They have no idea about how the company is positioned in the market.

POSITIONING IN THE MIND

Positioning is about a special kind of focus. This focus is about aiming at a psychological target inside the mind of your ideal customer. That psychology is a significant part of industrial-grade, high technology products. Focused positioning is not just for products advertised on television to consumers. Focus is about aiming at the thinking of your most important customers and ignoring the rest. Focus is about appealing to the emotions of the people at whom you are aiming. Focusing on the mind is not easy, but without it, you will waste precious time and wastefully burn up cash in a new enterprise. You need to pick a narrow, focused target because what you are about to do is very difficult.

Your goal is to fit your product into the mind of the prospective customer. Many engineers mistakenly position the product with numbers and spec sheets for products. However, that is not how the gorillas of tomorrow do it. Positioning is done in the head of the customer, not on a spec sheet. It is a psychological thing, about perceptions and minds. That is very hard to do, especially for technologists who are not good at comprehending people behavior.

When you have positioned with success, you will have created in the mind of the prospective customer the perception that there is no other product on the market quite like yours. It is unique. It slides neatly into a slot between two other competitors in the mind of your ideal customer. No other company can fill your slot. If they do, you will not be able to fit uniquely into the mind of the customer. That is why uniqueness and focus are so important. Investors want to immediately see your positioning when you present your business story. So do reporters and employees.

To position, you require two things: an ideal customer and your competitors. Let's begin with the ideal customer.

THE IDEAL CUSTOMER

Choosing your ideal customer is your next task. You begin by picking (focusing on) your first (very narrow) market segment. That is the one you must become leader of. After that you will add related market segments and use them to continue to grow the company.

 Think as if you are setting up bowling pins, each representing one market segment. Your goal is to begin with bowling pin 1 and become the dominant seller in market segment. Quickly follow with pins 2 and 3, and so on. Knock down the first pin so it knocks down two more. That is efficient. It builds momentum. It accelerates your business. It increases your unfair advantage.

However, picking the first bowling pin (narrow market segment) is trickier than it might seem. It is rare that first-time entrepreneurs get it right on the first try. They typically are not focused enough. They believe big is best, and that means they have to appeal to everybody who owns a cell phone or has heart trouble. But that is a big mistake. It lacks vital focus and bogs the company down. Competitors quickly race past such a defocused company. Try my fictitious example below and then see how focused you are.

Example 10-2   Ideal Customers and Bowling Pins: Downhill Luge Racing

Think about it this way: the techies in your core team have invented a new fabric and have found it is ideal for preventing skin abrasions caused by accidents to participants in extreme sporting events. In the form of outerwear, it takes on a sexy, wet look. The question is, To which customers should it be sold first?

You decide to begin with some basic market planning. You remember that each market segment is represented as a conceptual bowling pin but is actually a real person, a special person who fits a tight demographic profile. You have your core team spend a week talking to a lot of people in the twenty-something crowd. Everyone comes back enthused, with lots of information. You sift through it, and suddenly it hits you! "Our number 1 bowling pin should be eighteen- to twenty-three-year-old females with green hair who are left-handed and do downhill summer luging in southeastern Oslo!" They all cheer. That is focus!

"So what will our second bowling pin be?" asks your chief engineer.

"That's simple," you answer. "It will be the nineteen- to twenty-five-year-old males who chase them down the hill! They are related, have similar interests, and read much of the same materials. They meet in similar venues. They'll be reached by nearly the same messages we use on the number 1 group. That's awesome!"

That is also a great deal of efficiency. It is what builds momentum. It all starts with focus on the ideal customer.

NEXT CUSTOMERS

You must also carefully pick the follow-on customer segments. Who are the best customers to be numbers 2 and 3? In what sequence will you line up your bowling pins? Why is that important? Because if you pick wisely, life becomes much more efficient for a fledgling start-up with limited resources. For instance, buyers representing numbers 2 and 3 read and talk and think and behave like their friends in group 1. They share the same sports, same magazines, same trade shows, same television shows, same, same, same. They are related yet unique. There is overlap of each of the three groups, each subset, each market segment. Together they make up the larger overall market that your company is targeting, the one it is serving. The smaller pieces fit together to make the big picture. They belong together. They are your source of momentum and lift-off.

After you have identified your first bowling pin, you can move on. Find pins 2 and 3. Line them up in a careful sequence. The first pin must hit the next two pins, building your momentum: pin 1 becomes pin 3 becomes pin 7 and so on. Then you are on your way.

THE POSITIONING ROLE FOR YOUR COMPETITION

Next you must prepare to position your product offering in the mind of your ideal customer. You must position against a competitor. Your product will be compared with alternative offerings. Remember a new enterprise has competitors in two basic categories:

- Existing companies doing things "the old way."

- New enterprises that come in two flavors:

  - Me-too copycats (They will quickly try to do the same thing you are doing, but a bit better.)

  - Stealth start-ups (They are secret businesses focused on the same customers you are aiming at.)

Choose who the market leader is in your new market category. It may be a large public corporation selling old products made with old technology. Or it may be a new enterprise that has pioneered the new market category you are seeking to dominate. You must pick one company, by name, as your competitor to position against.

Then create a message that describes the value your product, service or solution will add to the ideal customer. Your positioning message must be unique. It must excite your customer to act. When it works well, it will cause the customer to decide in your favor. For instance, upon reading your positioning message on your company web site, the customer would be motivated to send your business development manager an email requesting contact by a salesperson.

Your message will position your offering in the mind of your targeted person. It is very psychological. It fits an empty slot in the mind of your ideal customer. That slot cannot be occupied by a competitor. You must fit an empty slot. Your positioning message should not be me-too or better. It must be unique.

The more you know about the market leader that is your prime competitor, the better your positioning message will be. Especially keep in mind that, as you launch your products, your positioning message will begin to shift because your competitors react to it. Review the earlier sections about competition, especially Chapters 1 and 2, and the materials on strategy. Focus on figuring out how the CEO of the market leader will react after you announce your first product. Learning how the CEO behaves under competitive attack will add a very powerful element to your unfair advantage.

Do not worry about stealth start-ups. Just keep listening to the rumors and try tracking down the sources. Typically where there is smoke, there is fire. But many new enterprises never get funded. However, accept the possibility that you may be second to market with your wonderful idea. Or that the stealth start-up that follows you may leapfrog your technology. Deal with such problems when they arrive. Work on finding facts, not feeding on fiction. Meanwhile, pick the existing market leader as your prime competitor and stay focused on building your unfair advantage.

VALUE PROPOSITION

Next on your list of to-dos is to figure out your value proposition. This was discussed in detail earlier, so a brief reminder will suffice here. Recall that your objective is to make your product so appealing to your ideal customers that they rush to purchase it. Exactly what will make it wildly compelling? What is it that will get the customers excited? Is it only the blue paint? Or is it better service? Is it extremely handy? Is it a huge time saver? Just what is it that gets customers panting for more?

Discovering the value proposition is definitely not intuitively obvious. In fact, history suggests it is intuitively nonobvious. If it is hard to see, that gives you another advantage (because you see it and your competitors don't). That advantage is good, but it will require extra effort to help your customers see it with their own eyes.

Your goal is to create a value proposition so attractive that the products leap off the shelf. "Our products sell themselves!" To write a compelling value proposition, consider these tips from the ranks of the start-up veterans of marketing wars:

- Be clear about precisely what the product or service will do. "How does it work?" is not what you want to hear after you finish your sales presentation. Draw pictures. Give examples. Do demonstrations. I have found out the hard way that even the most simple-sounding new device (such as a new kind of ladder) may be clear to you, but it rarely is to first-time listeners. What is "way cool" to you is typically "way unclear" to someone who has never before seen your invention. Take time to be very clear what your product or service will do to benefit the end user.

- "Save me time or save me money." Most value propositions can be boiled down to one or both of two benefits: saving time or saving money. Potential customers demand at least one of those two. Find out which is compelling to the end user of your first product.

- Value propositions have numbers. Translate the compelling words to quantified benefits: "It will save you over 40 percent of the current hospital cost to replace an artificial hip." Or "The cost to upgrade your existing systems is greatly reduced: half the time to install and one-quarter the monthly maintenance cost."

- Continue to advance your value proposition so it becomes even more attractive to the end user. Once you have crafted the first version of your value proposition, work hard to make it more compelling. "Our PDA screen is the only one in the world able to display purple!" is not a strong value proposition. This one is stronger: "Our PDA shows DVD streaming movies for less than the cost of going to the movie theater." Keep pushing for modifications that resonate with customers. That adds a great deal more to a competitive advantage.

In competitively crowded markets, value propositions that are strong and unique are difficult to create. In a commodity market, it is nearly impossible to invent a compelling one. For instance, by 2000, the disk drive market had become a vast offering of products from many suppliers. To consumers, all disk drives were alike; they wanted only the lowest price per gigabyte. The only value proposition in a commodity market is lower price. That is a very difficult situation for a start-up to try to compete in. Another crowded market is PDAs. By 2002 PDA marketing wars were being fought between entrenched and emerging competitors, many of them struggling to gain an advantage over others. Start-ups were not eager to enter the ruthless battleground. In such competitively intensive conditions, weak value propositions become common even from the most famous and revered corporations. Consider the following statement from a press release of a respected world giant about one of its new PDA products.

Example 10-3   Value Proposition: Sony Personal Digital Appliance
Press Release

Announcing the NZ90 Color CLIÉ™ Handheld w/ 2 Mega-pixel Camera PEG-NZ90. The new Palm Powered™ PEG-NZ90 CLIÉ™ handheld pushes the envelope of handheld computing, featuring the new Palm OS® v. 5.0. as well as an ARM-compliant 200 MHz CPU for enhanced overall performance and exceptional multimedia experience.[2]

That is more of a list of technology and features than a value proposition. It has buzzwords, a few numbers and techie-sounding acronyms. But the message does not tell potential buyers how much time or money they will save by using this new PDA. This product may be way cool, but the appeal is not obvious from the words chosen in that value proposition.

TALK TO POTENTIAL CUSTOMERS

How can you avoid such bad mistakes? I recommend you do sample tests of value propositions on potential customers. Talk to them. Ask them questions. That will tell you how compelling your value proposition really is. Remember that by the time you launch your first product, you want the dog so eager to eat your dog food that he starts tearing at the bag before you get it open. Ask real people—your potential customers—what gets them excited (or bored) about your idea for a new product. Listen. Take notes. Don't forget to ask the customers about the "whole product." Experts take weeks of intensive effort to craft the questions and diagnose the responses. The findings are a source of power. Cisco asked customers what was needed, and that led to its end-to-end solution message. Remember to keep modifying your proposition like the sculptor shaping a clay statue. The more you learn, the more you alter the message. Continue the hard work until your value proposition gets a lot of your targeted customers very excited. Then you are ready to go on to use additional marketing tools to strengthen your unfair advantage.

POSITIONING MESSAGE

With your value proposition completed, you are ready to create a specific message for the ideal customer. That is central to your marketing communications plan (marcom). Your message will consist of the words and graphics that excite and especially appeal to your ideal customers. It is a powerful, compelling message. That short declaration is called your *positioning statement*. It is like a brief story about your differences compared with your competition. It is very, very important. It is hard, hard work. Do it with excellence. It is one place that outside experts, professional marketing communications specialists, can earn their keep. The following example is based on material from a real start-up. It shows careful crafting of a message focused on the targeted customers of a new enterprise.

Example 10-4   Positioning Statement: Notiva

"Notiva provides Trade Settlement solutions that streamline and optimize the financial settlement processes between retailers, wholesalers and manufacturers. With Notiva, trading partners are able to:

- Make and receive optimal payments
- Collaboratively and immediately resolve disputes
- Reduce costs and cycle times
- Improve trade relationships

Find out what Notiva can do for you."[3]

Note how the Notiva positioning message emphasizes specific benefits to the customer. It includes a value proposition in words. The precise numbers needed for a strong value proposition will be left for the salesperson to work out in private consultation with each customer. Every business plan needs both a value proposition and a positioning statement. After you have finished crafting your own position statement, you are ready to choose the best way to communicate it to your ideal customers.

MARCOM CHANNELS: PUBLIC RELATIONS, ADVERTISING, AND OTHERS

When you have completed your positioning statement, you need to get it in front of prospective customers, strategic partners, and recruiting candidates. That is what marketing communications, marcom, is about. There are many creative choices. Pick carefully. Start by choosing the best channel or media for your carefully crafted message. Choose wisely because an error can weaken an otherwise strong positioning advantage. Let's examine two of the most popular: public relations and advertising.

Your prime marcom objective is to get people talking eagerly about your company and its products. That is what is meant by getting the word-of-mouth working for you. Good products get talked about because they are exciting and appeal to a lot of new customers. News about great products spreads like a wildfire. Great marketing starts the fire and fans the flames. As word flies around the world via email, at lunch talks, during gossip at the fitness center, on Internet news reports, from trade show panels, and so on, your marcom results get cheaper and cheaper by the minute. Soon your competition is depressed, envying how easy it seems for you to reach new customers. That is what you want your marketing people to accomplish with marcom, very quickly, very inexpensively.

So what does a CEO have to do? You spend millions on advertising to spread the word. Right? Wrong! Just the opposite. First-time entrepreneurs have not learned the secret.

Serial entrepreneurs know they win most often when reporters jump to write stories about a cool new product. Other reporters see the story and jump in to report about your company and its new product. They don't want to be left out, missing the next great thing. That starts a media wave that can become a feeding frenzy. Soon news races around the globe about your new enterprise and its cool products. Customers take notice. Strategic partners are pleased. That does not happen if reporters are bored. If it is not worth writing about, it means your ideal customer is also going to be bored. Huge amounts of spending on advertising cannot overcome that. A dull product is not improved with megabuck media spending. Trying to use million-dollar media campaigns to overcome market rejection of boring products is like spending money for a cover-up paint job on an inferior car that no one wants to buy. It is still an inferior car.

The other alternative is to use public relations. That choice begins by creating products that customers are eager to buy. You can use testimonials of your first customers (reference accounts) to "prove" people love your product. The exciting news is spread using public relations. PR is the preferred marcom tool of choice for veteran high tech CEOs. It is quick, affordable, and reliable.

There are two reasons that experienced leaders of new enterprises favor PR over advertising:

- Public relations efforts are more efficient than advertising. PR is much less expensive than advertising too. New enterprises in the United States can get world-class PR firms to do a good job for a monthly cost equal to a half-page of advertising in the back of a single high tech magazine. PR generates more bang for the buck.

- Public relations results are more certain with less waste. With PR, you know exactly when you have gotten the results: "Wow! We were quoted as a 'company to watch' in the front page article in *EE Times!*" With PR, you are sure about the results but cannot guarantee what the reporter will say about your company. But with advertising, it is the opposite: you are sure of the message and unsure of the results. You wrote the advertising words that were printed. However, you do not know if your ideal customer read your advertisement. The trick with PR is to get mentioned favorably. That is why picking a great PR firm is so important to serial entrepreneurs. They have their favorites. Great PR firms learn your story, help make it even more compelling, and know which reporters will be interested. Some PR firms are especially good at getting results for new enterprises.

Of course, your start-up will advertise in some way, but be careful not to use advertising for the wrong purpose. Research in consumer marketing during the past decade shows advertising is best for defending a brand, not building it; PR is best for building a brand.[4] Picking the reverse is like burning money: it is expensive and generates only a little heat for a short period of time. Perhaps you remember how hot advertising was during the Internet boom. Try to name any of the advertised products for the million-dollar advertisements on television for the American Football League's SuperBowl of 1999 or 2000 or 2001.

MORE MARCOM CHOICES

Besides PR and advertising there are many marcom tools to choose from. You can assemble a collection of them to create a marcom plan that overwhelms competitors. The italicized terms in the list of popular marcom choices in Table 10-1 have been used with success by high technology start-ups.

Table 10-1 Marketing Communication Tools

Backgrounder	Personal letters
Public relations	*Brochures*
Trade shows	Classified advertisements
Magazine advertisements	Newspaper daily advertisements
Television commercials	Radio spots
Yellow Pages	Events
Direct mail	Advertising specialties
Seminars	Sampling
Circulars	Signs on bulletin boards
User groups	*Internet ads*

SOURCE: *Nesheim Group.*

MARKET CALENDAR

Now create a calendar for the two years after your first product launch. Use a time line with events and dates, spelling out how, when, and where you will use each of the marcom tools you have chosen.

MARKET NUMBERS

With your marcom plan finished, you are ready to proceed to answer one of the most common questions asked of founder CEOs: How big is your market? That's a tricky question to answer because the market does not yet exist. But veterans know how to measure it and forecast its growth without blindly guessing.

New enterprise marketing people love numbers. They like to count the largest number of potential customers over the next three to five years. They use a top-down approach. They work down a funnel, from the top of its large opening to the bottom with its tiny opening. They narrow the market by dividing it into slices, and into smaller and smaller segments. Then they count the number of users in each market segment, estimate the average price customers would pay for products in each segment, and forecast how fast their new business sales will grow and what portion (share) the sales are of the narrow, targeted market.

Let's demonstrate that with an example of how to count a market that does not yet exist. Though the characters are fictitious, it shows how I observed serial entrepreneurs measure their new markets.

Example 10-5   Measuring the Size of a New Market: Avi and Surlock

Avi has an idea for a new enterprise that he has named Surlok Inc. It will sell a new kind of electronic security key to users of wireless devices concerned with loss or theft of their handheld cell phones and personal digital assistants. Avi thinks he can sell a hardware key for the handheld device that works through a server-based Internet service to authenticate the user. How big is his potential market?

Avi starts with rough estimates. He begins by estimating the largest thinkable industry segment. He looks for the number of wireless devices: about 400 million were sold in the world in 2003, according to several free reports he got from Wall Street research analysts. He calls this TAM (total available market).

Next, Avi counts the target ideal customers for the first product rollout next year. The customers use cell phones and PDAs and are mobile executives and sales personnel of corporations with annual sales over $1 billion. He calculates that 1,000 corporations × 5,000 employees × 10% of the target customers = 500,000, the number of units (i.e., people who might use his product). He calls this SAM (served available market). He thinks the SAM market segment will grow about 10 percent per year or more worldwide for the foreseeable future.

Then Avi estimates how fast his company will sell units each year and what portion his sales will be of SAM. He calls this SOM (share of market). Avi puts his first estimates of sales into a simple spreadsheet model. He thinks that 5,000 end user keys will be sold in Year 1 for a small share of the market (5,000 units sold / 500,000 units of SAM = 1% SOM). After a bit of additional thinking, Avi estimates he can sell 50,000 in Year 2 (10% SOM), and 100,000 in year 3 (20% SOM).

As for the servers, Avi believes he can sell one server for every 100 users and get $25,000 for each server. He thinks that if he prices the keys at $1 each, he will attract lots of end users.

He returns to his spreadsheet model and calculates dollars of sales. That includes sales of servers and keys for each year.

For example, Sales in Year 3 = (100K users / [100 users/1 server]) × $25K/server + (100K users × $1.00/user) = $25M + $100K = $25.1M of total sales for the company. (K means thousands and M is for millions.)

Avi adds those numbers to the marketing section of his business plan. After a few days, he returns to the forecast and decides to do more research aimed at improving the realism of his first estimates. He will focus on how fast SAM will grow each year and will look for better industry and geographical segmentations (new bowling pins).

Meanwhile, he tells his core team to begin to start a spreadsheet model of the market forecast for product family number two.

FOCUSING ON ZEROS

Avi and experienced entrepreneurs know they should focus on zeros, not the first digit. Getting the number of zeros right is more important than the first digit. Small markets do not attract money or top talent. Large markets have lots of zeros.

The market numbers must be large enough to create a company big enough to go IPO on NASDAQ within five years.

That requires at least $30 million of sales that will grow at least 30 to 100 percent per year over the next five years following the IPO date.

That level of sales will create at least $100 million of stock market wealth, the lowest size NASDAQ is interested in. How can your company get that big? That is up to you and your plan for creating an unfair advantage. Figure it out as quickly as possible. Small companies do not get venture capital backing.

The share of market sweet spot is between 3 and 30 percent in three years.

At 30 percent, you are a gorilla. You dominate. You are the leader of the new market segment. Below 3 percent, you are too small to be important and are not very interesting. Very small SOM percentages suggest you have overestimated your SAM and have to focus more. Very large SOM percentages suggest that you are not realistic; you are overly optimistic about capturing market share in the face of competition. Above 30 percent is king-of-the-hill country. It is hard work and takes a lot of time to get there. Domination is seldom attained before at least three years have passed.

Real entrepreneurs do not spend time doing sensitivity analysis.

There is too much uncertainty in the forecasts of fledgling markets and sales of start-ups to do what financial analysts call sensitivity analysis. The new enterprises frequently grow 100 percent and more each year in markets that did not exist last year. However, large numbers of MBAs do careful sensitivity analysis for giants that grow 3 percent a year in established markets spewing out tons of statistics. In contrast, founders of new enterprises begin with a rough model of their nonexisting target market and begin improving it day by day as more and more is learned. That never stops. That is how start-up marketing people begin quantifying something from nothing.

Modeling your market adds to your unfair advantage.

Knowing realistically how small or large a planned customer base might be is a key to planning how to hire and spend. It will guide you in tempering and moderating planned spending on expensive marketing and selling personnel and their activities. Modeling the workings of a market gives great insight about how much to spend on marketing. Modeling also helps you think methodically about how ideal customers will perceive your product offering (how fast they will begin to purchase it). It helps you sharpen your value proposition (what portion of early adopters will be eager to buy the first product). Keep in mind that your model is not a prediction of how your sales will turn out. Instead, it is a model of the possibilities of what could happen. It is part of your story. Take time to prepare the numbers well. Be realistic. Be creative. And please, don't be off by one zero, either way!

11

SALES

The sales function can add considerable strength to your competitive advantage. It is the intensive process that converts customers to invoices. Its power is founded on the (1) persuasive skills of the selling personnel and (2) choice of which sales channels to go through to reach the customer. Great selling skills have made many start-ups go world-class in spite of competitors' offering technically superior products. Clever choices of sales channels have propelled slow-moving new enterprises to leapfrog a leader and become king of a new hill. History has outstanding examples of new enterprises that used the sales function to become dominant in their new categories.

Example 11-1   Companies Founded on Sales Intensity

- **IBM** was founded on the bedrock of selling. Its founder committed to creating what became the finest selling organization in the electronic computer world. The upstart new enterprise quickly overtook pioneer Univac and left it in the dust.
- **Oracle** was launched by a CEO who was passionate about selling and attracted others who loved to sell. The company rapidly rose past technically superior software database competitors such as Sybase, emerging to become the dominant leader.
- **Cisco** was led by career salesmen. The board of directors chose successive CEOs from among highly competitive selling managers. The company rocketed ahead of other telecommunications competitors to become the global champion of routers.

SOURCE: *Nesheim Group.*

There are many clever ways to make selling more effective for your new enterprise. It is not just about how to pick the slickest-talking salespeople. There is a lot more to creative selling that can add to your unfair advantage. Consider the following; there are many more.

LEAPFROG THE COMPETITORS THAT ARE ALREADY SELLING THEIR FIRST PRODUCTS

An example of a way to do this is with a special deal with a selling giant like IBM. If it integrates your tiny product with its larger system solutions, you get instant access to a powerful worldwide selling force. That is how a start-up can create a global reach overnight via an established product and sales network. Sales will start almost immediately.

ACCELERATE THE CONSTRUCTION OF A WORLDWIDE SALES ORGANIZATION THAT WILL HELP LAUNCH YOUR FIRST PRODUCT

Let's say you are a start-up in Boulder, Colorado, and want to sell immediately in China and Europe. Try signing top independent sales representative firms in key cities in China and Europe. Your sales employees can then focus on North America. Outsourcing selling to established sales organizations has worked very well for new enterprises, wave after wave. You avoid the expense and hassle of recruiting an army of salespeople in cities flung all over the globe. Related to sales reps are distributors—the middlemen who not only sell for you but also buy products from you and deliver them to customers. Sales reps and distributors are quick ways to build a world-class sales staff.

Example 11-2   Choice of Sales Channels: BioKo Labs

Following is an excerpt from the real business plan of BioKo Labs, a private new enterprise planning on selling a new kind of intelligent, software-based, diagnostic tool to biotechnology laboratories specializing in genetic research applied to forensics. (I disguised the name of the company.)

Strategic Partners

Our first bowling pin is a collection of scientists working in one of the innovative American biotechnology laboratories. The best way to get our software to them will be through the already available distributors such as VWR Scientific and Fisher. These distributors reach out to all corners of our industry. By outsourcing our software distribution to them, we would ensure that our software would be accessible to many more companies than we could visit in one year with a direct sales force of our own employees. Distributors keep close contact with their customer companies, including the latest online real time customer response software systems. The distributors are very well positioned to meet our requirements for both sales and customer support. This channel will get our products to the doorstep of our targeted customers very quickly with top quality sales personnel.

Outsourcing our distribution would allow BioKo Labs maximum market penetration and greatest customer satisfaction from a purely product distribution standpoint. The disadvantage of outsourcing our distribution channel is that it will reduce our profit margin significantly. However, distributors would still be our most feasible option in terms of distributing cost as it would be more costly to have an in-house sales and distribution unit that reaches out to target companies to the scale of the distributors.

Here is another example of a new enterprise that focused on the sales function to build its unfair advantage. I learned the power of such focus while working as an executive for National Semiconductor.

Example 11-3   Sales Creativity Boosts Advantage: National Semiconductor

In the early days of semiconductors, the market gorillas were Texas Instruments and Fairchild Semiconductor. A new arrival, National Semiconductor, pioneered the use of regional distributors and independent sales representative firms. This expanded its market (reached more medium and smaller companies) and accelerated sales. National was able to "rent" instead of hire the best sellers in the industry. The gorillas followed, reluctantly, much later. In less than a decade, National rose from a small company to a world-class giant.

After you have chosen the best channels for selling your products, you are ready to pick the next sales tools. Besides sales channels, there are many other tools to use to create your sales plan. For instance, intensive sales training of direct selling personnel can distinguish sales representatives from those of competitors. And technology can boost the effectiveness of field salespeople.

SPEND EXTRA TIME TRAINING THE SALES FORCE.

Some veteran start-up CEOs insist on this. The objective is to sharpen the skills of the sales personnel before sending them to customers so they are more prepared than the competition. Those CEOs think it is an excellent investment because it helps also build an esprit de corps into the selling team that inspires the entire company to outperform competitors.

USE TECHNOLOGY TO BOOST THE EFFECTIVENESS OF SELLING PEOPLE IN THE FIELD.

Use of special communications systems can boost sales per person in the field. Examples include the use of wireless PDAs, cell phones, and laptops to speed information to your sales force when they are conducting selling presentations. The latest presentations can be downloaded at the customer site before the next presentation. IT systems can boost efficiencies when sending orders back to the factory by speeding the process and reducing errors.

There are many innovative ways to use sales to add to your unfair advantage. Gert Kindgren likes to dig into the details of the sales cycle and build a model. He begins with the selling time required from first step to the final step that gets the order. He uses the model to calculate how large a sales force will be required. He then proceeds to model early sales, starting with the first list of companies likely to purchase the first product. It has been his experience that "the sales cycle model is the one thing that binds all activities and processes together in a sales organization. It also gives investors and the CEO some comfort when judging the sales figures, sales planning and management of the sales activities."

A strong, creative sales function in your company will convert your value proposition into real orders. That's what it's all about. So get serious about your sales planning. In sales leadership, the saying is, "Failing to plan is planning to fail!" Get your core team together and figure out what you want to do to make sales a big part of your unfair advantage.

12

BUSINESS DEVELOPMENT

Where does the function known as business development (BD) fit? In-between marketing and sales. Dubbed *biz dev,* it is typically a separate function from marketing and sales. It has special characteristics and responsibilities.

SPECIAL MIX OF SKILLS

The BD person is the key to doing deals with giant strategic partners, early customers, and critical suppliers. The position also demands excellent selling skills such as convincing giant corporations to do contracts with a tiny start-up. The job is also part chief financial officer. BD requires a lot of knowledge about legal and financial matters, including securities law. The person doing BD needs to be a great communicator and strategist. It is a demanding job in any company. In some ways, the biz dev job is a jack-of-all-trades position. Few people are great at it. The job is best done by a veteran who is skilled at making quick contacts with key industry leaders and is clever in negotiating big deals with early customers and strategic partners, typically large corporations. Biz dev adds a lot of credibility to a fledgling organization when such deals are signed and publicized.

SCOUT FOR THE COMPANY

The BD job in a new enterprise is like being the guide for a hungry group of people anxiously looking to catch big fish quickly. "Where can we find a lot of eager customers fastest?" The BD goal is to rapidly identify a hot target market that the company can focus on. Then the marketing leader can decide how best to appeal to customers in that segment so that sales personnel have a better chance of getting sales traction with the first product. Remember that your ideal market does not yet exist, and it does not yet have a dominant leader. The BD job helps find the new market. The work is very demanding, and quite futuristic, and is filled with big unknowns. That is why it is both exciting and very hard to do. Some people love such responsibilities and do it very well, adding a lot to the unfair advantage of the new enterprise.

FUNDING

The BD leader often negotiates much of the terms of the seed round (first round) of the funding of the start-up. CEOs need help, and funding takes a lot of time. Lawyers negotiate details of each round of funding, working closely (cell phone calls every hour) with the core team. A CEO can offload much of that time-consuming work to a competent BD leader.

NEW BUSINESS DEVELOPMENT TREND

Over the past decade, I have seen a recent trend in BD in new enterprises: it is becoming common to see a VP of business development in the first days of a start-up. The BD job has become popular for an energetic cofounder who is soon flying, driving, calling, emailing, and meeting in a furious flurry of activity during the early formation phase of a new enterprise.

ORGANIZATION CHANGE ISSUES

Such people are instrumental in contributing to strategic plans, getting contracts signed by large corporations, and finding real customers for the first product launch. Later, a vice president of marketing will be hired. And a few months before product launch, a vice president of sales will be added.

Tip: The first BD leader can be threatened by the addition of highly competent marketing and selling vice presidents. If you are prepared for that emotional response, you can avoid an awkward transition. Most of the time I see the first BD leader very reluctant to give up responsibilities for marketing and selling to the new vice president, especially if the VP of biz dev is a cofounder. If you plan on such a transition, the hand-off will be less bumpy.

13

STRATEGIC PARTNERS

Strategic partners can add considerable strength to a fledgling enterprise. By working together, they increase the chances of outmaneuvering the competition. A new enterprise whose strategic partners have marquee names like Genentech ("founder of the biotechnology industry") and Qualcomm ("pioneer of code division multiplexing, CDMA") add instant credibility to a new enterprise. They remove doubt (about the survival of your start-up). They add credibility (that your products really work). They suggest you will be around for a long time (and that you are a real business). Research and development can be shared. Duplication of work and expensive equipment can be avoided. Industry knowledge can be exchanged and discussed. Time to set an industry standard can be accelerated. Any and all of those reasons should be explicitly added to your business plan.

Strategic partners should be seen as more valuable than simply famous names associated with your new enterprise. Earlier I mentioned how Good Technology used special relations with IBM and Microsoft to enlarge its competitive advantage. Adding strategic partners to the plan for a new enterprise has become a way of life for new enterprises.

The choice of strategic partners depends on what you want from them. Engineering can use strategic partners to integrate mutually beneficial technologies that become superior products. Sales can use them to gain additional channels to customers. Marketing can use them to gain access to larger customers more quickly. They help gain the attention of stronger PR firms and add a boost to the company's positioning as the new industry's new leader. Customer support can delegate to partners first-line contact with end users. The manufacturing department can leave the production headaches (of running a hectic factory filled with hourly paid employees) to an outsourced services partner so the new enterprise's staff can focus on quality and cost control management. Human resources can use strategic partners to recruit more rapidly. Finance can use strategic partners to do the simple, boring accounting work until the company is large enough to hire its own finance staff.

The following example demonstrates how to use careful planning and choice of strategic partners to build unfair advantage. The three founders were very deliberate and calculating in their selections.

Example 13-1   Choosing Strategic Partners: NanInc

NanInc is a new enterprise that plans to sell microscopic identification markers that protect brand watches and other expensive luxury consumer items. Here is its plan for strategic partners.

Strategic Partners

Our strategic partners will be companies specialized in laser and optical instrumentation for biotechnology and nanotechnology applications, especially Perkin Elmer, Beckham Coulter, and Applied Biosystems. We will outsource to them the manufacturing of NanInc hand held readers. This will focus our mutual resources on the first critical entry point into the new nano identification market segment. We will merge our R&D in nano identification devices with their specialty in customizing optical and laser scanners.

In addition, this partnership will further strengthen NanInc's potential to set the standard for covert identification systems. This provides our partners the special opportunity to get a virtual lock on the new hand held laser reader manufacturing market.

We will be committed to developing long-standing and meaningful relationships with companies who share our vision of achieving mutual success by delivering the best customer solution in this new market.

Our network of partnerships will include alliances and collaborations with leading universities. Cornell, Stanford and the National University of Singapore are the first. Their laboratories are leading several areas of nanotechnology research and will ease the engineering of our first products. They will also be part of our campaign to get industry to adopt as a standard our method of nano identification. We gain access to expensive equipment in their labs and research institutes and leverage their expertise. They benefit with monetary returns, our state-of-the-art applied technology, and the industry knowledge we possess. We represent a source of jobs and consulting work for their researchers and students. Most important, we both benefit from the experience of working together.

Finally, we will liaise with the International Anti-counterfeit Coalition towards building a standard in covert nano identification applications. We will leverage their broad industry networks and reputation in global anti-counterfeiting protection. In return, IACC will benefit from our sponsorship of their activities and using our technology as a platform to achieve more credibility for promoting anti-counterfeiting.[1]

BUSINESS MODEL

Assemble your business model using the strategic partners as building blocks. Surround your company with them, using arrows to show who delivers and receives what for how much. Add customers and outsourced services. Show distribution channels. Put it all together in a graphic something like this:

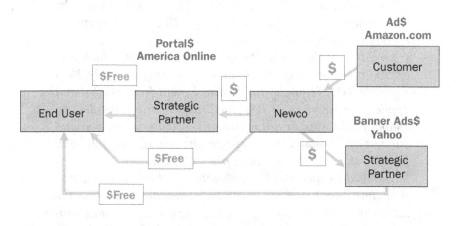

Figure 13-1 Graphic of a Business Model

You can get very creative with business models. However, as noted earlier, experiment with new business models only if it adds a great deal to building a powerful competitive advantage. One bold example is from Salesforce.com, the San Francisco start-up which chose an on-demand delivery model rather than the traditional sale and license model for software businesses. Here is how the company described their business model in the IPO prospectus:

> *The pervasiveness of the Internet, along with the dramatic declines in the pricing of computing technology and network bandwidth, have enabled a new generation of enterprise computing in which substantial components of information technology, or IT, infrastructure can be provisioned and delivered dynamically on an outsourced basis. This new computing paradigm is sometimes referred to as utility computing, while the outsourced software applications are referred to as on-demand application services. On-demand application services enable businesses to subscribe to a wide variety of application services that are developed specifically for, and delivered over, the Internet on an as-needed basis with little or no implementation services required and without the need to install and manage third-party software in-house. The market for on-demand application services is projected to grow from $425 million in 2002 to $2.6 billion in 2007, which represents a compounded annual growth rate of 44 percent, according to a May 2003 report by International Data Corporation, or IDC, an independent market research firm.*
>
> *We believe that the CRM applications market, which was approximately $7.1 billion in 2002 according to a July 2003 report by IDC, is one of the first to benefit from on-demand application services. CRM applications are intended to enable businesses to automate sales, customer service and support, and marketing. Despite the significant potential benefits that can be attained from CRM, many enterprises have failed to successfully deploy the CRM applications that they have purchased for a variety of reasons including the difficulty and relatively high cost of implementing and maintaining enterprise applications, as well as the historically low rates of user adoption and lack of ubiquitous access that have contributed to lower returns on investment in CRM deployments.*
>
> SOURCE: *U.S. Securities and Exchange Commission, EDGAR database, document 424B1, June 23, 2004.*

All functions of a new enterprise can find ways to use strategic partners. Partners can also be other start-ups that symbiotically benefit each other. Some experienced CEOs have even figured out how to make competitors into strategic partners. An example is the open systems concept used by UNIX and Linux server companies. Vice presidents of business development have learned how to seek out and craft deals that turn into mutually beneficial partnerships. Venture investors can bring access to giants that otherwise would not talk to you. As you can imagine, this is a field ripe for innovation and power building. It can greatly boost your unfair advantage.

The next section in the business plan examines how to use customer service to boost your unfair advantage further. Customer service often includes strategic partners and is an exciting area for partnership collaboration as well as for creative innovation. New enterprises increasingly use it to leapfrog competitors that have a head start, particularly when a new market does not yet have a leader.

14

CUSTOMER SUPPORT

Dell is famous for its customer support, and it has become a cornerstone of the company's unfair advantage. Customer service has enabled many new enterprises to get to IPO and become established as outstanding emerging-growth companies. New enterprises have often achieved fame by relying heavily on their customer support function to boost their advantages. In the following example from the health industry, note how the Boston-based start-up Health Dialog, a strategic partner of giant Siebel Systems, used customer support to launch a new enterprise with a competitive advantage.

Example 14-1 Customer Support Boosts Advantage: Health Dialog and Siebel Systems

Health Dialog is a venture-backed start-up that provides educational tools to help its customers make health care decisions. Its integrated suite of products and services comprises health care knowledge that enables health care institutions and employers to effectively reach and engage their members with a fresh form of collaborative health care management. By helping patients and doctors communicate more effectively, Health Dialog products and services focus on helping improve the overall quality of health care while lowering the costs of delivering that care.

The business model of Health Dialog is to make money by integrating into health service customers a new customer response software system provided by Siebel Systems. Health Dialog focuses on adding value by providing competitively superior customer service, particularly offering access to special medical information for health professionals.

Health Dialog is featured by the giant Siebel Systems (strategic partner) on the Siebel web site, where it trumpets the partnership as an outstanding example of a mutually beneficial success:

> Health Dialog: Siebel Alliance Partner. In a mere 90 days, Health Dialog deployed Siebel Call Center in its rapidly growing customer service center, enabling health coaches to better focus on the patient. Health Dialog says: "At our call center, health coaches want to focus on the caller. They don't want to be distracted by multiple screens or have to weave their way through multiple web sites. With Siebel Call Center, our health coaches can view complete customer profiles on our 26,000-page knowledge base from a single, intuitive screen.
>
> - Improves member satisfaction through more effective call handling
> - Increases staff productivity
> - Scales to handle projected membership base of 30 million members
> - Reduces user training time.[1]

This example is one of many innovative ways to use customer support to boost an unfair advantage. Taking time to carefully craft a superior advantage using customer support is worth the required time and effort. If you are looking for differentiation, try customer support. That can work especially well if other companies already occupy key positions and are already entrenched as the market's leaders of technology, or selling, or marketing. Your company can then compete as the outstanding customer support leader in the new market.

Next, let's proceed to Operations. The Operations section of your story includes the following:

- Engineering and Technology

- Legal and Intellectual Property

- Manufacturing, Outsourcing and Internet Operations

- Information Services

- Management and Key Personnel

- Facilities and Administration
- Financial Plan
- Valuation and Ownership

15

ENGINEERING AND TECHNOLOGY

Creating an unfair advantage by using the engineering function means you will be a master of the art of exploiting technology. Real engineers make real products for the real world. They use technology but don't worship it. Veterans of high tech new enterprises tell us repeatedly that there is a trick to building advantage with the engineering function: remember that your technology is in the heads of a handful of key techies. And never forget: engineering is both technically and psychologically intensive.

BEYOND TECHNOLOGY

To some scientists and engineers, technology is everything. It is "way cool," the only thing that counts. Serial entrepreneurs have a different version of how important technology is to a new enterprise. They tell me that, yes, technology is a critical key to what high tech start-ups build. Without it, the companies would not be high tech. But when used unwisely, technology, like other powerful tools, can be dangerous to the health and even survival of a new enterprise. Building a better mousetrap is not how great companies became great. Relying mainly on a better black box usually results in the end of a start-up. The great CEOs of new enterprises have learned how to use technology to add to the unfair advantage of the company without relying on it.

High tech companies are organizations that must have a trained engineer or life science expert as CEO. They have to be able to explain to technology-intensive customers how new products work. They talk in the same high tech language. They share a love of technology. The trick is to not fall in love with the technology. World-class high tech start-up CEOs are passionate about their technology but have learned in the school of hard knocks that technology is there to be put to work for the company, exploited to help create a great enterprise.

METHODOLOGY AND MANAGEMENT

Experienced engineers know there are many other things that can be done with the engineering function to add to the strength of a new enterprise. For instance, serial entrepreneurs have stressed to me something time after time: how engineers are managed is a vital part of unfair advantage founded on engineering. The veterans see the engineering function as more of a people game than a mathematics game. They know that engineering work is filled with headaches and trials triggered by trying to make new technologies work. They have experienced many challenging days trying to motivate sensitive technologists to do very hard things in very short periods of time. Engineering managers also know it is very hard to get excited start-up engineering product teams to do the inevitable boring tasks. Your approach and methods of managing your technical staff are part of a wonderful opportunity to add to your unfair advantage. Let's dig into this opportunity by first looking at technology, which encompasses important people aspects.

MAKING TECHNOLOGY WORK

A classic error is to get excited about a technology before you find an application for it. "It's a technology looking for a market" is the death knell for a start-up looking for funding. A classic example is artificial intelligence. Intellicorp got going and never did become great except for a final mention in the technology history books. A more recent example appears to many doubters to be nanotechnology. After about a decade of "nano-hype" by techies, futurists, and reporters, the nano market was still not "the next great thing" measured by sales from new enterprises. But the nano jury is still deliberating. By 2005 some nano start-ups have shown signs of getting traction with their first sales of early products, so keep watching—but be cautious. Great start-up companies rarely begin with a generic technology as their unfair advantage. Those that do seem to end up in the techie grave-yard.

Also beware of trying to do a start-up based on a new science that has yet to be proven. You must have a science ready to be engineered into a never-done-before new product. Only a rare few life science companies have succeeded getting funded to prove that a science will work and that real pharmaceutical products can be produced from it.

Instead, focus on using existing technologies to make great things that excite a lot of customers. The objective is to use technology to achieve proprietary breakthroughs that solve big problems and are converted into hot new products. Solving technological problems for the sake of solving them is not the purpose of a new enterprise. Start-ups need sales as fast as possible. Plan to use technology to create products that get the stakeholders raving about how valuable they are to end users.

The goal of the CEO is to get great products out of the engineering staff in spite of how hard or boring the technology is to do. Often the first few members of a technical staff begin working on solving a problem that initially sounds easy and trivial but ends up being very difficult to do. Hard can be good but also bad. "Hard to do" will be good for challenging an eager technical staff. It also erects barriers of entry to competitors. But overcoming technological snags and hard problems takes a lot of precious time. It is very bad for marketing and sales staffs to have to wait many months for the hard technological problems to be solved before the final details of real products can be decided on. Delays also worry investors and nervous employees. Your opportunity is to assemble the core technology staff and leadership that has encountered and overcome such tough times. They can tell you how to put technology to work to build great products.

Everything Has Technology

Do not overlook using even the simplest technology to add to your unfair advantage. Simple technology is not worthless; in fact it can be very valuable. *Technology* in its original Greek means literally "how to." So describe how you build your products and if you give it a proprietary name, "We use XaJamZonic293,"™ your technology becomes unique and puts your competitors (who claim no proprietary technology) at a disadvantage. Furthermore, you might be surprised to find that some of even the most mundane technical ideas can be patentable. I cover patents and other intellectual property in detail in Chapter 16. For now, let us caution the first-time techie CEO that unless you are going to be in the business of licensing patents (such as Rambus, Inc., which dominates licensing memory technologies to semiconductor manufacturers), do not rely on patents to become a great start-up.

Now let's turn our attention to a common danger of high tech start-ups: the features trap.

Features Trap

As you conceive of and start shaping your first product idea, beware of sliding into the features trap. Features are things such as lower power, faster compile time, a stronger metal case, a quieter-running blood analyzer, and so on. Instead, I strongly suggest that your core team work hard to focus your engineers on delivering products that fulfill a compelling value proposition to your ideal customer. Yes, features will be part of the product offering. But do not rely on a long product specifications sheet to try to win the competitive battles. You can use features—once in a while—to win a battle, but not the war. It is not easy to explain that competitive principle to a first-time entrepreneur.

The next example is my depiction of one of the sessions I have observed where an experienced investor tries to patiently explain one of the facts of life to an eager founder.

Example 15-1   Features Trap: Robert Runs Faster

"We will build better products that run much, much faster than the competitions' clunky products! Our technology will fly past them!" exclaimed Robert Lee, the enthusiastic techie guru of information processing at SowE Corporation. He sat down, and DT, the respected venture capitalist leaned back in his chair and quietly began to speak.

"Lee, I think there is a pony to ride here somewhere. I sense you have come up with something very important. Your idea may be the sign of a new market. But as an old guy who has learned the hard way, pushing speed or some other feature or two is not going to get you funded.

"Reliance on features pushes the company into a box. History is not kind to fighters of feature wars; they die a thousand deaths as competitors leapfrog each other. They dance in step together, singing that old anthem, 'We Are Faster Than You Are (Today).' To win the competitive wars and emerge as the dominant winner, you will need more than that.

"Starting with your ideal customer, you must take the time to find out what features bring the targeted customer the greatest benefit. Then choose the set most desired, and build those into your products. Then get your marketing hat on, and begin to position your product against your prime competitor. Emphasize how you deliver with your value proposition. Value propositions are much more than 'ten times faster.'

"We want you to build a great unfair advantage that includes your technology but does not rely only on it. In this century of instant exchange of information over the Internet, it seems as if someone else in the world is working on nearly the same idea using nearly the same technology. Investors and great employees want a stronger advantage than just great technology and a couple of outstanding features."

Use the technology innovated by your engineers, but do not over-use it. In addition to technology, there are other things from the technical staff that can boost your unfair advantage.

ENGINEERING ELEMENTS OF UNFAIR ADVANTAGE

The engineering part of your unfair advantage story needs to be plausible, that is, believable and practical. Let's begin by examining a short list of suggestions assembled from engineers who are veterans of high tech new enterprises. They have earned PhDs from the School of Hard Knocks. Their tips are based on experience gained while leading technical staffs racing to create the first product of a new enterprise. The list is not intended to be exhaustive. Engineering is rich with opportunities to innovate and boost your competitive advantage. Examine the tips I have chosen, and then innovate some yourself.

Document your key engineering milestones.

A Gantt chart works wonders here. That is one of those colorful graphical exhibits with a horizontal line for each of the important tasks you must finish to prepare your first product for launch. Each line is marked with the dates (month and year) when you expect to start and complete key engineering tasks. It especially helps the reader of your business plan see how deeply you have thought about the design of your first product. Think of it as a map of the path your technical staff will take to arrive at the date of first product launch.

Support key milestones with engineering details.

How will investors know that what you plan to build can be finished in time to win leadership of the new market? People with money to invest are skeptics. So are potential employees and the media. They want details supporting your broad claims and time schedule to complete the first product. They are especially sensitive when what you are going to build has never been built before. It is hard to be convincing if your technical staff has not done a lot of work thinking through details of how you plan to create the first product. It is not a good idea to try to invent answers during your first presentation. If you do, you will understand what it means to be a spear-catcher.

Table 15-1 First Three Versions of the Product

1. **Proof of concept (Product 1):** This version of the product is used to raise the seed round of funding (the *A round*). It is what the technical staff creates to clarify to itself exactly what the mysterious technical problem to be solved is all about. Typically the problem turns out to be at either extreme: too trivial (boring to engineers) or too hard (nearly impossible to solve). Engineers are filled with a mixture of wonder and trepidation at this stage.

2. **Demo (Product 2):** This version is used to raise the next round of multimillion-dollar funding (the *B round*). It is a demonstration model used to resolve the business case (how to make money after all the hard work). It can be used to recruit missing talent. Engineers use it to get feedback from potential customers and make modifications to further shape the final-product-to-be. In this stage, the technical staff is creating proprietary technology. Each day they are learning more and more about the technology they are working with. Tough technical problems are being encountered and overcome. Engineers are very excited and work long hours during this stage.

3. **Launch (Product 3):** This version is used to raise money to finance the first sales of the first product in the first product family (the *C round*). The technical staff is consumed by completing the first product for launch. Execution becomes paramount. Creative technical problem solving takes the back burner. Engineers find businesspeople taking over more and more of the leadership of the company. The technical staff is much calmer, and some are bored. A few of the very early engineers begin to look around for a more stimulating company to work for.

Source: *Nesheim Group.*

Do an excellent job of planning the completion of the first three versions of your first product.

The first version is dubbed *proof of concept*. That term refers to a laboratory model or an experiment that more or less proves that your technological dream can become a reality, that it will work. In its embryonic form, the proof of concept requires some form of mockup, screen shots, breadboard, or model. After proof of concept comes the *demo product*. It is a thing that really works but is not ready to be converted into a commercial product. The third version is the *launch product*. It is what you will sell to your first customers. Be sure to include all three in your business plan Gantt chart. Table 15-1 goes into more detail on these versions.

There are many other important engineering milestones on the road to first product launch. Add them to your Gantt chart. Then document the supporting details. How many people do you need for each task? Who must do what to accomplish each milestone on time? What special equipment and software are required? What strategic partners must be signed up to help design the first product? Digging into such details will confront you with reality. That will help your technical staff raise issues and resolve them before they become rude engineering surprises.

Be prepared. You can be sure that your interested investors will hire experts to scrutinize your plan. Those independent technologists review your engineering plan in detail, looking for errors of judgment and lack of realism. The goal is to reduce the unknown technology issues to a few that practical engineers can manage. The shorter the list, the better. Veterans know all too well that technical surprises will occur, and most of them will be bad ones. By the time they become ready for sale, few first-time products run faster or perform better than they were planned to.

How have you coordinated engineering milestones with your funding requirements?

Plotting engineering milestones on a time line improves planning the timing of important funding events. For instance, I find a common error is to plan to try to raise a fresh round of funding (typically the B round) before the demo is finished. That reduces the value of the new enterprise and makes the cost of the B round much more expensive, a very painful experience.

The following example is a stinging tale of why it is so important to think through the timing of funding events and match them with the uncertainties of engineering first products. I saw initial reports of a hot new enterprise, PolyFuel, turn cool as significant engineering development challenges slowed completion of the first product.

Example 15-2   Missed Milestone Hurts Funding: PolyFuel

Reporters began with stories admiring PolyFuel, an aspiring new enterprise aiming to deliver a prototype of a fuel-cell-powered cell phone. But as time wore on, cash began running low, and it was time to get another round of funding.

Vanguard Ventures, a respected Palo Alto–based venture firm, was interested and began to dig into the company's plan. It visited the company's laboratory, called in industry experts, and kept on doing its due diligence for two months. The partnership concluded it was unclear that PolyFuel could win the position of leader of the new field. Vanguard declined to invest.

Some time later, a venture firm familiar with energy deals agreed to lead a round of funding. Ventures West began to prepare a term sheet for negotiation. Intel agreed to join the $15 million funding round that was looking like being oversubscribed. But the bad news arrived while the deal was being investigated: PolyFuel missed a product development milestone. The prototype would have to be significantly reengineered. The good news was that PolyFuel completed the round, but at a substantial drop in valuation, which sharply increased the dilution for prior investors and employees. Missing milestones is very painful to funding efforts.[1]

Plan on missing milestones.

To say you should plan on missing engineering milestones may at first sound shocking. But that is what is most likely to happen. Entrepreneurs are born optimists. They are never early. Anticipate trouble. Plan on retaining enough cash reserves to survive missed milestones. Your objective is to avoid having to raise funds while the prototype continues to fail and the technical staff cannot meet key dates. Keep enough cash on hand to feed your company until well after you finally achieve the missed milestone. Then you will have added value to your company and can raise the price per share of stock sold to the next round of investors.

Carefully plan your early technical staff hires.

Veterans want the company to begin with a small team of experienced technologists. They will do both product development work and steer the rest of the technical staff (who are not yet hired) through the inevitable potholes in the road ahead. They especially want a lead engineer with a track record of recruiting outstanding techies (especially from among engineers he or she has worked closely with). They want the rest of the technical staff to be a handful of can-do veterans who have built great products that sold very well. Together that group is counted on to lead the way to completion of the first product for sale. They will act as both individual contributors and team leaders.

The veteran investor is especially interested in a complete team of technologists. The dream is to find a team walking en masse across the street to a new enterprise. That is not common but has happened. It can add a lot to your unfair advantage. More likely, you will be recruiting people who have been working in several companies. I find serial engineering leaders do not expect to have a complete team ready to go to work on the day the start-up gets its first round of funding. In fact, senior managers often tell me they prefer to hire fresh talent as it is needed, as problems are discovered. It is hard to anticipate in advance each of the specific technical skills that will be needed. Some can be hired by the hour to solve specific problems and leave. Others will be contractors who will become full-time employees.

However you decide to do it, this is an important part of your story. When you get it right, it will sound exciting to the stakeholders. You will be confident about how you will assemble a world-class technical staff that have been to hell and back a few times and delivered products that became winners.

Plan the culture for your technical staff.

The early technical staff will form and shape the culture of the company's technical personnel. Top engineers prefer to work with people they know and respect. They seek to be close to people who have working habits similar to their own. Like choosing roommates, they can be very fussy about such matters. They prefer not to join a staff of complete strangers. They are more motivated to work the hard, long, and often boring hours with people they have seen do the tough work. They want people they have seen in action, on the job, in person. They insist on being able to count on strong contributors who know that when the technology does not work, each person will have to jump in and get it fixed quickly, and with a minimum of fuss. How you plan on building that social and values-enriched part of your company is an important part of your story. The more you work on building a deliberate culture, the stronger your unfair advantage will be.

Document the methods you plan to use to design the first product.

That involves many choices and lots of detail. For instance, are you going to outsource some of the technical work? Will you use a great product design service? Jeff Hawkins contracted with a firm to help design much of the first hardware for the original Palm PDA. He did it again to design the first Handspring. What special equipment will your staff require to accelerate their work? How much equipment could you rent by the hour, and how much should you purchase? Addressing such questions is important before you try to raise funds or start recruiting. A team of experienced engineers who have answers will stand out to investors. That team will know where to and when not to do shortcuts. They are wise about workarounds. They know how to decide on trade-offs. They understand deadlines. They know their personal limits. They have become wise technologists. They are invaluable during the inevitable crunch times the technical staff will encounter.

The following disguised example, related by a veteran of several new enterprises, explains the value of assembling a group of engineers who know how to work through tough times.

Example 15-3   Engineering Phases: RakSaw Engineering

"Looks like it'll be a two o'clocker tonight," said Ken to Mandy on the phone. "Our key beta customer ran the demo and did their own benchmark. They are challenging our ability to scale from 100 to 100,000 users. We'll need to twist some dials and squeeze some code. Need a throughput boost of at least two. Four would be better. I'll grab some pizza and work late. Kiss Jack for me. See you in the morning."

That is what the VP of engineering said from work to his wife as evening arrived. A month ago, his RakSaw engineering team had delivered an almost finished version of the first product. It had gotten the first key customer very excited. Then the customer gave it a workout and came back to the vice president of marketing, saying that to go further, they needed evidence that the product would be able to eventually handle a very large number of users. That is when Ken realized it was going to be another one of those long nights. Mandy said she understood, hung up the phone, and went to prepare dinner for herself and their two-year-old son.

Ken walked to the conference room where his technical staff was assembling. They had made similar calls to home. Now the time had arrived to pull another rabbit out of the hat. The first customer product had gotten the juices flowing, but the hook was not yet set.

Ken knew through two decades of experience that the engineering staff must deliver a finished product that met most of the specifications set by the marketing staff. Together they had agreed on how the first product would perform. Yet in spite of promises that the specs were "set in concrete this time," the constant problem was that the specs were a moving target, and a potentially large customer had just moved the bar higher.

A long time ago, Ken had learned that the sketch of first product would be greatly altered by the time it was ready for sale. Like other veterans, he expected new products to have to go through phases as they are crafted into a final product for sale to real customers. RakSaw was entering the launch phase. That is how life works for the technical staff of a promising new enterprise.

Remember to plan the testing of the first product.

Someone has to do the testing and document the reliability data. Customers will demand it. That is how new products get qualified. Exactly how will your product be tested? What are your plans to produce a quality database? How long will it take? Who will do it? What will it cost? What special equipment will be needed? Dig into the details and resolve the issues now. Make it part of your engineering plan.

The following is an example I observed during the early part of 2003 at a real start-up in Silicon Valley.

Example 15-4   Test Plan: Rick's Test Board

Rick took over as the first vice president of engineering of a well-funded start-up. It was attempting to produce a new piece of telecommunications hardware that had run into serious product development snags. He found himself leading a demoralized technical staff that believed they had produced a very sick product. Early tests found the product frequently failed near the end of 1,000 hours of testing in the burn-in oven. The failures were unexpected and catastrophic, and the first product launch had to be aborted. Customers were angry. Disaster loomed. The core team wondered if the product should be scrapped.

Rick began with the nervous board of directors. He got them to agree to give him up to four weeks to find the problem. He then calmed the technical staff who were nearing panic. He showed the engineers how to put more care and discipline into their diagnostic work. They began to methodically conduct experiments aimed at discovering the fundamental problems with the underlying technology. There was some early indication that there might be trouble from electrostatic discharges in the product. Rick called friends who knew friends who were specialists in electrostatic physics and hired them as contractors to assist the testing team.

In less than two weeks, Rick's staff discovered that the troubled product was actually working well. The culprit was the method of testing the product. The testing procedure was generating random electrostatic discharges near the end of the 1,000-hour test period. The test board and sockets were the wrong ones for the type of product being tested. That caused even more failures.

A new test board with the proper sockets was substituted and the test procedure modified. Three weeks later, the product passed with flying colors.

Digging into the details ahead of time can circumvent serious problems such as Rick encountered. Testing is just one of several aspects of engineering new products. Each can become a part of your unfair advantage. The people side of engineering a new product can be a powerful source of more advantage. Engineers have to be managed. How that is done can add to or detract from your company's strength.

Deliberately build your technical team's working methodology.

Some engineering managers stand out because of the working methodology they use to build new products. Each technical team seems to morph its own special form of how they do things from the collection they bring to the company. Team leaders greatly influence the methods that emerge as a way of life in a new enterprise. The working methodology is grown like a garden. Its seeds emerge as flowers within the confines of company infrastructure, disciplines, policies, and values that contribute to the company culture. Your technical leader should be able to describe the initial methodology he or she will use to deliver the first product. Learn to tell that part of your story well. It is a key part of your unfair advantage. To some technical veterans, it is religious.

To conclude this chapter I will weave together parts of a recent interview I had with an engineer who has worked with a lot of new enterprises and their teams. I found KT working in a start-up that has a fighting chance to become the leader of a new IT market segment. His company is well funded with blue-chip venture money and has assembled an outstanding technical staff.

Example 15-5   Engineering Management Advantages: KT Responds

KT is a serial entrepreneur and engineering leader I have tracked for more than a decade. I asked him to tell me how to use engineering in a new enterprise to increase unfair advantage. Here is how he responded:

Q: Do you prefer beginning with a complete technical team?

A: Whole teams? Having tried that a couple of times, I'm not convinced this is true or even desirable. I think a better plan is to mix the gray cells from several prior companies to try to breed a better team. That lets you add lots of missing second-hand experience that way. You don't know on day 1 what snags you will encounter in day 2.

Q: How can engineering work with marketing to create unfair advantage?

A: Wow, a new product plan agreed to by engineering and marketing! I would love to be at just one company where there really was such a plan. In start-ups, interaction between engineering and marketing continues to be more of a drive-by shooting than a strategic plan. Marketing constantly arrives with new requirements from the last big deal put in front of them by a potential customer. Engineering is often sidetracked by fascination with product implementation details that are not market driven. Neither talks to the other in any sane way.

Q: What creative ideas have you seen to use engineering to add to the competitive advantage of a new enterprise?

A: I call it *engineering marketing*. It is the generation from the technical staff of items that support marketing, selling, and customer support—for instance, white papers, frequently asked questions, talks at conferences, and so on. They build the reputation of the company and guide the market proactively.

Engineering can do a lot more than deliver products. The product development process can add to (or detract from) your unfair advantage. Challenge your technical staff to get creative in preparing and telling their part of your story. It will boost the unfairness of your company's advantage.

16

LEGAL AND INTELLECTUAL PROPERTY

A plan to manage the legal matters of a new enterprise is part of your story. It can make a big difference in how strong your advantage is. A wisely crafted legal plan can add value through intellectual property, contracts, and great lawyers. Intellectual property includes patents, trademarks, copyrights, and a lot more. Contracts include legal documents for deals with strategic partners and early customers. You need lawyers who understand your business to help you make the most out of all of them. Some law firms specialize in patents. Others do only the nonpatent corporate and litigation work. Some law firms do it all. Great start-up law partners will show you how to create a stronger plan by creating, managing, and protecting intellectual property and negotiating better contracts. They assist the creation of stock options, manage labor disputes, and help you stay out of legal entanglements. Pragmatic lawyers will work closely with your chief financial officer doing rounds of financing and with your business development vice president negotiating deals with other corporations. All of those elements can be used to increase your competitive edge.

PATENT SURPRISES

Patents are part of a larger group of valuable items referred to as *intellectual property*. They are all based on trade secrets. For new enterprises, this family includes patents, trademarks, copyrights, Internet URL names, and more. If your company takes time to plan how to use each of them, they can boost your unfair advantage significantly.

Engineers and scientists often think a patent is the ultimate way to protect an idea, the ultimate unfair advantage weapon. Nothing could be further from the truth. Why is a patent not the all-in-all wonder for a start-up? Because if that is all the company has, it will have only one weapon to use to defend itself: it must use the legal system and go to court. That takes years and a lot of cash. The outcome of the trial is not certain. Lawyers do not know who will be the victor or when and how much the judge will award to which parties. It took decades to decide who owned the fundamental patents on the first intermittent automobile windshield wiper and the optical laser. Investors do not want to finance litigation. Employees do not want to work for companies that spend most of their money and time in court. Reporters like to write juicy stories about two companies fighting legal battles. Customers do not like to read such stories. Employees are not fond of joining them; they think something smells fishy.

BRAGGING RIGHTS

I suggest that start-up CEOs think of patents as bragging rights for their marketing department. Patents are evidence of something unique, valuable, and creative: "We have twenty-four patents applied for; our competition has none." That is the material marketing people love to use to position against less endowed companies. They can use the patent claims to fame immediately, without waiting for an uncertain trial to end years later. Patents add a sense of extra value to a company, even if the patents have not yet been granted or proven to be defendable in court.

In the long term, a start-up is wise to have applied for patents. Amazon.com used patents to later punish the me-too offense of Barnes & Noble (one-click ordering). In the semiconductor industry, patents have been traditionally used to create mutually beneficial cross-licenses. That avoids destructive legal battles and increases the size of the market competed for by the cross-licensing competitors. It helps the cooperating companies set the new industry standard. There are similar examples in the life science industry where patents are vital. But even in the drug business, new enterprises know they must not rely solely on patents for success. The lesson is simple: do not forget to consider patents for your start-up; just do not expect patents to be your ultimate weapon for your new enterprise in the first critical five years of its life.

The next example is based on several episodes I have observed with entrepreneurs and venture investors discussing strategic use of patents.

Example 16-1   Patents: Natisha's Expectations

"We will get our patents and rule the market!" exclaimed Natisha Karatchi, a revered biological scientist. "Doesn't that sound wonderful?" James, the gray-haired angel investor, waited for her to finish and then began to calmly explain to the inexperienced entrepreneur what really happens in a new enterprise that is based on life science inventions.

"Experience shows me that is not how the new enterprise world works, with some rare exceptions. For instance, a drug patent can produce a very powerful monopoly for a lucrative business model. That has been working well for new and old pharmaceutical companies for the past century. It is true that life science start-ups focusing on drug development employ the best patent lawyers and aim on sole dominance of a single drug. Yet that is not enough to ensure a winning company. The drug must first be developed in the laboratory. The testing and trials on animals must take place successfully. Then the drug must be approved in time-consuming, expensive clinical trials on real humans in countries around the world. And then doctors must be educated on why the new and much more expensive drug is better than the ones they have been using successfully for decades. And, of course, the copycats and illegal producers of the new drug must be dealt with. Meanwhile, new competing drugs will arrive. And your company must keep running by inventing second and third drugs. That takes a great deal of time and money and effort and skill. The outcome after the first patent has been granted is not certain. Patents do not make success guaranteed. They are a part of success, but they do not ensure it."

TRADEMARKS AND COPYRIGHTS

Besides patents, there is another important part of intellectual property to use as a competitive tool. Pay attention to names that you will trademark. Trademarks are part of your intellectual property. They become brands and standards. Your story should include when and how to file the legal paperwork in the important countries of the world. Copyrights are also valuable. They apply to words and pictures and more. Know where they will work and will not. In some industries, protecting intellectual property is easier than in others. Pirating of software is rampant in the digital era. As one wag put it, "There is only one copy of Microsoft Office in Asia." In spite of that, file the legal work, and add to your unfair advantage. Law firms specializing in international law can help you plan the defense of your intellectual property. Be sure your choice of patent lawyer has a track record that includes how to prepare plans for protecting intellectual property overseas.

FUNDING, CONTRACTS, AND BUSINESS-THINKING LAWYERS

Legal contracts that are well negotiated can be a powerful addition to competitive advantage. For instance, each round of your venture capital financing will be negotiated between your lawyer and the lawyer representing the investors. The fine print in the rights of the preferred stock owners can overweight the financial benefits and control of the company in favor of investors. Experienced lawyers also help craft those important early deals with strategic partners that create barriers to entry against follow-on competitors. Your terms in contracts with your earliest customers can determine the difference between booking the order and losing it. If you outsource manufacturing or customer service, you will have to live with the terms for many years of uncertainty and risks. Signing up to unwise prices and quantities can sink your ship.

Legal documents are crafted (with you) by business-savvy corporate law partners who are very familiar with new enterprises. They and their teams of legal assistants understand your business, the industry you are in, the companies that you are contracting with, and how the venture community works. They are well connected. Great lawyers make life a lot better for the core team of a new enterprise. Such people are more than lawyers. They think and act like competitive businesspeople. They have a strong sense of start-up urgency. They appreciate the intensity of the battle caused by the arrival of disruptive technologies. Great lawyers also help new enterprises lay out long-term plans for achieving dominance with intellectual property in countries around the world. The plan will include defenses against attackers and violators, small and large. You may be surprised to learn how different it is to get a patent in different countries. For instance, a single error in timing of filing documents in one country can ruin your right to be granted a patent in many others. So be careful about how you prepare your worldwide intellectual property plan. And be wise about your selection of the lawyer who will negotiate the terms of your next round of financing, the strategic partnership deals, and customer contracts. Your choices will significantly affect your unfair advantage.

17

MANUFACTURING, OUTSOURCING, AND INTERNET OPERATIONS

New enterprises can add to their competitive strength by using outsourcing and related services. That allows your core team to focus on what it does best, leaving the rest to experts.

It seems that nearly everything can be outsourced. Experts await your call. Examine the talent of your core team and find ways to use experts for hire to fill talent gaps. Contract engineering companies have skilled engineering staffs. Some know how to help your small technical team design for better manufacturing so that your first product not only will be produced at a lower cost, but will also do things your competitors' product cannot. Others can test your first product with their specialized, expensive equipment. Similarly, you can also outsource customer service and technical support. Companies in India can effectively respond to customer problems in excellent English at prices lower than in your home country. If you will be doing e-commerce, your Internet businesses will require a lot of bandwidth, very quickly. You need a service that can scale up with short notice when sales finally take off, but meanwhile one that is affordable to your tiny new enterprise. Such services can be obtained from several giant organizations specializing in such services.

The list of creative possibilities is a long one. A plan that wisely picks when and where to outsource, and is careful in choosing from among the best providers, produces a sizzling story. Your company can emerge much stronger and more attractive to your stakeholders.

MANUFACTURING

For a great manufacturing plan that gets respect, document the monthly details of how you plan to produce your first product. Use the same charts, care, and depth of detail as you did for the engineering plan to design it. Use a milestone chart with major manufacturing events. Link them to the engineering and customer service plans. Divide the key tasks into those to be done by employees in-house and those to be done by outside service providers. Contact outside vendors, interview them, and document your decisions. Include the details of their contracts and costs in your financial forecasts. Organize your company to include the staff that will be responsible for coordinating the outsourced manufacturing process.

Construct a detailed model of the parts and costs of your first product. Support your numbers in a bill of materials (BOM). Show quotes of prices from vendors for each important component. Explain how you will get enough of the scarce, expensive parts. Add the cost of labor to produce the first product. Predict the price drops per component over time as you ramp up your unit sales (the learning curve). Those numbers will be the basis for a model of the cost of goods sold and will be included in your financial statement forecast. Models of the cost of production will save you a lot of time. As the product design shifts (it will, for sure) and as pricing from suppliers varies during preliminary negotiations, a model lets you quickly redo your BOM cost estimates. It also helps generate issues to be dealt with before you are challenged by a caustic investor or a sharp employee candidate. Modeling the cost of the first product also increases insight about where to use creative manufacturing technology to gain a boost in your unfair advantage. Take advantage of manufacturing economics. Add it to your unfair advantage.

INTERNET OPERATIONS

Model the details of your Internet operations. Include everything from systems to equipment to maintenance to people. If you are planning on doing heavy amounts of e-commerce, extra time and detailed thinking are needed to complete this section of your story. Internet business stories need to show samples of screen shots, sketches of IT architecture, choices of software and hardware, services supplied by outsiders, and so on. Be sure to include telecommunications expenses in detail. Name all the key vendors and their pricing for software, servers, broadband pipes, and more. Be sure you talk to them to see if closer contractual deals can lead to strong strategic partnership benefits. Modify your organization to include the related Internet operations employees and their management. Put the expenses into your cost of goods (hardware or services) sold (shipped or supplied) in the income statement of your financial forecast.

Do you remember how Amazon.com used its Internet operations to gain a lead and keep in front of its attacking competitors? Try doing even better than it did. Detailed innovative thinking about Internet operations can be very powerful, especially for attracting creative technical talent and money.

OUTSOURCING AND STRATEGIC PARTNERS

Outsourced services from strategic partners are increasingly used to build unfair advantage. Outsourcing is evidenced by a contractual commitment. It is more than a legal document for an order to produce 100,000 units each month at a fixed price. It is a working business partnership that benefits both companies. Start-up CEOs can creatively use outsourcing to gain power that cannot be matched by competitors.

Signing up an outsourcing partner for a new enterprise is tricky. Most giant contract service companies are not interested in the low volumes that a start-up will begin with. The best outsource contractors are looking to do business with a few carefully selected new enterprises. Those are the fortunate ones seen as the most likely winners that can become future giants of their new industries. Therefore, you have to sell them by telling them your story, just as you do other stakeholders. When you get them excited, your established outsourced partner will be eager to assist your fledgling business in responding to surprises, good and bad. They can help you win, big time.

A strategic partnership for a new enterprise is a special relationship between partners of unequal size. It is a relationship that is delicate at first and later is awkward to control. It is not a "who you know" type of power, not the *guanxi* of China or the "great Rolodex of names" or "networking contacts" that some people think is pure gold. Instead this is a special business relationship marked by a mutual sharing of trust, risk, and reward. Some have labeled it enlightened self-interest.

Let's look at a good example set by Handspring, which chose an outsourcing partner to manufacture its first product. The details are my summary of looking in from the outside on a company I have studied closely. The story is about successful partnering during an exciting and complex series of events that were managed well (outstanding execution) by a world-class core team.

Example 17-1   Outsourcing Boosts Advantage: Handspring and Flextronics

I observed with great interest the construction of Handspring by its core team of serial entrepreneurs. They were the people who had created the Palm personal digital appliance business. Later they left that company to start a new one and expand the market.

Their business model focused on doing product design, marketing, and selling and called for outside companies to perform other functions such as manufacturing. Handspring chose Flextronics to be its outsourced manufacturer and a strategic partner. It was one of the largest electronic manufacturing services companies in the world. The core team had used Flextronics in their prior company.

The two organizations worked up a detailed one-year forecast for manufacturing the first Handspring product. It would be sold initially from the Handspring web site and later in retail channels of distribution. The business climate was strong. As consumer demand grew during the hot Internet boom days, cool new electronic products were flying off the shelves. That was good news. However, with the good came the bad. Soon the newest parts for PDA hardware, especially high-quality display screens, were in scarce supply. Extra quantities became unavailable at any price. Rationing by suppliers began.

Handspring realized it was in trouble with a new product that needed many of the scarcest parts. It turned for help to giant Flextronics. It stepped in and very quickly used its purchasing muscle to locate and secure enough of the scarce components for the first production run.

As the first product launch day got nearer, Handspring began to prepare to sell the product from the company web site. With just a few weeks to go, a handful of employees scrambled with some web site expert contractors, and up went the Handspring web site, ready to take customers' first orders. Launch day finally arrived. The Handspring server was fired up and waiting. A button was pushed, the press release went out, and the company went into business selling.

All went well—for a few minutes. Then the unexpected happened. Instead of the as-planned-for number of sales per hour, Handspring found its web site swamped with overwhelming numbers of orders. Its web server soon crashed. The company had grossly underestimated the first wave of demand. How would the tiny start-up respond to this difficult surprise? What could be done to produce enough PDAs to meet the overwhelming demand? Frustrated buyers were getting very angry, sending emails and phoning Handspring. The press began writing sour stories about the troubles of success.

While the web site team jumped to solve the order volume problem, the company core team rushed to confer with Flextronics. Together they came up with a fix. Once again Flextronics obtained the scarce components from vendors it knew well. It also found ways to divert other critical parts to temporarily fill near-term Handspring production run increases. Flextronics' production line managers juggled build schedules and added extra labor to fill the unexpected spike in demand.

Within a few months, sales estimates from Handspring became more predictable. Flextronics was able to settle down to less hectic responses. The first crisis was over. Handspring had chosen an outstanding partner for a lot more reasons than lowest-cost supplier. That paid off handsomely.

Manufacturing, Internet operations. and other forms of outsourcing are fertile grounds for innovative entrepreneurs to boost their advantages. Work on them before showing up to do your first presentation. Discussions with outsider vendors will enrich your knowledge, flush out issues, and reduce surprises. You will be far ahead of your competition after you do your homework.

18

INFORMATION SERVICES

*I*nformation services is the newest function ripe with opportunities to add strengths to your unfair advantage. It has become a critical and integral part of new enterprises. In the old days, the first engineers hired did the designs of new products and also connected the first company computers to a network. They pulled cables while fresh code compiled. They interrupted engineering work when servers crashed. It seemed smart ("We saved thousands of dollars of cash"), but it turned out not to be wise. It added stress to engineers and delayed getting the first product to market. "Penny wise and pound foolish" is the old British adage.

Today's new enterprises view the information services function much differently. They see it as a competitive tool. It is much more than an administrative headache. CEOs now plan to have their information service requirements managed by technical experts—systems administrators dubbed *sysadmins*. They are proficient at choosing equipment, installing it quickly, and keeping it running. That leaves design engineers and the rest of the employees focused on getting the company to first product launch as quickly as possible.

Start this part of your story with the person you are going to hire to manage your information services function. Go on to describe how information services will grow with the company. Explain where the webmaster and system support will fit into your organization. Describe in detail your choices of software and hardware and how they will work.

The information services function is used intensively in life and information science start-ups as well as in consumer-oriented e-commerce and service organizations. None should treat information services as an afterthought. Instead, get proactive about how you plan on using these services to increase your competitive advantage.

Make it part of your business model. Describe and name your information services strategic partners. Think creatively, looking for ways to increase your unfair advantage because of your information services choices. Dell online ordering and customer support services are outstanding examples of how a start-up increased its competitive strength by using information services. Be explicit with your information services plan. Show details similar to those in your engineering plan. Include the expenses in your financial forecast. You can combine information services, Internet operations, and information technology as you build your unfair advantage.

A burst of articles announced the arrival of two bold and very clever cell phone service providers. The following example describes how they built their unfair advantages beginning with innovative information services and then combined these with other elements. They were quickly successful in the face of apparently insurmountable, entrenched competition.

Example 18-1   Information Services: Virgin Mobile and Boost Mobile

A good example of using innovative information systems to create a new business occurred in 2003. Two upstart new enterprises, Virgin Mobile and Boost Mobile, used special combinations of information services, Internet web sites, customer interface designs, and crisp consumer brand marketing to focus on a fresh market category: prepaid mobile virtual network provider. They quickly emerged as leaders of the market segment focused on youth. The services let young people buy minutes on calling cards purchased at music and electronic stores without credit cards. That allowed people of all ages, including preteens, to use a cell phone. Their purchases built up minutes in their accounts, ready for use any time they made a call.

Instead of constructing their own expensive infrastructure, Virgin and Boost contracted for information technology services using the existing infrastructure of telecommunications giants. That got them into business quicker and gave them significantly lower capital requirements. They used proprietary designs of information systems to simplify their customers' sign-up process. That reduced administrative costs noticeably. Virgin Mobile claimed its service plan was so straightforward that in January 2003, 50 percent activated their phones online and 87 percent of subscribers added minutes to their account without speaking to a customer service person.

Other giant cell phone providers incur large costs for their older, person-to-person customer services.

Virgin and Boost focused on a segment without a market leader: high school and college-aged cell phone users. The image was hip. The message was fun and convenience, not cheaper pricing. Virgin especially leveraged its rebel reputation and positioned the service as something parents would never use. "The rock in our slingshot in this battle of David versus many Goliaths is focus," a Virgin Mobile executive said. "We built this from the ground up to focus on the youth market."

Virgin and Boost each had something unique. Virgin created a special service called "rescue ring." It let subscribers program their cell phones to ring during a bad date, setting up a convenient escape. Virgin Mobile partnered with MTV to allow its subscribers to use phones for video voting, audio postcards, and wake-up calls from reality show celebrities. Virgin's customer base included 55 percent females. Boost had tie-ins with surfing, biking, and other extreme sports events; its customers were in California and Nevada only, and they were about 60 percent male.

That is how to use information services plus a lot more to create a sizzling unfair advantage. Time will tell how well the two upstarts fare in the face of tough competition. The point is to get innovative about how to combine elements, including information services and its related functions, so your unfair advantage rises far above the competition's.

19

MANAGEMENT AND KEY PERSONNEL

We invest in people" is the often-quoted statement from venture investors. "Who are your people?" is what they mean. They want to know a lot about you. They will put millions of dollars into your hands. Who you are, individually and as a team, is the most important section of your story. Plan on telling it well. Serial entrepreneurs have a related adage: "We cannot afford good people because they make too many mistakes. We can afford only outstanding people." How will your core team be perceived? I believe that will be the most important factor in your ability to attract the best people. It is a shock to first-time start-up technical staff to hear that the management section is more important to venture capitalists than the technology section. So let's look at how to assemble a good story about the humans who will run a new enterprise.

MANAGEMENT PHILOSOPHY

Experienced entrepreneurs have become veterans by developing methods of managing people over long periods of time, working through difficult challenges and terrible disasters. They know what it is to fail as well as to succeed. They do not dwell only on the victories. Veterans are full of stories that begin, "I remember when that awful XYZ happened, and Karl said the most unbelievable thing to me! We went through hell but came out alive with some bitter lessons learned." Veterans can also tell you how they treat people and what they expect of top talent. They can describe what motivates an engineer, gets a salesperson enthusiastic, drives a customer to purchase or go away angry, and so on. That is what should be described in this people-centric section of your story. Describe your philosophy of managing people. Make it clear what you believe in. Talk about attracting and retaining top talent and how you work with customers and strategic partners. Tell what you expect to do with your board of directors and advisers. In this section, concentrate on what you feel strongly about when leading and managing your new business. That is what your management philosophy is all about.

CORE TEAM

In a presentation about your management, investors want you to address a very basic question: "Who are you, and why should we invest in you?" In this case, *you* refers to the core team, not to the entire company. The people with the money want to get to know the handful of initial leaders they have to trust with millions of their dollars: the CEO, the employees who report directly to the CEO (typically vice presidents or directors), and a few key individual contributors (such as the technology guru). What can you say that will give the stakeholders confidence that you are the right core team to manage this new enterprise through the launch of the first product or next phase of the business? What can you say that will convince the doubters that you are the CEO who can lead the core team through the good and bad times?

To respond, begin with yourself. Start by describing your own personal unfair advantage. Take some time to reach a conclusion about what your advantages are. You may be a brilliant product designer. You might have a world-class track record as a salesperson. Your laboratory work may have produced brilliant biological technologies that were patented and famous. But what evidence is there that supports your claim that you are the best leader of this small, select group of employees? "In addition to whatever guru engineering brilliance you have, whatever incredible new strategic marketing skills or whatever else you have, tell us how effective you are at managing people, through thick and thin," says DT to the founder and people he interviews. "How good are you at building teams to grow an idea into an incredible world-class enterprise?"

Leadership is the overriding requirement of the core team, followed closely by the ability to get people to work together to get the first product launched. The emphasis is on how to advance the company through the first big phase of growth. Can each member of your core team recite examples of his or her leadership? What in their track records shows each is a leader who knew where he or she was going and convinced others to follow? What examples can each of you cite about when you worked together on difficult projects that resulted in successes? What in your track records demonstrated you understand how to push a big project for a new product through all of its stages to launch? Prepare your responses to leadership questions such as those. That is a critical part of the company's unfair advantage.

Similarly, why has each of the other core team members been picked for their roles? Why did Ragnhild get chosen for the vice president of marketing? Is she vice-presidential caliber? How did you decide to put Rick into the role as vice president of engineering? And so on. Each person's unfair advantage needs to stand out. It is more than saying which of the great schools they got their degrees from. It is more than the number of years they have worked in the related domain. Instead, it is a mini capsulation, a short paragraph, of a human being in the role you have selected for them in this phase of the new enterprise. Short capsule stories are hard to write. But they must be written, and well. Like a product description, if you need to read a page of information (résumé) about the person, you will not get the sale (or money from the investor or acceptance of employment by a talented engineer).

Together, your core team should sound like a dream team of the next world-class enterprise, not just another start-up group. During the eleven years prior to doing the start-up that became Palm, Jeff Hawkins looked for outstanding people on the job and got to know them very well. They grew closer as they shared their dreams and prepared for the eventual day when they would leave employers and do their first start-up. Careful picking of the core team is one of your most powerful unfair advantages. That greatly boosts your chances of getting the money. It attracts the most talented people. Reporters are eager to write about it.

ORGANIZATION CHART

Include a chart of how the company will be organized the day it gets funded and how it will look by the time the first product is launched. You can get innovative with your graphical depictions of who reports to whom (circles, wagon wheels, upside down, whatever), but do not spend too much time on creative art. The main value in doing the chart is to get on paper what the core team has agreed to among themselves: who the boss is, who reports to whom and who is responsible for what. You would be surprised at how many core teams do not reach that point of agreement before looking for their seed round of funding. Do not try to decide on that in the parking lot before your first presentation.

RECRUITING

"The number one reason that start-ups do not meet their growth plans is that they cannot hire the good people fast enough!" That is a maxim I heard so often I wondered how true it was. After working with hundreds of companies and their stakeholders, I am a believer. The rate of recruiting dictates much of your success. How fast you get your people will be one of the most important processes you have to create, install, and manage as the company's leader. It is a great way to increase your unfair advantage—or weaken it. Recruiting is very time-consuming. My studies of start-ups indicate that founder CEOs spend at least 20 percent of their working time doing recruiting. The core team has to spend large blocks of time each day reading résumés, doing interviews, and preparing offer letters. It is a never-ending responsibility. It is always important. The entire company does it.

Let's quickly review the basic ways start-ups find new people.

Buddy System (Recruiting Phase 1)

To get started quickly, the core team immediately contacts people they respect and have worked with before, people they know and trust. The day the seed round funding deal closes and the money is in the bank, they leap into action. In a few days, they have hired a handful of the first employees. All of them are well known to the core team. The good news: the unknowns are few, and the time to hire is short. The bad news: there are not enough people in that pool of talent to fill the slots of needed employees.

Recruiters (Recruiting Phase 2)

Next come the recruiters—individuals and firms paid to find a big batch of missing talent. Contingent recruiters send a lot of emails and faxes of résumés for middle and lower managers and workers. Retained searchers (headhunters) are used for vice presidents and CEOs. The good news: recruiters know a lot of people who are looking for jobs in an exciting new enterprise (like yours). The bad news:

it takes time to get the recruiters going and to find the best people. And recruiters cost real money—tens of thousands of dollars per person hired, and perhaps even stock. Even worse, the top-tier recruiters are often so busy, in both boom and bust times, that when you solicit their services, you may not even get a response.

Company Recruiting (Recruiting Phase 3)

Eventually the company will begin to do its own recruiting. Studies show company recruiting costs are nearly the same as using recruiters. Your company posts jobs on its web site. It goes to job fairs. It advertises. A company employee is assigned the responsibility for processing the hundreds of résumés that are by now being emailed to the start-up by the hour from around the world. Temporary contractors are sometimes used. They are recruiters who come to the company to do only recruiting for your new enterprise. The good news: you get a lot of attention. The bad news: it still takes a lot of time and money, more than most people realize.

Tip: Do not forget to include the cost of recruiting people in your five-year financial forecast. The cash cost is real. Recruiters charge from 20 to 30 percent of annual cash compensation, and more for executives. Some recruiters take less cash and some stock, but they are still expensive. Do not forget shares in your stock option plan for recruiting new employees: reserve extra shares for expensive executives and their recruiters. You can model recruiting. Start by selecting the portion of all employees who will be recruited by each type of recruiting method. Calculate the cash and stock costs for each recruited employee. Predict those costs for each of five years. Pay attention to details. That not only reduces rude cash flow surprises, but also exhibits the kind of commitment to professional management that world-class investors look for in core teams.

Time is the enemy when recruiting. It takes twice as long as estimated to do each of the following: (1) find the best candidates to try to recruit, (2) coordinate everyone's calendar to get the schedules of interviews ready, (3) go through the interview process for each candidate and reach a hiring decision, (4) get the candidate through the process of negotiating and accepting your offer of employment, and (5) get the employee to give notice to his or her employer. Be prudent in anticipating how fast you can hire your missing talent. It always is much slower than you planned.

Respect the intensity of recruiting. As growth takes off, the whole company seems to be recruiting someone all the time. It is a thrilling but dangerous time that can sink your overworked staff. They are already slaving away, madly racing the clock to get the first product launched. So be careful about overcommitting to rapid rates of hiring. If you have never led a group that has recruited fifty outstanding people in a year, take extra time to work out the details of your hiring plan. Do not expect to get your money without explaining in detail how you plan on carrying out that awesome feat.

COMPENSATION

Plan to use compensation to help build your unfair advantage, but do so wisely. Find out how local companies in your industry are compensating their employees. Talk to specialized compensation consultants. Deliberately construct your compensation plan to include creative incentives. Do not leave it to be done after your business is started. Pick from the many choices you have: cash, bonuses, stock options, car allowances, vacation, personal time off, and so on. Some companies go for the golden handcuffs (Silicon Graphics used it effectively) by deliberately choosing to pay wages in the top quartile of their city. Others go for low cash ("Keep them hungry."). Others balance trade-offs of lower cash for extra stock options. Some emphasize perks like child care, PDAs and cell phones. Compensation is where creativity can be put to work to boost your competitive advantage.

COMPANY CULTURE

A plan for a deliberate working culture can add to your advantage. Start-up people are like other people: they want to work and have a life also. If your company's culture thinks that way, then declare it boldly. Make it part of your start-up from day one. Aristotle, the ancient Greek philosopher, said that people are made up of three elements: material, physical, and spiritual. The challenge in life is to keep the three elements in balance. Humans working in start-ups also want their lives to be in balance. Experienced entrepreneurs have learned painfully that you cannot put your life on hold and expect to succeed.

BAD BEHAVIOR

Here are typical examples of behavioral actions by naive start-up leaders: stop exercising, grab bags of junk food instead of healthy meals, sleep less, stop reading books, cut out time for entertainment, spend less time with family, put friends on hold, and skip religion. Especially avoid talking about what makes life worthwhile. Unless a balanced lifestyle is worked on, work will triumph. The stresses of a new enterprise eventually break down even the strongest entrepreneur. They end up burned out. Eventually even the toughest leaders find they need physical stamina and human supporters to succeed with a new enterprise. Start-up life is more than working extra hard for a short time. When you understand that, perhaps you can alter the story about the plan for the culture of your company.

Your goal is to build a working culture especially attractive to outstanding people who understand that a start-up is a grueling marathon, not an easy sprint. Experienced people will not sacrifice their lives for you, the great leader. They have many other choices of work. Instead, the best are going to join for the long term because they believe you will be working with them on the exciting start-up while also working hard at balancing lives. If you want to attract people with a culture that works hard on winning in business as well as with the physical and spiritual elements of life, make it part of your story about your unfair advantage. That will make your company a very attractive place to work. It will attract the best.

David Rex, an enthusiastic Texan and veteran lawyer to entrepreneurs, points to a great business cultural example in Southwest Airlines: it has a Department of Culture. The latest president was the prior head of that department. The company stands out in stark contrast to giants like American Airlines. In 2002 Southwest was the sixth largest U.S. carrier but had a market capitalization equal to the total of the combined market capitalizations of the five largest airlines. Company culture can be very powerful to new enterprises.

20

FACILITIES AND ADMINISTRATION

Facility is a lot more than a building. It means: "(1) Anything that increases physical comfort; Also: amenity, comfort, convenience; (2) The ability to perform without apparent effort: ease, easiness, effortlessness, facileness, readiness."[1] It can be used to increase your advantage.

Some CEOs choose to save money by leasing the cheapest facility and furnish it with the cheapest chairs and cubicles because they believe lowest cost is vital to winning. Others insist on the most expensive facility, believing a high-class image is critical to impress customers and other company visitors. I find the extremes are seldom the best choice, for several reasons. For instance, a successful, rapidly growing start-up quickly outgrows its first location and must move, forcing a second choice of facility. Another reason for moderation is due to the importance of location. Choice of location can produce deeper, more powerful advantages than fiscal choices. For example, the commute hassle from home to work is a big part of an engineer's decision to join companies located in large cities. Engineers often work strange hours and appreciate less wasteful commute times. The distance to restaurants and health facilities is important to social and health styles of outstanding employees. A restful campus setting with trees and waterfalls attracts people and contributes to stress reduction. The list can go on and on. It is a very basic way to add unfair advantage to a new enterprise. Following is one of the most creative ideas I have seen up close on how to use a facility and company culture to boost competitive advantage.

Example 20-1   Facility Choice Leads to Number One: The Benjamin Group

Sheri and Steve Benjamin started their fledgling public relations firm, the Benjamin Group, in a simple rented space in a first-class, high rise building in Silicon Valley. They had done their research and felt that the local market was underserved by existing firms. Sheri was the PR wiz and Steve the sharp numbers guy. They saw an underdeveloped opportunity to make a major contribution to high tech companies seeking to make better use of PR in their marketing campaigns and new product introductions.

Sheri and Steve had entrepreneurial drive and a great deal of innovative spirit. They also had something special: they were a devoted couple committed to raising a warm, loving family, balancing both business and work and without sacrificing excellence in either.

Soon after they opened for business, Sheri and Steve decided to bring the kids to the office. Their experiences with care providers did not meet their standards for excellence. As the business grew, employees were hired. Their children joined the Benjamin's children in the office.

As the number of children rose, it became clear that more than additional office space was required: the children needed a playground. Furthermore, the Benjamins wanted full certification for the operation as a child care facility. The high-rise building was not suitable.

Not to be thwarted, the enterprising couple made a few phone calls, did some research, and began to get creative. It was not easy, but in about a year, they came up with a novel solution: the Benjamin Group would do what no other PR firm was doing: buy a building of its own, convert a portion of the parking lot to a playground, and open up a private day care center large enough to accommodate many more employees' children. Steve and his family were familiar with industrial real estate investing. Sheri had confidence that a new facility would enable her to attract more PR account managers. The business was growing fast, and the firm needed more space very soon.

As soon as the ink was dry on the purchase contract (and the mortgage payments began), Sheri and Steve held an all-employees meeting to announce the move to the new building. They also told their staff to bring their kids to work.

As the Benjamin Group sign went up on the side of the building, the firm's innovative plan became reality. Soon Sheri was adding more to the competitive advantage, such as introduction of new methods of managing client relations, including novel methods of tracking and communicating project expenses to clients. Clients applauded. Meanwhile, Steve kept the cash flow positive and checks flowing to make the monthly building mortgage payments. Top talented PR professionals began knocking on the door, eager to work for the Benjamin Group. They began exiting competing public relations firms and joined the Benjamin Group to help develop new accounts. In a few years, the child care facility was fully licensed, and the Benjamin Group rose to become the top-ranked public relations firm in Silicon Valley.

Asked how the Benjamins viewed the competitive benefits of the child care facility and other innovations, Steve said succinctly, "We figured we didn't have to be wildly different, just different enough." It is also a fine example of how a self-funded (bootstrap) company can succeed. The choices of facilities made a powerful contribution to the success of the Benjamin Group. There are many other ways to pick a facility and thereby increase your advantage. Think before you choose.

21

FINANCIAL PLAN

Outstanding financial forecasts build great advantages. Your company needs good numbers because they are an important part of your story. You tell it in words, pictures, and numbers. Think of financial statements as a numerical reflection of the unfair advantage of your business. That is one reason future employees want you to tell them about some of your numbers. The right numbers, plus the words and pictures, grab the attention of your listeners. They expect the financials to be as exciting as the words and pictures. They want to feel the power of your competitive advantage emerge from your financial forecasts. That can make the difference between getting your funding or not, attracting that outstanding employee, or exciting the reporter. Let's take look at what you can do with numbers to increase your advantage.

NOT A PREDICTION, JUST THE ZEROS, PLEASE

You are not required to predict with precision the future financial outcome of a start-up. That may surprise you, but the veterans agree. The financial forecast is not a prediction of an outcome that will happen, plus or minus a small percentage. In a start-up, there is too much uncertainty to expect anyone to come up with forecast numbers that will be realized within a small margin of error. That is one reason real entrepreneurs do not use MBA techniques such as sensitivity analysis.

How good do your numbers have to be? I tell the people I coach, "Just get the number of zeros right; we are not concerned about the first digit." Serial entrepreneurs agree. What does that mean? Simply this: "Our start-up will launch our first product early in Year 2, double sales and employees each year thereafter or more, and be profitable with at least $70 million of sales by Year 5." With a rocket ride like that, you will not be concerned with "plus or minus 15 percent." You just hope the wheels stay on. You do not need to calculate alternative financial forecasts depicting several probabilistically weighted alternative scenarios such as "most likely" plus "most conservative" plus "most optimistic." Giant public worldwide corporations hire MBAs to create those cases and mix them with a probabilistic distribution of outcomes to generate expected values. Entrepreneurs just want the number of zeros to be right.

A new enterprise uses financial numbers to tell the story about how the business model—the economics of the business—will work. For instance, Dell's business—selling directly to end users—called for a fresh business model, and the financial forecast reflected that: it did not look like the financial statements of other personal computer companies. If your start-up is going to try to dominate a new category, your financial statements will reflect that originality. Your business will be attempting to do a financial first, something never done before.

Financials of start-ups will also reflect the industry they compete in. But each new enterprise will look different in a few important ways. For instance, a new "fabless" semiconductor company designs semiconductors but outsources their fabrication to specialized factories. Fabless companies will have financials that look similar to other large semiconductor companies, but the "fabless-ness" of the new enterprises will make their forecasts look different in special ways (no factories or production equipment).

In your case, the financials of a new enterprise will reflect your verbal story about how your unfair advantage will produce sales, profits, and cash flow. The numbers must show how you plan on making money (the business model). They should show growth (number of employees and sales). They must show success (profits and positive cash flow). They will show efficiency (sales per employee). Think of the financials as if you are saying to stakeholders, "If our assumptions work out, more or less, our business will generate financial statements that will look something like these." A good story is reflected in a good financial forecast.

WHICH NUMBERS ARE MOST IMPORTANT?

You need a lot of numbers to weave your story together. Each recipe has many. They include a complete income statement, balance sheet,

Table 21-1 The Big Five Financial Questions

- "How big will your sales be in Year 5?"
- "How many people will you require each year?"
- "In what year will your profits turn positive?"
- "In what year will your cash flow turn positive?"
- "How much capital will you need each year?"

SOURCE: *Nesheim Group.*

and cash flow statement for each of five years. That may sound overwhelming, but there is good news for new enterprises: I have found a small handful of numbers especially stand out. These five, listed in Table 21-1, are the ones used most frequently by serial entrepreneurs and veteran VCs whom I have observed. The numbers answer key questions. When you have the answers, you have the numbers needed to demonstrate your unfair advantage.

What are investors looking for in response to those questions? Some of the answers I found classical venture investors looking for most often are set out in Table 21-2.

Table 21-2 Classical Start-up Financial Goals

- Sales in Year 5 must be at least $25 million, preferably much closer to $100 million or more.
- Sales should be growing very fast per year, doubling or more each year.
- Profits should be nearing break-even by Year 3, at least break-even by Year 4, and turning a modest profit by Year 5.
- You should turn cash flow positive by Year 4.
- Capital required should be at least $5 million, include two or more rounds of funding, and generate a return on capital consistent with the risk taken in each round, at least an average return of ten times in five years.

SOURCE: *Nesheim Group.*

QUANTIFY YOUR BUSINESS MODEL

Serial entrepreneurs talk a lot about their business models in financial terms. They focus on answering the question, "How do you plan on making money?" The veteran CEOs explain how their business models work with numbers as well as words. They show the flow of cash between the business partners. They make it clear what the start-up's flow of cash will be doing between the date the company is created, the date the first product is shipped, and the years of subsequent growth. They show details of how each dollar of sales will be spent (on operating expenses and equipment) and how large the leftovers will be (net income). They explain how fast the company will be paid by customers (accounts receivable) and how slowly the company plans on paying their suppliers (accounts payable), particularly strategic partners.

FIRST PRODUCT FINANCIALS IN DETAIL

Your first product must succeed, or you will have a disaster on your hands. Everyone knows that, especially your chief financial officer. Therefore, be sure to work especially hard on forecasting the detailed financial statements that explain how much money it will take to get the first product family launched. Start your work with monthly numbers. Then step back from the monthly forecasts and go on to do a more general analysis of the long-term picture, the five-year forecast, by year.

Table 21-3 Important Numbers

- Number of engineers needed to finish the design and construction of the first product
- Amount of equipment needed by employees to get to first launch date
- Cash flow to key suppliers, especially outsourced manufacturing services
- Cost for marketing and sales to launch the first product
- Sales forecast of the first product, particularly the rate of acceptance by the early-adopter category of customers
- Number of shares for stock options for the first fifty employees
- How much cash is needed to build the first product and launch it

SOURCE: *Nesheim Group.*

Table 21-4 Long-Term Numbers Needing Special Attention

- When sales would exceed $25 million
- First year of profit before taxes
- Operating profit as a percentage of sales in Year 5
- First year of positive cash flow
- New capital required each year
- Speed of payment of invoices by customers
- How late to pay suppliers
- Head count by department, especially marketing and sales
- Sales per employee
- What public companies Wall Street investment bankers and research analysts would use to compare the start-up
- Stock market valuation of the start-up at the time of the IPO
- Ownership (percentage owned by stakeholders, dollars of absolute wealth per employee, size of the employee option pool)

SOURCE: *Nesheim Group.*

Your financial statements covering the time to launch your first product should also include a few important numbers investors are very eager to see. I found CEOs especially clear presenting the parts of their financial forecasts listed in Table 21-3.

Over the five years forecast, there are other numbers that are especially important, such as how much cash the start-up will need, year after year. Veterans thought through each of the classical phases of a start-up listed in *High Tech Start Up* and attached numbers to each phase (head counts, expenses, equipment, sales, and cash flow requirements).[1] They understood what a balance sheet is used for and how to calculate the funding needs of the company. The longer-term numbers that CEOs paid special attention to are included in Table 21-4.

NUMBERS AND GRAPHS CLARIFY UNFAIR ADVANTAGE

Your numbers and graphs paint a picture of your unfair advantage. The story must be a balance between plausible and exciting. *Plausible* means the numbers are believable and realistic. Only during the mania phase of a boom period do core teams get away with presenting numbers that are otherwise unthinkable. Remember that you are telling a colorful story, just like the storyteller speaking to an enthralled group of children huddled around the cozy campfire on a dark night. The firelight reflects the speaker's excited face and enhances the emotional color of the story. As the moving hands of the storyteller emphasize key points, they trigger imaginations that paint pictures in the minds of the audience. Graphs are powerful pictures of numbers. They reinforce your unfair advantage. When you sketch numbers and pictures that are believable, your story will be even more attractive to the audience. Good numbers make good graphs. Serial entrepreneurs especially use a few colorful graphs of selected portions of their financial forecasts to point to strong unfair advantages.

- Figure 21-1 focuses on growth in sales and how efficient per person the company gets as it matures.

- The profit march from early stage losses to breakeven to profitable growth is described in Figure 21-2.

- Cash flow from operations and financing is depicted in Figure 21-3 as the burn rate swings into positive cash flow.

Sales growth, people efficiency, profit and cash flow are what a new enterprise leadership focuses on during its march to create a great company with strong financials. That is how value is measured by the stakeholders. The story told in graphs paints an exciting picture of an unfair advantage unfolding in financial terms.

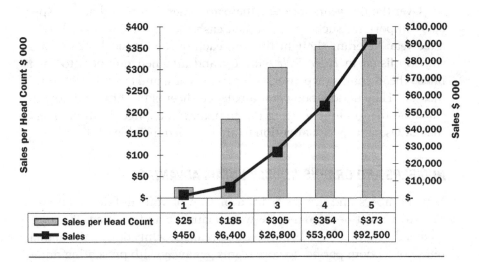

	1	2	3	4	5
Sales per Head Count	$25	$185	$305	$354	$373
Sales	$450	$6,400	$26,800	$53,600	$92,500

Figure 21-1 Graph of Sales and Head Count

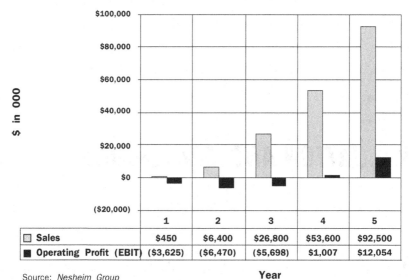

	1	2	3	4	5
☐ Sales	$450	$6,400	$26,800	$53,600	$92,500
■ Operating Profit (EBIT)	($3,625)	($6,470)	($5,698)	$1,007	$12,054

Source: *Nesheim Group*

Year

Figure 21-2 Graph of Profit Growth

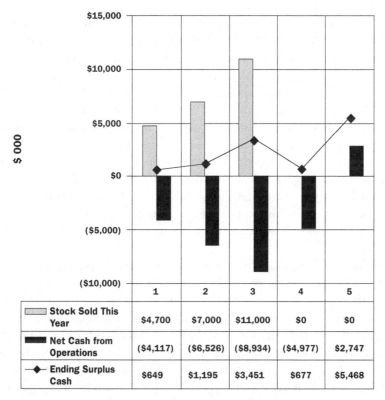

	1	2	3	4	5
Stock Sold This Year	$4,700	$7,000	$11,000	$0	$0
Net Cash from Operations	($4,117)	($6,526)	($8,934)	($4,977)	$2,747
◆ Ending Surplus Cash	$649	$1,195	$3,451	$677	$5,468

Source: *Nesheim Group.*

Year

Figure 21-3 Graph of Cash Flow

22

VALUATION AND OWNERSHIP

Valuing your company wisely can add to your unfair advantage. How much is your company worth in millions of dollars? What portion should be sold to investors, at what price per share? The trick is to get the value just right—neither too high nor too low. If your valuation is too low, it will be seen as a tiny business, too small for a first-class investor or veteran employee. It will look like a mom-and-pop company that is led by a naive founder. If your value is too high, it—and you—will be viewed as unrealistic and not worth arguing about. You have to find the golden middle (from an old German proverb). If founders and management get too greedy (hold on to a fat percentage of the ownership), they will not be able to attract the funding they need, and key employees will not work for them. If investors in one round of funding either overprice the shares or grossly underprice the shares (too greedy or exploitive), that will block the company from attaining required follow-on financing. And if in the future years there are any drops in the per share stock price (needed to get the next round of funds), it is a signal to employees that the business is in trouble (and time to get their résumés updated and look for a new company).

So how do you find this magical valuation, the golden middle? I like to think of it as a balancing game. It is not a zero-sum game where the clever founder outnegotiates everyone else and ends up with the largest portion of the pie, a billionaire, and everyone else gets just peanuts. Instead, it is a task that demands careful planning and thought. It must cover the ownership for each of the investors and all of the employees for each of the next five years. Each of those stakeholders will be looking for an expected return on investment over the next five years. You must forecast the financial numbers in detail and come close to satisfying each person. When you do, you can rest

Table 22-1 Company Shareholders

- Founders
- Management and employees
- Advisers, boards, and groups of technical and business experts
- Consultants and contractors
- Strategic partners, including customers, suppliers, and selling organizations
- Recruiters
- Investors
- Board of directors

SOURCE: *Nesheim Group.*

assured that your company will have enough wealth to share with the people and investors you need to attract to make the company a success. The list of shareholders (see Table 22-1) is longer than some first-time entrepreneurs expect.

FINDING THE GOLDEN MIDDLE

How do you find the golden middle, the number of shares for each stakeholder? Here are some tips from serial entrepreneurs who have done it before.

Find comparable companies.

Financial statements of large public companies are easy to find: *www.sec.gov* lets you access for free the EDGAR database with all the historical financial statements you could ever want, including those of IPOs (Form 4246). The data are for many companies—American and overseas headquartered—whose stocks are traded on exchanges in the United States. Use EDGAR to get the historical financials of a few comparable public companies, the ones you want to have your start-up compared with at the time of IPO. The valuations of private companies are a bit trickier to get, but it is done every day in cities around the world. You too can get on the inside track of the confidential world of start-up valuations. Begin by gaining the confidences of other entrepreneurs: talk to them, and start sharing your numbers with them. Then do the same with lawyers, accountants, angels, and, even venture capitalists. Your goal is to find the valuations of privately funded start-ups similar to yours—new enterprises seeking money to launch their first product.

Do your stock option numbers with care.

Create a spreadsheet model of how many shares you plan on granting by stock options each year over five years. Name the first twenty employees and the number of shares for each. Then add the other stakeholders who will get shares. Set a value of the stock options per share (the *strike price*) for each of the five years. Add the shares to get the pool of shares reserved for stock options. Combine them with the founders' shares and shares sold to investors for each round of your financing. Total the shares for the entire company for each of the five years.

Value your company for each of the five years.

You need to know how to value your stock for each year of your company's life. One way is to review Chapter 9 of *High Tech Start Up*, which explains how valuations are set for high tech companies. Appendix D also contains tables of the valuations and capitalizations of real companies in several industries. Or ask for assistance from a serial entrepreneur or start-up accountant or lawyer. The secret trick they have learned is that you value a new enterprise by working backward. They start with the date of the predicted IPO and then work backward, year by year, to the seed round, valuing each year as they work toward the seed round. An investor in each year must be able to get a return on investment high enough to attract the investor. That ROI will be the cost of capital for that investor. As the risk goes down each year, the required ROI goes down. Then use the price per share each year to calculate the wealth for each employee. Each employee will be expecting an amount of wealth at IPO time that reflects his or her risk in joining the new enterprise. You must also forecast that in detail.

Valuation planning can go a long way to strengthening your plan and its inherent unfair advantage. The audience will see the possibility of a large amount of wealth to be created and shared fairly by the stakeholders. When you complete that portion of your story, you are ready to present it to anyone. They will get excited about how you plan to convert your idea into a remarkable unfair advantage.

- Figure 22-1 shows how dilution works as shares sold to investors and employees are added to the total shares of the new enterprise. Founders own less and less as a percentage of the company. Investors are eventually also diluted by increasing stock options for new employees that help the company grow larger and larger.

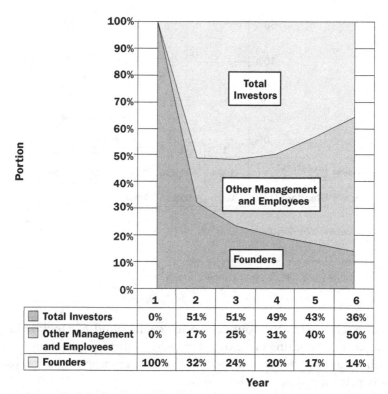

	1	2	3	4	5	6
▨ Total Investors	0%	51%	51%	49%	43%	36%
▨ Other Management and Employees	0%	17%	25%	31%	40%	50%
▢ Founders	100%	32%	24%	20%	17%	14%

Year

Source: *Nesheim Group.*

Figure 22-1 Company Ownership Graph

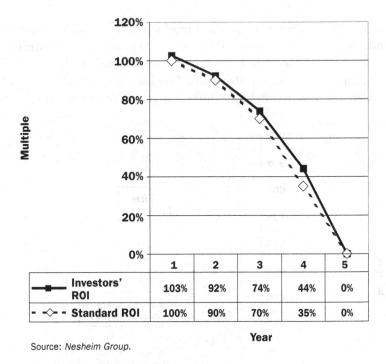

	1	2	3	4	5
Investors' ROI	103%	92%	74%	44%	0%
Standard ROI	100%	90%	70%	35%	0%

Source: *Nesheim Group.*

Figure 22-2 Investors' Return on Investment Graph

- Figure 22-2 helps the founders price each round of stock sold to investors. By coming close to the expected return on investment for each round of risk capital raised, the new enterprise can realistically price the shares of the company.

- The valuation of rounds of financing can also be shown as in Table 22-2. There the numbers are clear for each deal proposed for investors. For instance, it shows the value of the company after each round of financing (post-money), the price per share of the shares, how much cash was raised from the sale of shares, and the relationship between the value of the company and its sales in dollars.

Table 22-2 Company Valuation Table

	Year 1	Year 2	Year 3	Year 4	Year 5
Sales	$450	$6,400	$26,800	$53,600	$92,500
Multiple of Annual Sales (000)	4	4	4	4	4
Calculated company valuation post money[1] (000)	$2,400	$25,600	$107,200	$214,400	$370,000
Chosen company valuation post money (000)	$10,000	$32,000	$91,000	$220,000	$380,000
Total company shares[2] (000)	9,300	12,581	15,187	17,512	21,000
Value Per Share[3]	$1.08	$2.54	$5.99	$12.56	*$18.10 IPO*
Investors' ROI multiple = risk curve[4]	16.8	7.1	3.0	1.4	1.0
Investors' ROI[5] (percent per year)	103%	92%	74%	44%	0%

SOURCE: *Nesheim Group.*

1 Post money and pre money are terms for the company after and before a round of financing.
2 Total company shares = Founders' shares + shares sold to investors + shares reserved for stock options
3 Value per share = ($Post money company value)/(Number of shares fully diluted, including all shares reserved for share options)
4 Investors' return of investment multiple is also an index of the risk of the company. It is calculated as follows: Multiple = (Year 5 $/share)/(This year's $/share)
5 Investors' ROI = $1 grows to IPO value (Year 5 $/Share) at this interest rate per year.

DETAILS INVESTORS WANT

After your presentation to interested investors, you are nearly finished. But there is one more thing to prepare for: expect to have experienced investors follow up by asking for a lot more detail. The following example is a disguised version of an actual email sent the afternoon following a final presentation by a core team at Newco to the partners at North Venture Capital Partners.

Example 22-1   Information Required by Investors: North VC and Newco

—Original Message—

From: dick@northvc.com

Sent: Monday, December 17, 2003, 6:48 PM

To :tom@newco.com

Subject: Newco Presentation Follow-up

Tom: Thank you for your overnight package. Although the materials you sent do generally address the areas in which I had questions, we need more concrete information to move forward. These are some of the questions I am looking to you to answer and specifically what information will help me.

1. What does your sales pipeline look like? The materials you sent do tell me who you are talking to, but I would like to know where you are in the sales process with these companies and what the size/structure of the sales deals by customer may be.

2. Where are your detailed financial forecasts? (cash flow, balance sheet, cap tables, etc.) The numbers you presented were a good sketch. We want the entire set in detail.

3. What is your go-to-market strategy? The materials you sent indicate the markets you will attack, but I would like to know more concretely about timing, anticipating how much in sales and to whom, as well as how you might hope to attack these first customers and other types of customers.

4. In your slide on mobile phones in Japan you note the share of market for DoCoMo (Kyocera, Sanyo, Toshiba, Hitachi), Panasonic, NEC, MEC. Where did you get this information?

If you would like to discuss my questions, please don't hesitate to give me a call. I am in North America a week from Wednesday. As I will be on vacation this week I probably will not answer immediately, but I have my cell phone and definitely will give you a call back.

Regards, Dick

COMPLETION

Congratulations! Now you know the elements used to craft a strong unfair advantage. There is only one step left: put your story into your own words. Write your business plan. It is your statue to mold and shape. It is your new enterprise story. You can do it. Others have preceded you and succeeded. So can you!

PART III

APPLYING UNFAIR ADVANTAGE

23

SURFING DISRUPTIVE TECHNOLOGY WAVES

Unfair advantage is used to surf waves caused by disruptive technologies. A disruption triggers the next wave of new enterprises. Technical minds never stop thinking. Innovative people create opportunities that use disruptive technologies to start fresh waves.

Serial entrepreneurs have learned to spot the new waves. They look for swells beginning to rise, hoping to spot the next great ride before others do. That is one reason they are so secretive. They are technology wave experts. They have learned to surf the boom-to-bust high tech waves. Let's examine a few waves so you can begin to analyze them and prepare to ride one. I will show how to use unfair advantage to surf to win.

WE HAVE BEEN HERE BEFORE

Waves such as the Internet boom-to-bust are not new. The PC era was also a huge wave with a tiny beginning, an exciting rise to stardom, and a crash ending. So were the giant genetic engineering and monoclonal antibodies waves. Other large waves include semiconductors, workstations, personal digital appliances, cell phones, digitization of movies, and high definition television. More recent ones include genome biotechnology, cancer therapies, global positioning systems, wireless networking, and nanotechnologies. Fresh waves are arriving as you read this. Each wave is new and yet shares important characteristics with prior waves.

Each wave has its own starting point, and as soon as it is spotted, countless technical minds spring into action like eager surfers waiting in the ocean balanced on their boards. They push off and begin to ride the new wave. Most will fall off before reaching the beach, but that does not stop them. They are even more determined to get more out of riding the next wave. The now-experienced riders will again paddle out and join others looking for the next great wave.

Each disruptive technology triggers a wave by itself. But several of the waves bump into each other as they begin to move forward. Sometimes several combine to create tsunami-sized waves such as the Internet. Each wave starts, rises, moves forward, gathers speed, crests, begins a rapid descent, and finally crashes on the beach. That ends the life of the wave. That is how they work. Waves are not new. They are a way of life. We cannot avoid them. They are neither good nor bad. They just are. Entrepreneurs learn to surf them.

WHAT A WAVE LOOKS LIKE

Waves that follow the boom-to-bust cycle look similar. Kindleberger's classic study, *Manias, Panics, and Crashes: A History of Financial Crises,* looked back over centuries in which different kinds of eco-

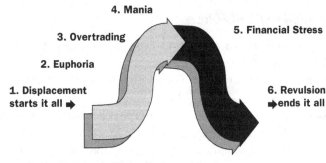

Source: *Charles Kindleberger,* Manias, Panics, and Crashes *(New York: Wiley, 2000). Nesheim Group.*

Figure 23-1 Wave Pattern: Kindleberger's Phases

nomic cycles and business waves came and went.[1] From tulips to oil to foreign currencies, he concluded that these waves go through sequential phases and form the same distinctive pattern (Figure 23-1):

1. **Displacement:** Something arrives to upset business as usual.
2. **Euphoria:** The first excited investors begin to put money into related new enterprises.
3. **Overtrading:** A rush starts to get in on the ground floor, and money flows into many new companies.
4. **Mania:** A wild rush to get in before it is too late sends a river of money flowing into anything related.
5. **Financial stress:** Reality arrives as new enterprises begin to crash and optimism turns to pessimism.
6. **Revulsion:** Investors depart, many with nothing.

I find the same pattern in high tech boom-to-bust cycles. Let's look at Kindleberger's description of a wave and use it to explain a classical high tech wave created by a disruptive technology. As you read, try applying each phase to a wave you are familiar with, such as the Internet.

1. **Displacement.** Innovation begins a new high tech wave by giving birth to a new technology. Entrepreneurs get wind of the new technology and begin to dream of making cool new products with it.
2. **Euphoria.** As soon as the pioneering companies get funded and their first products are launched, a group of start-ups led by experienced entrepreneurs enters with business plans that also get funded. The media begin to write stories about an exciting future for this new wave.
3. **Overtrading.** Investors race to fund exciting new start-ups, and suddenly there is money for nearly anyone. A herd of me-too start-ups rushes in. Everyone is talking about the new wave.
4. **Mania.** Word spreads fast, and overnight everybody wants in on this next great thing, regardless of how wild its business claims are. Suddenly anyone is an expert about the new wave.
5. **Financial stress.** Competitive battles become intense. Individual companies begin to stand out, taking commanding leads over competitors that are falling further and further behind. Reality sinks in that only a rare few will thrive, with the rest doomed to slide into oblivion.

6. **Revulsion.** In the final phase, a few victorious gorillas and chimpanzees emerge, and the last of the struggling start-ups succumb. Venture investors celebrate their few winners, count their losses, and start looking for the next great thing.

WHICH PHASE OF THE WAVE ARE YOU RIDING?

Each phase of the wave calls for different riding skills. If you want to try a ride, begin by identifying which phase you have chosen to start at. Then modify your plan to fit that phase. If you enter at the displacement phase, your plan will look much different than if you enter in the mania phase.

Table 23-1 Phases of a Wave Through Investors' Eyes

Phase 1: **New technology arrives, but the opportunities are unclear, foggy.** *Technology gurus* get the attention of seed-round investors, preferably ones experienced from the last great wave. Technology is king.

Phase 2: **Some think they see a large potential market has been discovered.** *Core teams with plans* for a new business rise to the top popularity charts of investors with deep pockets. Market insight is king.

Phase 3: **Infinite-sized dreams billow upward.** *Incomplete core teams with better ideas* get funded by a growing herd of very excited investors. Business models are king.

Phase 4: **Mania.** *Anyone with an idea* using the new technology qualifies as "management," and investors of all kinds stand in line begging to invest. Anything is king.

Phase 5: **Reality is conceded.** *Only experienced, complete core teams* who can walk on water get funded, but few try. Tough management is king.

Phase 6: **Gorillas emerge.** *No one gets funded.* The wave is over. Bankruptcy is king. Investors count their losses, celebrate a few winners, and begin to look for the next wave.

SOURCE: *Nesheim Group.*

The movement of a wave from phase to phase changes which elements are best to use to build an unfair advantage. That is why serious entrepreneurs become wave experts. They have learned that what works well in the boom phase is bad in the bust phase, and vice versa. Become a student of start-up waves. Learn to recognize which phase a wave is in and which are the best elements to use in each phase to build an unfair advantage. Study how to keep modifying your competitive advantage as the wave rolls forward. Finally, like a fast-swimming seal maneuvering to get away from attacking sharks, be prepared with moves that will keep you ahead of your competitors and put them at a disadvantage in their attempts to attack you during your ride.

To get you started analyzing the phases of a wave and picking the best elements for an unfair advantage, look at Table 23-1 which shows how investors change their interest in management during the phases of a wave. Management is always at or nearly at the top of the list of what is important to stakeholders. It is what attracts the best people and money. Yet each phase of a wave changes the flavor of what is meant by "attractive management."

Adjust your plan and its management team according to what phase of the wave you are in. The modifications will add greatly to your unfair advantage.

TIMING YOUR ENTRY

There is an old saying, "The rising tide lifts all boats. But it won't raise a stone." It is attributed to everyone from an unknown caveman to presidents. Applied to new enterprises, it means the rising wave will not compensate for an inadequate business plan. You must have an unfair advantage. Without it, you are a stone.

Everyone expects the next wave lift to lift them like the tide. However, serial entrepreneurs appreciate that it is very hard to be exact about the arrival date of the next great thing. I found experienced entrepreneurs very sensitive to the dangers of the lure to rush into a new market too early. They resist premature entry. Before hopping on their boards, they spend extra time to confirm there is a wave to ride. That is why they believe in second-mover advantage. They have seen many attempts that proved to be too early. Several have experienced the painful disappointment of jumping on what they expected to be the next giant wave but which turned out to be small and quickly washed out. That is why doing market research by talking to potential customers is so important. If the tide is large enough, a new market will grow, splinter, and open up lucrative segments for entrepreneurs to ride to victory.

Although entering a later phase has its advantages, dominant leaders begin to emerge during later stages, making it more dangerous to enter the competition. It is hard to come up with an unfair advantage if you are going to be the twelfth company trying to build a similar mousetrap. And if you are thinking about entering during the mania phase, the wave will already be peaking by the time you get funded. The crash will follow shortly after. Similarly, if the downward phase has already begun, it is unwise to expect even a great idea with great management to get funded quickly. Even the so-called start-up gods, the serial founders of world-class start-ups, find it nearly impossible to get financed after the mania phase starts sliding into the crash phase. This is the kind of anticipatory thinking that the venture community thrives on. It is part of their daily lives. Time your entry wisely.

DIFFERENT MOVES FOR DIFFERENT PHASES

The wise entrepreneur knows that strategic and tactical mistakes cause high tech wave riders to crash on the rocks. Picking the right moves depends on knowing which phase the wave is in and what works best and worst in each phase. Following are some examples.

Raising money is difficult and time-consuming in all phases, except during mania.

Plan on needing months (I recommend about nine months) to get experienced investors to reach for their checkbooks. Be ready to answer very tough questions, so do your homework, complete your business plan, and construct your unfair advantage. Be prepared for a long time to transpire before you get your money.

Easy mania money lures core teams into dangerous planning behavior.

Hot times make it tempting to grab the money and run with it. "We will construct a business plan later." But my analysis of waves such as the Internet era tells me that the winners were dominated by people who took time to craft an unfair advantage before going for the easy money. Because they had unfair advantages, they soon outdistanced and outlasted the competition (still trying to figure out a good plan). They became stronger by the day, successfully rode the rising wave, and survived the inevitable crash that consolidated the new industry. Those leaders did not simply let the tide lift their businesses. Instead, as the tide rose, they continued to add more and more power to the company's unfair advantage. That is what enabled them to thrive, not just survive. They went IPO and emerged as gorillas.

Plan to exploit the shortage of outstanding people during the mania phase.

In overheated days, it is hard to hire. Make the problem an opportunity: create a special "hot times" recruiting program that will overcome intense competition for top talent. Craft the story of your unfair advantage so that it is so compelling that even during the wildest of times, top talent will flock to your door instead of to the one down the street.

The mania phase intensifies pressure to compromise on the quality of people hired.

Start-up history shows me that your hiring rate is going to be even slower than you, the ever-optimistic entrepreneur, anticipate. That will make it tempting for you to fill jobs with anybody and everybody. Even during the easy-to-hire phases, hiring delays will pressure you to compromise on quality of personnel. Resist those temptations. Seek only world-class talent at all times. Do not succumb to the pressure to settle for the first average people that you find.

Plan to reach profitability before the market peaks and starts its downward plunge.

Profits are hard to attain during boom times because your company is growing so fast and everyone says the good times will go on indefinitely. The temptation is to go on spending at a high negative burn rate, leaving profits until sometime in the far future. But every wave eventually peaks and crashes. I find the companies that became world-class planned to generate a profit and attain positive cash flow well before the crash phase began. Their leaders were passionate about becoming profitable. They did not listen to industry gurus and the media touting that profits were not important.

"Thou shall not run out of cash" in any phase is the first financial commandment of start-ups.

Manage your burn rate prudently and differently for each phase. The mania phase encourages wild spending, while the other phases focus on how to ration it. Pioneering founders learned it is wasteful to promote a company before the prototype works. It is not wise to start selling before the first product excites the ideal customer. It does not pay to start spending on PR before reporters understand what the new market is all about. Plan on hiring professionals who know how to spend wisely. Employ people who can monitor and control your cash flow as well as your profits. Set your key milestones with some time to spare. That demonstrates that professional managers are in charge. Then you will increase your company's valuation and attract the next round of financing.

Your plan will have to shift gears, particularly in response to the inevitable unexpected events.

Remember the start-up adage, "Doing a start-up is like building a bicycle while you are riding it." Your company will sequentially go through the classic phases of the high tech wave. Everything will change a great deal. Your business plan will need to be updated every six months. In two years, you will not recognize it compared with your first plan. As the wave shifts unexpectedly, you have to react. That is what "execution" is all about. Lay down your strategy, and then shift to tactics. Modify your plan as you find out what works and what does not. Your stakeholders will be expecting you to be continuously altering your choice of elements to boost your unfair advantage, build momentum, and emerge the leader of your new market category.

PICKING POWERFUL FORCES TO PROPEL YOU

Earlier I explained how different phases alter what investors look for in core management teams. Let's look at some of the other choices to add power to your advantage. I will show you how to alter them to fit the special needs of each phase of a boom-to-bust cycle. In each phase, there are powerful forces that you can create. The power comes from making wise choices from among the many elements used to build a strong unfair advantage.

During the earliest phase, your visionary and proof-of-concept skills are priceless.

During this phase, the CEO raises seed money based on a conceptual story. It is not easy because not much seems real or concrete yet.

- Venture investors are intrigued but are very big doubters in this phase. You need links to a few partners of the world-class venture firms who will give you the benefit of the doubt and open their schedule for a presentation.

- Angel investors become especially attractive in this phase because of their domain skills and patience. They are willing to spend extra time to help you "find a pony to ride" with your idea, that is, to figure out how to make a big business out of it.

- Technology is big in this phase, but so is a special kind of engineering staff. You need a tiny group of practical technologists who are craftspeople able to translate dreams into prototypes that work. There is no product yet. It is in the twinkle of the eye of your technical guru and marketing brain. Your engineers must be more skilled as experimentalists who build prototypes than technical staffers who build products to specification. Many of the technology risks are unknowns in this phase.

- Your marketing people should be skilled at thinking up a first product that customers will be eager to use. There are no customers yet.

- Core team members must be skilled at talking to and analyzing potential customers and enticing powerful strategic partners.

- The company works hard on choosing a clever entry strategy.

- The existing ("old-fashioned") way of doing things is the competition and market leader.

- Marcom works to position the company as a leader of an exciting but not-yet-proven-market. Naming and messaging choices become very important because they set the stage for future branding and standards setting.

- Founders who flourish in this phase come from the ranks of respected serial entrepreneurs, but include very clever promoters and often highly charismatic communicators. First-time entrepreneurs find getting attention very difficult.

- In combination, those skills contribute forces that add advantage during the earliest phase of a new enterprise.

Product marketing skills rise in importance during the euphoric or second phase.

As word spreads and the new market opportunity becomes clearer, the decision to enter the competition gets easier. But the best elements of unfair advantage are different from those used for success in the prior pioneering phase.

- Start-up money becomes easier to obtain. Founders find themselves having choices of investors. The best start-up ideas find VCs beginning to compete to invest in the better new enterprise ideas.

- Skill in picking the first twenty employees becomes especially important in this phase. The clock begins ticking down to the time to launch the first product, increasing the sense of urgency. However, talented people are eager to leave a good employer to join a start-up core team. They can see the new market opportunity and want to hop on board a promising new enterprise.

- In this phase company leaders are builders who attract the money and a batch of real managers. They take the spotlight away from the visionary leaders of the prior phase. They have outstanding track records as leaders who launched successful businesses. They are capable of forming core teams that convert ideas to real products that sizzle.

- Technology takes a back seat to other functions like marketing. Compared with the earlier phase, technology becomes one of the elements of unfair advantage, not the most important one.

- New products are refined starting with the end user instead of with technology. Technology problems are smaller, reduced to a difficult but manageable set of challenges. The first products are built by engineers who watched pioneers make product mistakes. The new hires are skilled at crafting a real product from a soft set of specs set by practical marketing people who refine a real product based on daily talks with potential customers.

- The first twenty employees form a team that is especially skilled at rapid construction of simple infrastructure to take orders, deliver new products, support customers, collect receivables, pay suppliers, and keep up with the rapid growth of the new enterprise.

- Marketing focuses on finding a hot market segment to try to dominate. The by-now-floundering pioneering companies showed the way by discovering where the market was not.

- Preliminary selling skills rise in importance. Customers are curious and willing to listen to laptop presentations before the product is ready for delivery. Marketing or business development staff take responsibility for this job during this phase.

- Finance has a plan calculated to manage the burn rate well beyond the second round of funding. The five-year plan is ready and supported with many details.

Great people are your ace card during the mania phase.

In this phase, the entire world is rushing to get aboard the wagon. The gold rush is on. Everyone is running as fast as they can to find a market—any market—to dominate before the boom comes to its inevitable halt. The thunderous herd of competitors ignores the reality that a start-up is a marathon and behaves as if it is a sprint.

- Money is easy to get. People are hell to get. They are outrageously expensive. CEOs must have enormous courage and skill recruiting outstanding employees as fast as they can. Compromising on people in this phase is a great temptation. Pick people and investors wisely; you will have to live intimately with them for half a decade or more.

- The core team in this phase consists of balancing artists who run very fast. Everything has to be done instantly.

- Marketing focuses on differentiation and media messaging management. The core team is especially talented at using marcom to get the attention of the media. The objective is that their company can appear as very different, very clever, and very certain to be very successful. Fighting for media attention dominates marketing fights during this phase.

- New products are invented in the heads of the core team instead of starting with the end user or with technology. The first product is already known, and follow-on products are created in the minds of innovative employees.

- There are no more difficult engineering problems to overcome. The new employees are good at testing and quality control.

- Selling in the crowded market becomes highly aggressive, clawing for orders from customers besieged by a wild frenzy of competing new enterprises.

- Fresh business models are used to gain competitive advantage and access overlooked market segments.

- The core team is very skilled at doing everything on the fly, immediately.

- It seems as if anyone can be a founder and get a company funded.

- Finance staff sweat the first forecasts of sales. Cash burn rates rise beyond plan and are ignored. An experienced chief financial officer is hired and begins to install the first systems and procedures.

During the peaking phase, leaders shift business models to ensure profitability and growth.

This is a dangerous phase in which to try to enter the game. Serial entrepreneurs usually skip doing a start-up in this phase. Existing new enterprise core teams find themselves becoming fearful. They sense big changes are coming rapidly and unpredictably, and they are going to be unavoidable. Confidence begins to melt like snow in the desert. The hardest part is anticipating when the peak will arrive and the plunge will begin. People begin to look for the edge of the cliff.

- The primary objective is to confirm the company has become the dominant leader of a new market category before the next, very dark phase begins. By then, management will have given its all to establish the company as king of its hill. If they are successful, the first signs of victory will be clear—the competition begins to wilt in the competitive heat.

- Fiscal measures of success, including profits and positive cash flow, become clear and manageable.

- The trick is to have already built a strong unfair advantage by the time your company arrives at this unpredictable phase. Your goal is to have built a strong foundation during the preceding euphoric and mania stages.

- The best core teams in this phase are the growers. They grow sales, profits, and cash flow in spite of sensing the bubble will burst and doom will arrive. They create more new products, add sales in new countries, and find fresh market segments. They are often referred to as professional managers.

- Leadership moves to preserve surplus cash. The enterprise has attracted large sums of money raised in multiple rounds of financing. Management has earned the respect of the media, the local community, and investors.

- Finance reduces hiring and spending plans, preparing for the arrival of the storm and plans on helping the company leave the last phase as a big winner. IPO dreams begin to surface.

Cash reserves are king as you head into the crash phase.

Your company has attained its vaulted goal: it has become a gorilla of its target market segment. Attackers are weakening. The market continues to grow, but at a slower rate. Your company is a winner. No one with any wisdom tries to enter the competition in this phase.

- Do not plan on raising fresh capital until the funerals are finished. You might get lucky raising a fresh round, but don't count on it. Its cost of capital will be very high, and you will learn the pain of "cram-downs" (where distasteful terms of a financing are forced upon your company, i.e., crammed down your throat).

- Do not wait to cut back on spending. Cutting back too late will add your company to the funeral pyre. Yes, the company still needs cash to compete. That is why the finance staff is very skilled in this phase at managing the burn rate.

- People who know how to manage well during the crash phase are defenders. They keep the company on the top of its market, fiscally healthy, and highly respected. As the wave crashes on the beach, they emerge as one of the few big winners and look forward to years of long-term prosperity.

Those are a few examples of skills that can add power to your unfair advantage, depending on which phase of the wave you are riding. There are many more choices and opportunities to use to step ahead of your competition. Try reviewing your plan and modifying it according to what you had planned to do during each phase of riding your wave.

ANALYZING COMPETITIVE RIDERS

Take the time to analyze who will be your toughest competitive surfer. Figure out how your market leader is most likely to ride this wave. Look for common mistakes, such as choosing the wrong elements to emphasize during each phase. Study the psychology of the CEO and core team, especially if the competitor is another new enterprise instead of a giant. Analyze the people, the management, and the competitor well enough to predict with confidence how they will react to the next shift in the wave you are both trying to surf to victory. A very strong, but mostly overlooked, element of an unfair advantage analysis is the insight gained about the very soul of your archrival. How will the CEO respond to competitive duress (especially the kind your company will cause)? How does he or she like to surf high tech waves?

EXECUTING THE RIDE

When you ride your wave, you are executing your business plan. You have to ride, make it happen, and hope you will do it very well. The market may appear wonderful and very large, and the times ideal for your new enterprise. But the surfboard will not carry you effortlessly to victory. You have to do a lot of hard work paddling, fight to stay balanced, and make many difficult decisions so that you gain and keep the lead while you ride this new market category wave. Note that this book is not about the execution of your plan. That is a subject to be worked on in the future. But be sure you use the management section of your story to present your case for how your core team will be outstanding at executing your business plan during each phase of the wave. The core team must be attractive to the stakeholders as competent wave riders. Each core team leader must have a compelling story of managerial excellence based on a documented track record. In other words, present why your core team is ideal for this phase of the wave you are planning to surf. That will increase the eagerness of each stakeholder to participate in your ride.

GORILLAS EMERGE ON THE BEACH

By the time the ride is over and the wave has crashed onto the beach, one company has emerged as the dominant winner of the new industry. It once was a tiny start-up. Now it is referred to as a gorilla. It is not from the herd of slower-moving giant corporate elephants. Yes, a few large, existing corporations will decide—slowly—to try to ride the newest technology wave. But history is not kind to them: most of the time, they arrive too late and either crash on the rocks or give up and bail out.

Some corporate giants choose to remain watching from the beach, preferring not to attempt to ride. Instead, they bet their money on a deal with a hot-looking start-up rider. They either become a strategic partner or eventually purchase the start-up rider and company. Such deals do not produce gorillas. Gorillas are pure start-ups that rode the new market segment to domination. The gorillas of tomorrow learned the secret from yesterday's gorillas: you become a gorilla by creating and developing a strong unfair advantage that propels your company and transforms it into a gorilla by the time it reaches the beach.

SUMMARY OF WAVE RIDING

To ride a disruptive technology wave, create an unfair advantage that enables you to become the gorilla of your targeted new market segment. Ride new waves whenever possible, avoiding attempts at being a cheaper-faster-better competitor of an old wave. Try very hard to enter at the most lucrative time—neither too early nor too late (either extreme is death). Each wave has distinctive phases. Study them so you know the phase you will be in when you enter the competitive fray. Pick the right moves and best elements to build unfair advantage for the phase of wave you are in. Be sure to spend lots of time talking to real customers. They are critical to choosing your moves. Wrong choices will prematurely crash you on the rocks. Become the expert at knowing how your competition will surf the wave, trying to beat you to the beach and emerge as the new gorilla, dominant king of the new hill. Be especially wise about how competing CEOs will respond to competitive stress. Take extra care to assemble an outstanding core team. Pick your dream team based on how they have ridden waves in the past. Assemble your story in the form of a compelling unfair advantage. It will attract the stakeholders you need to surf to IPO victory as the gorilla of the next great land rush, the next great thing.

24

GOING WORLD-CLASS

*I*n my global travels, I found two mottoes central to the mind-sets of experienced entrepreneurs: (1) "Think world-class only." (2) "Never say you are a Brazilian or Chinese or American company; instead, say you are the leader of a new category." Veterans feel strongly about running their new enterprises according to these mottoes. Let me explain why. You can use them as part of your unfair advantage.

THINKING WORLD-CLASS

Battle-scarred veterans admonish their core teams to think like world-class champions from the day of birth of the new business. They do not think, "I'll start very small and someday grow larger." They have painfully learned that if you don't start by thinking world-class, then they will quickly find themselves overrun by world-class-thinking companies. Goodbye to you, world-class to them.

Never say you are a Brazilian or Chinese or American company.

Times have changed. Gone are the days when success was ensured by exploiting local political clout and business connections with friends. That used to be the way to get special benefits for new enterprises from governments—financial subsidies and tariff walls that prevented painful attacks by powerful world-class competitors. It used to be how you got the sales order. But today such business methods are derisively dubbed crutches, a sign of weakness. More important, the forces of free market globalization are too strong; they break crutches. The important markets of the world are open to entry by any competing enterprise from any country. Your company cannot expect to use crutches and learn to run like a world-class competitor. Today's new enterprise must learn—quickly—how to fight and win in the large, open global markets of North America, Europe, and Asia.

Culture barriers are not strong enough to hide behind.

"But we are Chinese and understand China. Our competitors don't." I have heard that argument in every country I have visited. The flaw is simple: as soon as you show there is a new market in China for some new gadget, world-class competitors rush into China, hiring your Chinese cousins. You lose your cultural advantage. No longer is it possible to become a significant company if your team sees its advantage as being the only company that understands the local culture.

Instead, think of yourself as the leader of a new category.

Wouldn't it be great to be known as *the* leader of a hot, new global market? Like Xerox or FedEx, your company name would be synonymous with the new category (plain paper copiers or overnight package delivery). Intel means microprocessors and Cisco means routers. That is winning big. You do not get there by saying you are a Brazilian company. You get there by focusing on dominating a new market category.

Competitors will figure out how to get around barriers.

This century is marked by intense, rapidly shifting tectonic plates of industrial competitiveness. The shifts are evidenced by increasing competition between groups of aggressive companies, young and old, headquartered in many countries. They are rushing after the same new worldwide markets that you are: waves triggered by the latest disruptive technologies. As soon as new enterprises spot the new market segment popping up in another country, they rush there. They figure out clever ways to leap across border and cultural barriers. Soon they start selling in the new country. They cannot be stopped.

The important new markets are world markets from their beginning. That is why start-up founders keep their passports handy and a bag packed, ready to fly on short notice to any country where there is an eager potential customer. They think, talk, and act world-class from day 1.

LESSON OF THE BUTTERFLY'S PROTECTIVE COCOON

Remember the lesson of the butterfly: biologists teach us that if you try to help a butterfly avoid its violent struggle out of its protective cocoon, the butterfly will die. It needs the struggle to strengthen its beautiful wings so that it can fly. Avoiding the struggle will not work.

Some entrepreneurs look for a lot of help from their local government. I find that is a big mistake. Such companies grow up distorted and become weak competitors. Once a new enterprise becomes accustomed to the crutches of cozy government support and subsidies, it is very difficult to throw away the crutches and run as fast as the rest of the highly competitive world. Singaporeans call it the cocooning effect. Safe, cozy, protected business environments produce weak companies. Safety enclosures do not expose start-ups to the rough and tumble of the capitalistic world. Modern entrepreneurs agree: new enterprises must learn to get tough while taking big risks. They need to learn how to compete with the best in any market in the world. That should start on the first day of the life of the start-up.

LESSON: ISRAEL 1-2-3

World-thinking new enterprises are not just in the United States. I have found outstanding examples in other countries, small and large. Proportionate to population, Israel is the world leader of successful high tech start-ups. That tiny country of 6 million has over 150 new enterprises that have gone public on the NASDAQ stock exchange during the past half-century. This is second only to Canada. They are black-belt masters at creating unfair advantages.

By contrast, European and Asian countries with similar-sized populations are seen as outstanding if they have more than two start-ups that went IPO on NASDAQ. In Europe during recent decades, the new enterprise momentum has dwindled to nearly zero in the large, mature countries. Their labor laws, taxation, social systems, and cultures inhibit creation of new businesses of any size. However, the smaller countries in Eastern Europe are eagerly starting new enterprises. They might be able to renew a badly needed wave of world-class start-ups headquartered in Europe. Similarly, there are a lot of eager entrepreneurs in Asia, especially in giants like India and China. Time will tell how successful they are as measured by the number of IPOs on NASDAQ. Today's low number of NASDAQ-listed companies that were started outside the United States reflects how hard the struggle is. It is very difficult to create something from nothing and triumph in competition against companies of all sizes from any country around the globe. Companies that figure out how to think world-class from birth have the best chance of becoming world-class winners. That thinking converts an idea for a small local business into a competitively healthy new enterprise with an unfair advantage.

Example 24-1   World-Class Start-ups: How Israel Does 1-2-3

Over the past two decades, I have had the delightful opportunity to work with and observe high tech entrepreneurs from Israel. They have contributed to a wave of unprecedented new enterprises that should inspire eager entrepreneurs in any country. They have shown how new enterprises from a tiny country can create an astounding number of successful high tech start-ups. That is second only to Canada. Over decades, its entrepreneurs have figured out how to build unfair advantages that quickly transform fledgling companies into competitive giants selling around the world.

Israel is not an attractive place to start a new enterprise. At the country level, the size of the local Israeli market for anything is minuscule. Violent hostilities of the Middle East make the country unattractive to invest in compared with Asia, the United States, or Europe. In spite of such serious disadvantages, the government has not tried to protect local start-ups or provide easy money. Instead it has created incentives to entrepreneurs who wish to start new businesses locally and become world-class competitors. The government has solicited and encouraged venture investors to establish offices in Israel. There are also attractive financial incentives for companies that spend money on early-stage product research and development. Other inducements include competitive labor laws and low taxes on long-term capital gains. Local financial securities laws encourage venture capital deals similar to those done by American investors. Universities and government laboratories encourage spinning out applied technologies to new enterprises. A pool of well-educated technologists comes from students trained at local universities and government institutions. Ambitious immigrants with special talents, a keen desire to work hard, and fresh from training courses add skilled people to the working pool. Military service produces leaders who later become experienced in industry, often after working for multinational corporations, particularly those headquartered in the United States.

At the company level, Israel's new enterprises have learned to practice what I call "the Israeli start-up 1-2-3." Israel's new enterprises repeatedly follow a simple path to world-class success. The beginning step is to (1) form the core team in Tel Aviv, get the seed round done, and have the technical staff finish the proof of concept. Next they (2) fly to the United States and finish filling the management team, especially picking the marketing and selling vice presidents from successful companies. That makes it easier to attract the next rounds of funding that finance the launch of the first product in the United States. In a year or so, the growing start-up has proven to the world it can compete with the best on the planet. Finally, the rapidly growing start-up will (3) go IPO on NASDAQ in order to feed the growth of the company as it expands to markets around the world.

Start-ups from Israel follow that simple 1-2-3 pathway to success. It is a process that start-ups from other countries can copy. I highly recommend it.

MOVING FROM LOCAL TO WORLD-CLASS COMPETITOR

Some new enterprises begin by focusing on their home country because it is a market they feel safe starting to compete in. But soon they realize that their plans that focus on the local market compromise their long-term potential. Focusing on the local market does not produce the world-class greatness its founders dream of.

An interesting example is the Li-Ning Sports Goods Co., a new enterprise in China. I learned of it through students from China and researched its roots and progress. The new enterprise's first-time entrepreneur, Li Ning, began his business by dreaming of becoming a great company selling sport products made by Chinese to the consumer market in China. After all, China's fast-growing economy is going to be huge someday. And even if the Chinese economy today is only about the size of Italy's, China is growing at double the rate of economies of the Western world. Many of the 1.3 billion peasants will want sports shoes and related gear someday soon.

How did Li-Ning Sports Goods Co. do? After a successful beginning, the founder concluded the hard-earned results were below his expectations. In order to prosper, he decided he must change his mind-set from thinking local to thinking world-class. Here is a short description of what the highly respected founder learned and how he changed his company.

Example 24-2   Going World-Class: Beijing Li-Ning Sports Goods Co.

After winning three gold medals in gymnastics at the 1984 Los Angeles Olympics, Li Ning decided to use his name to start a business. He founded Li-Ning Sports Goods Co. to produce sneakers for the market in China. Nike had succeeded as a foreign supplier, and the Chinese consumer market was growing fast.

Initially the shoes sold quickly based on the founder's name. In China, Li is as well known as Michael Jordan is in the United States. The company sold more shoes in China than any other company, including Nike. But soon more Chinese brands appeared on store shelves along with more foreign names. The company could not command the same price premium as flashier foreign brands of sneakers and apparel. Li-Ning products sold for two-thirds to half that of the premium brands and became positioned as a low-quality sneakers company selling dated styles.

The results prompted Li to make some bold changes. He dismissed his relatives who worked as employees and hired professional managers. He added more fashion and flair to products by contracting with Italian designers. He spread the word about the changes by hiring a French advertising firm. Soon his sports products showed up on the Spanish women's basketball world champion team, while the Chinese team wore Nike uniforms. He also sponsored teams in France, Spain, Russia, and elsewhere. He began to spend a lot more on advertising aimed at establishing his brand, a stylized L, as a rival to foreign brands. His goal was to dominate the category of Chinese-branded sporting goods. Li Ning said, "The whole world is globalizing. If we want to be No. 1 in China, we have to be international as well."

Being branded as world-class from day 1 is easier than shifting out of being branded as a small local company in your country. Get it right the first time. Your objective should not be to become market leader in your home country. Instead, it should be to become the leader of a new world-class market category. Your home market will then be included as part of your global market.

LABOR FLIES BETWEEN COUNTRIES

You can take advantage of the world's mobility of labor. As you read this, thousands of entrepreneurs are moving to new jobs around the world. The movements are epitomized by ambitious thirty-somethings: they spontaneously fly to places like Hungary and Shanghai. In 2002, there were estimated to be over 30,000 English-speaking expatriates in Shanghai. Such people are leaving stagnating economies and stifling job markets such as Germany and France, where cultures inhibit and discourage entrepreneurs and the young cannot find jobs worth doing.

Another opportunity comes in the form of the wave of expatriates returning to their home countries. After leaving the country of their birth and succeeding in thriving economies like the United States, entrepreneurs return to create new businesses that compete on a world-class scale and benefit the local developing economy. India has become a center for outsourced customer service centers and related software. Many of the leaders of the new Indian enterprises learned their skills in other countries and moved back to their mother country after spotting the next great opportunity. China has had a similar return of the diaspora in recent years. Budding Chinese entrepreneurs have created companies doing mainly light manufacturing assembly, but some notable high tech–related start-ups have popped up in recent years, and consumer branding companies are on the rise. There are countless similar stories from other countries. I found a delightful example in a telecommunications entrepreneur in New York City who saw an overlooked opportunity in his home country, Afghanistan.

Example 24-3   Afghanistan Unfair Advantage: Telephone
                Systems International

Founded in 1998 in New York as an international reseller of telephone services, Telephone Systems International grew in a hotly competitive market. With the opening of Afghanistan a few years later, founder Ehsan Bayat saw a flanking opportunity: an uncontested new market for mobile phone services in his home country, Afghanistan. He is an example of an entrepreneur who thinks world-class. Here is how the company's web site announced its expansion to world markets.[1]

About Us: Telephone Systems International (TSI) is a resale service provider with its own international gateway switch in the United States, and is licensed by the Federal Communications Commission of the USA to provide phone service between the USA and international points. TSI, a privately held company, was registered in New Jersey in June 1998, and is headquartered in New York, NY. TSI was founded by Afghan émigré, Ehsan Bayat. Telephone Systems International Inc, Afghanistan became a member of the GSM Association at the April 2002 plenary meeting held in Rome, Italy.

That information was followed by a press announcement explaining the company's entry into Afghanistan.

10 December 2002. Argent Networks awarded convergent billing and customer care contract in Afghanistan. Argent Networks has won a coveted convergent billing and customer care contract that will help reconnect Afghanistan with the outside world, following decades of wartime separation. The US$2.25million contract was awarded by the Afghan Wireless Communication Company (AWCC—a joint venture between New York-based Telephone Systems International, Inc. (TSI) and the Afghan Ministry of Communications.

The press announcement concludes with this telling paragraph that reveals the world-class mind of the founder:

AWCC will be converted into a fully integrated mobile carrier, able to interconnect with all major networks around the world. Subscribers will be able to use the service when traveling overseas, just as visiting subscribers will be able to roam in Afghanistan.

The next time you are traveling in Afghanistan, you will know the cell phone service you are using is from the mind of a world-class thinking entrepreneur, Ehsan Bayat.

25

WHY GIANTS FAIL TO CRUSH NEW ENTERPRISES

*H*istory reveals that giant organizations lose to new enterprises most of the time. Giants have poor track records of competing in new markets that are brought to life by disruptive technologies and exploited by new enterprises. Rarely does an existing gorilla win the dominant position in a new category. Instead, start-ups are victorious, the first to capture the lion's share of the new customers' orders. That may seem surprising, but research reveals it is true.

Why do the thriving, large public corporations, the gorillas of their domains—with much more cash, people, and resources—not crush every tiny new enterprise that springs up? I have observed several reasons. So have serial entrepreneurs and veteran venture investors. Many of the reasons have been very well documented in Clayton Christensen's work, *The Innovators' Dilemma: When New Technologies Cause Great Firms to Fail.*

DIFFERENT EXPERTISE

Giants have become experts at keeping huge organizations alive. But entrepreneurs are experts in starting something from nothing. The leaders of new enterprises are skilled at quickly creating an unfair advantage that puts a giant at a significant disadvantage. Nimble start-up core teams figure out clever ways to use their advantages at the expense of the floundering giants and become the overwhelming victors.

"THE LAW OF NOTHING" PREVAILS

The Law of Nothing is this: "For a market that does not exist today, when that market is at its peak, the companies that dominate at the peak were not there at the beginning." Try out your own memory. Name a company that is a gorilla of a new high tech market category. Did it begin as a start-up or as a gorilla? The list of examples is very long: Intel microprocessors, Cisco routers, Amazon.com e-commerce books, Google Internet search engines, and so on. Start-ups win, becoming the new market gorillas. Gorillas of yesterday do not also become gorillas of the new space. Instead, they typically opt to watch the competing newcomers from the sidelines or wish they had.

"LEAVE US ALONE!"

"Leave us alone!" is the cry of the start-up team that has to struggle inside a giant corporate structure. Large companies fund internal teams assigned to respond to disruptive technologies. They form new business units inside giant parent corporations. If the parent leaves the child alone ("Here is $5 million. Come back rich or broke"), the child has a chance to grow up healthy and emerge as a respected new enterprise in the form of a new product family, new division, or new subsidiary. Sadly, in spite of good intentions, the father never seems be willing to let go of the steering wheel. Instead, at the first signs of things going wrong, the father grabs control away from the entrepreneurs ("Father knows best"). The result is typically an end to the new enterprise, a press release about a special one-time charge to profits for "discontinued operations," and an embarrassed father with some disappointed, angry children.

JEALOUSY: ENEMY NUMBER ONE

Jealousy raises its ugly head when the CEO forms fresh teams and commissions them to do the next cool thing for their giant company. Jealousy is a negative emotion that translates to hostile reaction. I see this as the number one danger to internal start-up teams. Long-time employees left behind complain, "The new enterprise team gets to have all the fun, fame, and fortune, while the rest of us remain as slaves, put up with all the political crap, struggle through long, dull hours, and try to keep sales rising 2 percent a year." This happens whether it is a new business unit, fresh group or division, or even stand-alone subsidiary.

Human jealousy is a powerful drive that clouds wisdom and dulls kindness. I have seen lawyers at headquarters take months to respond to contract approval requests by internal start-up teams begging to get the first sales contracts approved and in front of waiting, eager customers. Test facility managers have demanded months of prior notice before checking out early prototypes. Finance staffs have demanded instantaneous extra paperwork important only to headquarters. Requests by the new enterprise for relief were denied in nearly every case. Even intervention by the parent CEO did little to relieve the situation and change people's behavior. I found this pattern of jealousy-invoked actions to dominate and inhibit the leaders of internal new enterprises started inside large corporations.

FIXATION

Fixation on serving existing customers well made the giant corporation famous. But it is also the root of why start-ups dominate the new market. Long ago, when it was a tiny company, focus on filling the needs of targeted customers brought the giant success. It rose to dominate its market category. It is king of a new hill. It is the victor. It is secure. The competitors are weak and not a serious threat.

After becoming king, all goes well for a few years until the arrival of a disruptive technology. Then the king hears the thunder of the hooves of a herd of new enterprises. At first, the king is not concerned because his customers are not very interested in the consequences of the new technology. But eventually the king decides this new thing is serious and must be studied and analyzed. A special task force is assigned to scout out the phenomenon and return with a report. In a few months, the report is finally made: the threats are real and serious, something must be done soon. Top-level executives hold somber meetings. A few months later, they make a decision about how to respond, but by then the herd of new enterprises has ridden far out of sight.

DEFENDER MENTALITY

This mentality or mind-set is consistent with the defender strategy discussed earlier. By the time the giant makes its first move into the new market, a new enterprise has already become the leader. Some giants see that and decide to remain on the sidelines. Intel stuck to microprocessors but invested in new enterprises that helped develop markets for products made by Intel. Other giants choose to strategic partner with one of the stronger new enterprises in the new space. IBM supported Good Technology's wireless email service. But some giants do choose to attack the new enterprises. Siemens entered the cell phone business well after Nokia was dominant. If one of the late-entering giants is able to achieve a significant level of success (that is rare), its degree of success is less than most observers expected: the successful giant achieves a much smaller share of the new market than the leading start-up. The new enterprise takes the lion's share, with crumbs left for the giant. Nortel and Lucent also tried to do routers, but Cisco became king. In rare cases, a giant can earn a significant share of market, but even then, the portion will be far below that of the dominant (start-up) leader. Nokia became number one and owned more than a 30 percent share of the cell phone world market while giant Motorola owned about half as much. Giants like Sony were far behind and rumored to be losing a lot of money trying to gain market share.

The media are especially harsh on the giants that fail to crush tiny new enterprises. Reporters seem to think that the giant has failed if it does not overtake the leading start-up and become the new and permanent king of the new hill. I disagree. Surely it is respectable for any giant that chooses to compete and ends up ranked in the top five in market share compared with a dominant start-up in a new market category. That is very hard to do and end up with profits. I respect any established corporation that achieves such a result and earns a positive return in its investment.

FLEXIBILITY

There is much greater flexibility in a new enterprise. Start-up veteran Daniel Wong notes that giants have layer on layer of management, all of which must be communicated with when making strategic decisions. He and others know that the process of creating an annual plan for a giant is an agonizing, time-consuming chore, involving thousands of communications with different divisions scattered around the globe. The resulting three-hundred-page document is completed over months of hard work. After that, every employee is expected to stick to the plan for the next twelve months. In contrast, a start-up updates its plan every month. It is completed in a few days and has a tenth the number of pages. New enterprises respond much more quickly to sudden shifts in the new market.

FLAT ORGANIZATIONS AND RESPONSE TIMES

The lack of many layers of management enables new enterprise managers to make instantaneous decisions while they walk down the hall.

Giants have complex matrix organizations that must conduct meeting after meeting, slowing decision making and forcing simple choices into weeks and months of response times.

PROCESSES

Rigid processes are established and religiously followed by employees in the giants. Managers move decisions through people and time using the methods and practices that have been documented in large manuals. The processes are based on the deep values of the very solid culture of the organization. Giants have recorded in concrete "how we do things around here." In contrast, start-ups use processes found to be helpful and discard those that are not. They document as few pages as possible. They move quickly to adapt and change according to what gets the job done the best, the fastest. As new employees arrive, new processes are tried and others modified. A start-up is an organic, ever-changing organism.

SPEED

The speed rate for decision making by giants is glacial speed—it seems to take forever. But it happens in nanoseconds in start-ups. Giants can be counted on to move slowly and are thus very predictable. New enterprises are full of surprises. They jump the same day onto opportunities that they spot. The giants begin to ponder such situations, emerging months later with a decision to begin a task force to investigate a possible opportunity.

DIVERSIFICATION

Diversification is a must for giants and a must-not for start-ups. Research over the past half-century about the risks and rewards of business shows the giants do best when they focus on how to reduce risk. That is what they hire MBAs to do. But start-ups do best when maximizing risk. That means they focus on doing one thing better than any competitor and do nothing else. They are eager to enter one new market. Giants shy away from taking singular, large risks. New enterprises thrive on them. They love high-risk environments. To them, diversification is death by boredom.

EXCEPTIONS

There are a few rare examples of internal start-ups that won. They are cases where the parent isolated the new enterprise and left it alone to live or die as a real start-up. That is a cold reality that is very hard for the culture of a giant to accept. CEOs who do that are brave. Art Money did it at ESL, a subsidiary of TRW. The entrepreneurial program he started inspired several businesses, including Corsair, which later attracted top-tier venture funding and went IPO.

26

VENTURE CAPITAL FIRMS APPLY UNFAIR ADVANTAGE

Venture capital firms compete intensely for the very best—but rare—deals each year. There is an old saying among veteran investors, "In a given year, there are only forty deals worth doing." Those are the start-ups with the greatest potential. Partners of the finest venture firms eagerly wish for the first contact with their founders.

To attract the best deals, the top-ranked VCs have learned to make unfair advantage work for themselves and their firms. Some are so famous that they have become branded. Unfair advantage distinguishes the revered firms from the others.

The venture investing business is a very difficult way to make money. Behind the bright stories of glamour, wealth, power, and adventure is a darker story. The business is intensely competitive, with easy entry: anyone with money to invest can say he or she is a venture capitalist. It is very high risk. One venture wag put it this way: "I've been at it for six years, and I think it will take me another ten to finally feel like I have learned to play this game successfully." Another VC said, "I believe it takes about $20 million of losses to make a real venture capitalist. You make a lot of mistakes along the way to maturity." It is a very long-term game: investors wait half a decade and more before they know their profits.

FOUR CLASSES OF VENTURE CAPITAL FIRMS

VC firms mature in the four predictable phases in Figure 26-1 as they try to climb the venture investor ladder to greatness. Depending on how mature they are, venture firms offer different resources to core

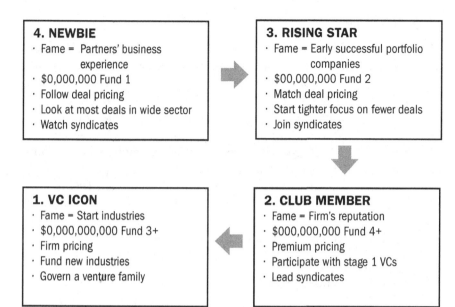

4. NEWBIE
- Fame = Partners' business experience
- $0,000,000 Fund 1
- Follow deal pricing
- Look at most deals in wide sector
- Watch syndicates

3. RISING STAR
- Fame = Early successful portfolio companies
- $00,000,000 Fund 2
- Match deal pricing
- Start tighter focus on fewer deals
- Join syndicates

1. VC ICON
- Fame = Start industries
- $0,000,000,000 Fund 3+
- Firm pricing
- Fund new industries
- Govern a venture family

2. CLUB MEMBER
- Fame = Firm's reputation
- $000,000,000 Fund 4+
- Premium pricing
- Participate with stage 1 VCs
- Lead syndicates

Source: *Nesheim Group.*

Figure 26-1 Venture Firms Mature in Four Stages

start-up teams. Similarly, the reactions by large corporations to calls from VCs depend on the status and maturity of the venture firm. The press alters its interest in venture firms depending on what phase of maturity they are in.

I found experienced entrepreneurs consistently recommend picking an investor for more than money. The investor's experience with start-ups, wisdom in decision-making, and connections with industry can be more valuable than precious cash. Veteran CEOs of new enterprises also have strong opinions about what type of venture capitalist is best for a startup. I could find no consensus. Some advised picking only from among the top tier venture capital firms. Others said founders should focus on an individual, find a famous partner that will sit on the board of directors. Others said to choose a venture firm small enough so your company gets the most attention and assistance from the entire firm. What you can get from your venture capitalists in addition to money is an important part of your unfair advantage. Let's begin your selection process by classifying venture firms and give examples of how real venture capital firms use unfair advantage to distinguish themselves from other competing venture firms.

Stage 4: Newbie

The first-time venture firm, a Newbie, is formed by two or three business friends. They were successful general managers from outstanding high technology companies. The partners make the firm famous. They come with track records of more than a decade of successes in an industry. They began as technology contributors who climbed the management ladder in giant public companies and then moved on to the challenges of higher-level responsibilities in smaller public companies. Often their last job was as either CEO or vice president of a venture-backed start-up that emerged a winner and went IPO or was acquired.

- Their first fund is typically less than $10 million.

- They set valuations for each deal in accord with terms set by the more mature venture firms.

- They mostly react to deals that arrive on their doorstep. These are deals in a wide range of industries. They also use their industry contacts to seek fresh ideas in sectors they know well. Fresh from the corporate battlegrounds, they may spot new ideas before more mature venture partners do. They especially try to find good deals in early stage start-ups using technology related to the intrinsic skills that the Newbie partners gained while working in public companies.

- Newbies are relegated to observer status for most of the hot deals flowing between the top venture firms.

Stage 3: Rising Star

The fame of the Rising Star firm grows based on the success of each partner's investments in successful start-ups funded during the Newbie phase. Early investments have resulted in successful companies. Some have been acquired in their early years while at least one has gone IPO. This lifts respect for the venture firm to the next higher level. The firm begins to be mentioned by its name almost as often as each partner is mentioned by name. Reporters looking for quotes for articles begin to call on some of the Rising Star's partners.

- Their second fund is typically $10 to $50 million. An additional partner is often added to the firm to add a missing domain expertise.

- They set valuations for each deal that match the terms set by the more mature venture firms. Their cost of capital is about the same as that of a Newbie.

- They look at deals in an increasingly narrow range of industries. They especially seek start-ups using technology in industries where their prior investments were successful.

- Rising Stars are invited for the first time to join deals syndicated by VC partners from more mature venture firms.

Stage 2: Club Member

The Club Member has become a venture firm known by its name. Fame has shifted to respecting the firm more than individual partners. The media write about "the arrival" of the firm. Individuals are famous for being a partner of a famous venture capital firm. The fame of the firm is based on the successes of several of the partners. Several new investments have resulted in IPOs and valuable acquisitions. The start-ups have become leaders in their markets and are known around the world.

- Each new fund of the Club Member is quickly followed by others. The total rises to at least four. Institutional investors are cordial and respond promptly when invited to invest in the next fund. The total portfolio size, as measured by total capital raised, rises to and sometimes exceeds nine figures, typically around $100 million. First distributions begin as limited partners are sent stock in start-ups that either go IPO or are purchased by a public company. Several of the funds of the Club Member have resulted in handsome returns on investment. Club Member partners become multimillionaires, some tens-of-millionaires.

- The Club Member firms set premium prices for each deal. Their cost of capital has risen. Founders of start-ups say they are expensive. The firm will negotiate valuations aggressively with founders but do not like to walk away from an attractive deal based solely on a pricing disagreement.

- Club Members know what industries they want to invest in. They have begun to look for core team leaders preparing to start next companies. New partners are added to bring special domain expertise into the firm.

- Club Members are invited to join deals led by the most mature venture firms, the revered VC Icons.

Stage 1: VC Icon

Fame has put this firm on the top rung. It now sees itself as starting industries, not just companies. The name of the firm has become a brand known around the world. Some of the firm's veteran partners are dubbed "icons" by the venture community and an awed media. There is a hierarchy of many partners, from senior to junior. Associates have been hired. Multiple office locations are common, some outside the home country.

- The active portfolio sometimes exceeds the billion-dollar range. They can raise as much money to invest as they choose to.

- They set firm prices on valuations for each deal and will turn down entrepreneurs who insist on higher valuations.

- They see themselves governing a venture family. The family consists of allied venture firms, wealthy executives, corporate investors, portfolio companies, universities, and even governments.

- They are aggressive in trying to start new industries. Partners are confident of the names and arrival times of new waves of disruptive technologies.

- VC Icons create their own syndicates of venture firms to do large deals. The syndicates often include large multinational corporations.

Those are the four stages of maturity that venture firms aspire to. A few have earned their way to the top rung of the ladder. Many are trying. It is a very crowded, intensely competitive market. The distinguished VCs understand the power of unfair advantage. They look for it in start-up ideas. They are experts at using it in their firms to make first contact with the best founders.

VENTURE FIRMS APPLY UNFAIR ADVANTAGE

Some venture capitalists have become very skilled using unfair advantage. Many have not. The top firms have learned how to achieve the ultimate win for a venture capital firm: to get the first contact with the founder or lead investor of the next Cisco or Amazon.

An aspiring veteran partner said, "All I need to succeed is first contact. To me, that means that either I get the first email from the founder, or the VC partner with the deal calls me immediately." Because earliest contact gives a powerful competitive edge, investment firms work hard to open their arms to entrepreneurs. It is so important that it can be seen on web pages of outstanding venture firms. For example, in February 2003, the home page of giant Sequoia Capital quoted Vani Kola, CEO of nthOrbit, saying, "Sequoia Capital was my first choice at RightWorks and now at nthOrbit. We have aligned goals, building great companies that last."[1] Fresh names appear on the Sequoia home page monthly. Such flattering testimonies were gained through hard work that resulted in mutual success for the founder and investor. It is not just a game of words. There must be winning companies behind the words. The testimonies must be real, not PR fluff.

Testimonies are used to position firms in a very crowded market of investors. Each VC wants to offer a very personal, very special reason for entrepreneurs to call him or her first. The positioning statements of each firm are chosen to entice founders to do exactly that.

Each venture firm tells a version of the same story: how its unfair advantage can bring more than money to outstanding entrepreneurs. It is a very serious marketing communications game. Some venture firms have learned to play the game with outstanding success. I will clarify my point with Kleiner Perkins Caufield & Byers, a firm I have had the privilege of getting to know since my first days in Silicon Valley.

Example 26-1   Icon VC Unfair Advantage: Kleiner Perkins Caufield & Byers

When it comes to the world of venture investing, Kleiner Perkins Caufield & Byers owns the term *public relations*. KP, as the firm is dubbed, started in the earliest days of modern venture investing. Over several decades, it rose from the ranks of first-time venture firm and now is one of the finest. KP has earned such a strong reputation that the firm has become a brand. It broadcasts that brand through aggressive PR about the successes of the firm's investing activities.

From the home page of the KP web site, you can see many of the elements that contribute to the unfair advantage of this respected venture firm.[2] It began investing in 1972 and has built over 350 companies, including such household names as America Online,

Amazon, Sun, Genentech, Compaq, and Juniper. Each has become a leader in a new market and a branded corporation.

The specialty of the KP is tapping resources from what it calls a *keiretsu*. By that, the firm means it manages a wide-ranging group of individual contacts, investors, partners, and corporations. The resources of the *keiretsu* are available to the companies KP invests in. That positioning creates uniqueness for Kleiner Perkins Caufield & Byers. It is attractive to founders who want to build unfair advantages. It is hard for other firms to match the skill of KP as it articulates why you, the next great start-up leader, should contact KP first. KP understands how to build and use an unfair advantage.

That is a gorilla of the venture community, a true icon. There are others, and they compete aggressively. Each has uniqueness in its unfair advantage. Competitors have grown gradually in number and quality as the pool of venture capital has grown, particularly during the Internet boom. It is a tough business, where a sustainable unfair advantage stands out.

Emerging from the Internet era are a few outstanding examples of new venture firms. One of the rising stars is BlueRun Ventures. In 1998 it was formed as Nokia Venture Partners with a vision for a new generation of venture firm. It is backed by the resources and money from a collection of special corporate and institutional investors. In its short number of years, BlueRun Ventures has already been a successful investor in several famous new enterprises. The firm grew quickly from Newbie to Rising Star. And in less than a decade it has achieved Club Member status. By 2002, BlueRun Ventures had become well known in venture circles. It is especially attractive to entrepreneurs in mobile and IP-related (Internet Protocol) markets and technologies. I got to know it during a funding round for a new venture I was coaching.

Example 26-2   Rising Star to Club Member: BlueRun Ventures

To brand its position, BlueRun Ventures combines the cachet of Nokia with the rising demand for global wireless services. BlueRun's home page makes it clear who should call on it first: mobile and IP-related start-up businesses.[3] It has positioned itself as "the largest venture capital firm to invest exclusively in the mobile and

IP related start-up businesses and technologies and has global investment scope."

The firm manages over $650 million. It is based in Menlo Park, California, in the heart of Silicon Valley, with satellite offices in Washington, D.C., London, Helsinki, Hong Kong, Seoul, and Tokyo.

The firm especially looks at the leadership abilities of the core teams invited to present their ideas. It "places a great deal of emphasis on the experience, talent and commitment that a company's management team brings to the table, as we assess the team's ability to lead a portfolio company through the rigors of growing a successful enterprise and attacking market opportunities. The team must be committed to the hard work and dogged determination that is required to make an enterprise successful." BlueRun goes on to emphasize that it works "to build a relationship of mutual trust and to support the company's management team. Such support consists of the additional value provided by traditional venture capital firms including access to the [firm's] vast network of contacts, assistance in building the management team, and guidance for the myriad of strategic and tactical issues faced by entrepreneurial enterprises. In addition, portfolio companies can benefit from the Fund's access to the immense network of individuals, resources and technical expertise of our value added limited partners."

BlueRun Ventures is a good study of how to combine elements to create an unfair advantage and use it to produce stunning success rapidly in an intensely competitive market. The rising tide of the Internet helped, as did ties to the famous Nokia, the world's cell phone gorilla. Yet it was not just good luck. The September 1998 founders, Peter Buhl, John Gardner, Antti Kokkinen, and John Malloy, made some outstanding investments, built an organization with world-class reach, and helped build some significant new companies. They were able to advance their initial unfair advantage and develop it organically during the wild ride up and down the last wave of disruptive technologies. They emerged with results that earned the respect of the greats in the competitive venture community.

Now let's shift our focus from California and Finland to Norway for an example of a Newbie that has already established its unfair advantage. The firm is Alliance Venture, located in Oslo. I got to know the founders through their support for a new ventures summer intern program for Norwegian students in Silicon Valley.

Example 26-3   Newbie: Alliance Venture, Oslo, Norway

Alliance Venture is synonymous with international connections to and from Scandinavian start-ups. The firm is a crisp example of careful thinking done by its partners. Alliance built its unfair advantage on the international managerial experience and business connections of its founders: Jan-Erik Hareid, Bjørn Christensen, and Erling Maartmann-Moe. It is benefiting from increasing interest from venture firms looking at deals flowing to and from the Scandinavian region of Europe. Alliance avoided getting caught up in the Internet era investing mania. It learned from the errors of its predecessors. Here is what greets you on the Alliance Venture home page:[4]

> We put the power of our experience and international network behind all our investments. Alliance Venture invests in Scandinavian and U.S. emerging technology companies at an early stage and supports their global expansion through alliances with leading technology corporations and international venture capital firms.
>
> We invest in companies where we can add value with our operational experience and extensive international network. Our main competitive advantage is the core team's competence, experience and network which are used for investment evaluations and active follow-up. The experience includes a good balance between operations and business, applied research, finance and entrepreneurial backgrounds.

Further examination of the web site also reveals a careful assembly of first-class business partners, advisers, Silicon Valley resources, and board of directors. Each adds to a strong network of accessible people, venture firms, market leaders, and businesses. Perhaps being of Viking blood is also part of its international skill set. In any case, if you want or need VCs with Scandinavian connections, Alliance Venture suggests you call it first.

Those are some examples of unfair advantage at work in venture capital firms. Next let's examine how large corporations use unfair advantage.

27

GIANT CORPORATIONS APPLY UNFAIR ADVANTAGE

Today's giant, industry-dominating corporations won their champion's cups by becoming masters of creating and strengthening unfair advantage from the day of their birth. They made it a lifetime passion. They are yesterday's tiny new enterprises. They began as infants and grew to become gorillas of their domains. They created the new industrial standards and became the brands consumers know so well around the globe. That is one of the hardest things to do in business.

INTEL BECAME THE GORILLA OF MICROPROCESSORS.

Intel is an outstanding example of how to advance an initial unfair advantage and become a respected global champion. Intel's initial unfair advantage was centered on the core team's rare skills, sharpened during the earliest days of the semiconductor industry. The company's core team chose to leave mother Fairchild because they wanted freedom to run a semiconductor company the way they thought it should be run, not like a stodgy parent dictated.

In 1968, the cofounders, technology guru Gordon Moore and Bob Noyce, coinventor of the integrated circuit, convinced Art Rock, the godfather of modern venture capital, to finance their start-up. Microprocessors had not yet been invented. The company would begin by designing memory semiconductors (the market was open and growing) and build them in a new factory (to gain technology and cost advantages). The turning point in Intel's history was the invention in 1971 of the Intel 4004, the world's first microprocessor.[1] Intel struggled and lost a few rounds in the early microprocessor battles, but finally emerged as the victor: world leader of microprocessors. From then on, it left the competition in the dust.

Intel's initial unfair advantage was deeply entrenched in the extraordinary skills of its core team. Gordon Moore guided choices of technologies and direction of research and development. Strategy-minded Les Vadasz thought up shifts that outmaneuvered the competition. Under the leadership of Andy Grove, tiny Intel advanced its microprocessor lead when it got giant IBM to cooperate on setting technical standards and designing new personal computer products. Bill Davidow used creative marketing methods, including Operation CRUSH, to outposition start-up Zilog and giants such as Motorola in the great microprocessor marketing war.

Intel's leaders were outstanding at advancing their initial unfair advantage. The late Bob Noyce had an uncanny ability for seeing the next great semiconductor family that Intel should produce. He guided the shift from commodity memories to proprietary microprocessors. That added significantly more value, profits, and cash flow to the company. The stronger balance sheet financed the next generation of very expensive, very high technology semiconductor fabrication facilities. Competitors could not afford such factories. Intel's intense investment in research and development produced a wafer fabrication staff held in awe by competitors. The company's techie culture grew even more attractive to the world's finest semiconductor engineers. Through it all, Intel's top management was able to stick together, developing ever more competent professional managers. They were always highly competitive people. Their unfair advantage kept growing and growing and by 2004 showed no signs of weakening.

ADVANCED MICRO DEVICES EXCELLED IN THE INTEL ERA.

The company was founded with $100,000 in 1969 by Jerry Sanders and seven other ex-Fairchild employees. Its initial unfair advantage was Jerry Sanders's charismatic leadership and his superb selling skills. Jerry, as he is affectionately known, was respected as the best semiconductor salesman in the world. Augmenting that advantage was the core team that had worked closely together at Fairchild. Jerry loved celebrations and flamboyant events and used them to shape the company's highly motivated culture.

During the company's first years, AMD focused on selling alternate-source devices, products obtained from other companies that were then redesigned for greater speed and efficiency. "Parametric superiority," AMD called it. To give the products even more of a selling edge, the company instituted a guarantee of quality unprecedented in the industry: all products would be made and tested to stringent military standards specifications, regardless of who the customer was and at no extra cost. Competitors did not match that move. Adding to the company's advantage was Jerry Sanders's reputation for overcoming sales adversity. He became famous for being able to hop on a plane to a customer and pull orders out of the hands of competitors who thought they had taken a big order away from AMD.

AMD advanced its unfair advantage by investing aggressively in proprietary product designs. Seeking more differentiation and financial gain, the company's engineers began to introduce products that were truly unique. AMD constructed modern semiconductor factories to build them. Factory operational skills became world-class. These advantages lifted AMD up to the next level of strength and size. The company was listed in 1984 in the book *The One Hundred Best Companies to Work For in America.*"[2]

In March 1991, AMD began attacking Intel's virtual monopoly of the microprocessor market. To do so, it applied the same know-how it learned in its first days as a strong number two competitor: delivering value-priced products whose performance was superior to the market leader's. Further strength came from outstanding field applications support teams and specialized sales groups. The company became a world-class name second only to Intel in microprocessor sales.

SINGAPORE AIRLINES IS CONSISTENTLY RATED THE BEST AIRLINE IN THE WORLD.

Singair's initial unfair advantage was a mix of home field advantage plus bold, unconventional thinking by its innovative core team. Although its roots can be traced back to the late 1940s as a fledgling airline flying a handful of ancient aircraft from city-state Singapore to nearby countries, the company we know today as Singapore Airlines was conceptually born three decades later. In the early 1970s, its leadership made a bold decision that forever transformed the backwater airline and changed the world's standard of first-class air travel. Management committed to becoming the top in quality air travel in Asia.

To gain an initial advantage, Singapore Airlines used technology to leapfrog its competitors. It purchased the latest fleet of new Boeing jets with financing backed by the airline's owner, the government of Singapore. That gave Singair the highest operating efficiency and most passenger comfort among Asian airlines of the day. Management also decided not to join the International Air Transport Association. The core team wanted freedom to innovate, including doing things that did not conform to the rules of the day. For example, Singapore Airlines wanted to experiment with creative seating layouts in each plane, not hindered by strict rules on the exact positioning of every seat as dictated by IATA. That nonconformist, innovative behavior established Singair as the one to follow. It emerged positioned as delivering air travel service second to none. The company's culture became known as a great place for creative people to work.

The core team advanced its unfair advantage by creating new forms of airline services focused on international traveling executives. The ideal customers were from American electronic multinational corporations, especially those in Silicon Valley, that had set up regional headquarters in modern, English-speaking Singapore. The visionary Singair management worked hard to transfer to employees their passion to be the best airline in the world. The by-now world-class leading airline especially paid careful attention to its choice of employees; they were intensely screened and carefully trained. Staff painstakingly planned the details of every flight. On-board personnel set the highest standard for perfection of service, from first-class to business to coach. On-ground operations employees delivered the best support known in the air travel industry. Ready to expand worldwide, Singapore Airlines cleverly communicated its superiority using a marketing advertising campaign based on the exotic Asian "Singapore Girl"—the on-board hostess who epitomized luxurious, hushed first class service for all classes of travelers who chose Singapore Airlines. The fledgling airline from a tiny country began with a creative nonconformist unfair advantage, used it to advance and strengthen its competitive strength, and became the envy of and role model for airlines around the world.

SOUTHWEST AIRLINES AND RYAN AIR DOMINATE DISCOUNT AIRLINES.

Two new airlines, Southwest and more recently Ryan Air, used nearly the same unfair advantage to become kings of discount air travel in the United States and Europe, respectively. Each had an almost fanatically intensive focus on a new, highly efficient business model. They mixed that with fun-loving company cultures to create powerful unfair advantages. They decided to deliver simple, low-cost air travel to people wishing to get from city A to city B faster and more economically than two people driving in one car. Their Texan (Southwest) and Irish (Ryan) founders thought they had ways to create economic advantages that would distinguish them from the expensive, complex airlines like United Airlines and British Air. The giants that tried to compete with their own shuttle services turned unprofitable. Me-too competitors followed each year, but the few that survived are more than me-too. Several went off the radar screens into start-up oblivion.

Southwest and Ryan stuck to what made their initial advantages unfair. They avoided temptations to "finally become a real airline" like the widely disbursed and unprofitable giant airlines. They grew by focusing on doing one thing well in more and more carefully selected, underserved cities. Southwest and Ryan flew only one model of jet. That simplified maintenance and kept costs lower. Meals were hand snacks, eliminating expensive catering and serving staff. Clever choices of routes (flanking moves to nearby airports in overlooked cities) exploited weaknesses of competitors ("Attention Boston Flyers! Fly Southwest Airlines: It is quicker door to door to fly from Providence, Rhode Island, than drive through bumper-to-bumper traffic and a clogged tunnel to Boston's Logan Airport).* Management took special care in labor relations with pilots and flight attendants. That led to attractive labor compensation deals with unions that boosted productivity: every employee was commissioned by the culture to do whatever was needed to get the planes full and keep them running on time. For example, when needed, pilots took tickets and air hostesses cleaned plane interiors. The cultures of Southwest and Ryan were lively and spiced with wry humor (pilot over the loudspeaker system: "If any of you can see San Jose out your window, let us know. We are going to land there in ten minutes."). Special care was taken during interviews of prospective employees: the interviewers looked for just a few new employees who shared the passions of the original founders. Southwest and Ryan airlines grew and remained profitable while giants and most me-too competitors were losing money. The two start-ups stayed focused on using the unfair advantage that delivered their initial successes and emerged as kings of their hills: low-cost air travel. They became role models for other regions of the world.

---

* Remember how dynamic unfair advantage must be: after the new entrance to Logan Airport opened, the bottleneck disappeared.

SAP IS KING OF THE ENTERPRISE SYSTEMS SOFTWARE MARKET.

SAP's initial unfair advantage was the sharp insight its German founders had about a special customer problem: managerial inefficiencies in worldwide corporations caused by poor information technology software systems. The core team thought the time was ripe for a single new system of unified software that could boost the efficiency of an entire global organization. SAP was founded by veteran German information technology consultants who understood the headaches of giant companies struggling with clunky accounting systems, hand-crafted operational modules, and expensive management information software that did not communicate well with each other. SAP used a contract for a customized software system for a multinational chemical giant in Europe as the basis for completing its proof of concept and prototype. It became the genesis for a new standardized SAP system to be sold to any global enterprise. The leaders were skilled in technology, selling, and execution. They had worked together and shared the same passion for the concept, confident it would excite the best managements of multinational corporations around the world. Their understanding of the fundamental need of the ideal customer was the bedrock on which SAP built an eventually insurmountable unfair advantage.

The first SAP system was positioned as the leader of a new emerging category, the enterprise software market. The architecture was based on a proprietary template concept. It was software that specially trained programmers modified to fit the unique requirements of each customer. During the first years of its introduction, SAP discovered that independent software programmers who were looking for new work were eager to learn, install, and customize the SAP system for giant customers. That was faster and had fewer headaches than doing code from scratch. Eager coders went to SAP training school, adding momentum to SAP, which eventually became the industry standard.

SAP advanced its unfair advantage by making clever sequential choices of industries (bowling pins). That let SAP designers create application templates fitted to related industries without making drastic time-consuming changes to the fundamental SAP software. Sales grew very fast. A few years later, the core team made a near-perfect move to get the SAP system working on client-server platforms. That left start-ups such as Baan behind. SAP continued to increase its sales momentum. Oracle and other software giants began to respond to the SAP threat but were late. SAP management expanded sales to Asia and soon became known worldwide. By then, several small me-too competitors had jumped onto the huge, rising wave of enterprise software systems. Some focused on midsize to small companies not yet served by SAP. Others went into giants not yet using SAP systems. However, they were late, and most tried to do too much with too little and crashed on the rocks. (Ambitious, aggressive Baan went bankrupt.) SAP landed on the beach as the winner, the start-up that emerged as the gorilla of a new world-class market.

These are but a few of the examples of how new enterprises became corporate giants. They used unfair advantage to begin, to grow, and to win—big-time.

28

MBA SCHOOLS APPLY UNFAIR ADVANTAGE

A few top schools have learned how to use unfair advantage to become world-class. They dominate market segments. Each owns a word or phrase. The battles for top MBA business school rankings generate good examples for studying how to use unfair advantage where we might not expect it.

HARVARD OWNS "BUSINESS SCHOOL."

Harvard University named its MBA school the Harvard Business School. HBS is revered for its graduates, several who have become world-class managers in public corporations and governments—the bigger the better. It teaches from the world's largest library of case studies of business problems. The school sells large numbers of copies of these case studies around the world, generating considerable revenue and spreading the name of the Harvard Business School. That attracts top students, who attract top faculty. HBS publishes a popular business magazine and is allied with a book publisher. Together, the elements combine to become an unfair advantage. Competing schools can demonstrate similar profiles of students, faculty, and publications but have yet to overtake the Harvard Business School's reputation as *the* MBA business school. For instance, over the past decade, I often asked business people to try to rank the top ten MBA business schools according to the latest *Business Week* rankings. Respondents rarely got the rankings of the top ten correct, and most started with Harvard on the top (even though Harvard has often not been number one).

HBS focuses on positioning itself as the leading trainer of the world's leaders. It does not emphasize one of the basic business functions such as marketing or finance. Instead, it sees itself as the king of the hill of MBA schools because it graduates the most outstanding business leaders. HBS has been on the top of that psychological hill for decades.

During its reign, HBS has followed one of the principles of the Defender strategy: it blocks strong competitive moves. This can be seen in a shift during the Internet era. That wave forced HBS to respond to the entrepreneurial tidal wave. It was a momentary opening for any of the other top-ranked MBA schools to exploit, but none acted fast enough or well enough. HBS finally reacted and closed the door. It rushed to add a large amount of entrepreneurial- and technology-related case studies and courses, particularly about companies in Silicon Valley. The move used a key Defender principle: attack yourself. By 2001 HBS had once again taken the lead in generating case studies about the latest wave, this time about the start-up world related to the entrepreneurial Internet era. The move is reflected in its marcom positioning statements. The positioning is clearly stated on the school's web site, as reflected in my observations in the next example.

Example 28-1   Defender: Positioning Harvard Business School

When opening the home page of the web site of the Harvard Business School, the observer is drawn to the picture of the dean.[1] When it is clicked on, a recorded message from the Dean begins: "The mission of the Harvard Business School is to educate leaders." He goes on to confidently cite the outstanding qualities of the faculty and then the special classroom experience that changes the lives of students forever. The message is short and to the point.

The web site expands the dean's message and adds this fresh paragraph: "But much about the School is changing as we embrace a rapidly changing world. We are educating students and building knowledge for a global community that is increasingly entrepreneurial and ever more reliant on technology—and therefore more dependent on its shifts. These times demand creative leadership."

Without altering its fundamental positioning, the school has neatly included small companies, high technology, and the entrepreneurial spirit. HBS behaves like the MBA gorilla that it is.

NATIONAL UNIVERSITY OF SINGAPORE IS "THE BEST SCHOOL IN SINGAPORE."

NUS is the first choice of many university applicants from Asia, regardless of which country they are from. NUS positions itself as the leading university in a respected city-state of 3 million people. Informally, its alumni proudly declare their school is "the Harvard of Singapore," and a few even claim it to be the Harvard of Asia. Operating as a traditional large Western university, it offers a vast number of courses in many disciplines. Its student population exceeds 23,000, and graduate students number over 9,000. The school has a number of high tech laboratories that attract faculty from around the world. In addition to its on-campus faculty, NUS is engaged with other brand name schools in joint research and teaching projects. Its students do graduate work at outstanding universities in North America and Europe. Graduates completing their studies at such schools usually return to Singapore to work for a few years leading some part of the local government. Then they depart for more lucrative positions, such as in multinational corporations. NUS is a key part of the economic and social fabric of Singapore whose economic results have been remarkable: in less than four decades Singapore became the second richest per capita country in Asia (Japan is first).

At the turn of the year 2000, leaders of NUS began to alter its positioning to retain its unfair advantage. The country's leaders shifted gears as the Internet boom burst and the country's business model went into recession. During the prior half-century, the country's leaders had focused on and succeeded in attracting headquarters for American and European multinational corporations' administration and manufacturing. However, the Asian economic troubles of the 1990s spurred the country's leaders to make big strategic changes. China was growing rapidly, making Singapore expensive for manufacturing. The tide of globalization was pressuring Singapore to open its protected financial services and other businesses. And the lack of entrepreneurial successes from Singapore was of deep concern to politicians, voters, and young people looking for a future.

NUS became a significant part of the country's fresh plan to make a world-class strategic move: the government decided to focus on creating a fresh culture in Singapore that would encourage the creation of new enterprises. One of the challenges was to educate leaders who could start new businesses in Singapore. NUS was given a key role. The school worked out a new positioning that combined entrepreneurial education and its established position as a world-class educational and research university. The marcom message was carefully crafted to reflect how NUS plans to ride the rising waves of China, globalization, and entrepreneurship. Since 1998 I have had the honor of working with leaders in Singapore as they added programs of teaching and encouraging entrepreneurs in their ambitious city-state. Some of the programs are reflected in the following new vision for the National University of Singapore.

Example 28-2   Position Change: National University of Singapore's President's New Vision

The web site of the National University of Singapore opens with the headline, "Fostering a spirit of enterprise."[2] Then a message follows from Shih Choon Fong, president:

> I envision NUS as a Global Knowledge Enterprise, which builds synergies between education, research and entrepreneurship.
>
> Let me give you examples of successful knowledge enterprises, such as Stanford, Berkeley, MIT and University of Pennsylvania. Because of their entrepreneurial culture, start-up companies and high-tech industries develop around them, creating jobs and wealth. Similarly, Peking, Tsinghua, and Fudan are moving in this direction.
>
> Likewise, NUS has taken steps to nurture a more entrepreneurial culture. We have established NUS Enterprise. You may have heard about our two overseas colleges—one in Silicon Valley in partnership with Stanford, another in Bio Valley with the University of Pennsylvania. In these entrepreneurial hubs, our students will work and learn from peers and entrepreneurs.
>
> Being a national university, our mission is to serve country and society. The NUS educational experience develops students' intellect, shapes character, and fosters lifelong bonds with peers, university and country.

NUS has made a significant move in response to a need and changing times. The rest of Asia will be closely watching what transpires.

LONDON BUSINESS SCHOOL CLAIMS IT IS "TRANSFORMING FUTURES."

The LBS web site opens up with a banner flashing "TRANSFORM-ING FUTURES." The greeting tempts readers to click to find out just what the school means by that. A formal mission statement gives some insight. A new dean puts a further spin to it in a special message to readers. The comparisons of the two messages reveal how determined LBS is to be different, yet how difficult it is to communicate a message that is unique. It is very hard to be more than just a top business school with students from many countries. The faculty and alumni I have met from the LBS are passionate about making it one of the best business schools in the world.

Example 28-3   Positioning: London Business School

Here is the opening from the LBS web site under the mission statement headline:[3]

> We want London Business School to be the most important and most respected international business school, a learning community of celebrated scholars, teachers, colleagues and alumni whose creative work has a powerful, lasting and worldwide impact on the learning and practice of management by important business leaders.
>
> Our Mission: To generate important new ideas, knowledge and skills that will transform management practice; to create and execute learning opportunities for current and future leaders and managers that will transform their futures; to communicate our intellectual capital worldwide.

A message from a new dean, Laura D'Andrea Tyson, reflects an attempt to attain a focused differentiation without losing the breadth of a top MBA school. There is extensive use of numbers and other citations of excellence. The long list is similar to a list of features used for a new product being positioned for battle in a very crowded market. The use of British spelling does create some uniqueness and a European sense of style, and the school chose an American female for its latest dean.

London Business School has the power to transform your future. London Business School is consistently ranked among the top ten business schools in the world, reflecting the excellence of its teaching and research programmes, the calibre of its students, and the diversity and reach of its intellectual community.

The faculty, students and staff represent a myriad of different cultures and backgrounds. More than seventy percent of the faculty is international, coming from 23 countries around the world. The diversity of the student body is even greater. Eighty percent of students are from countries outside the United Kingdom, and those students join us from 55 countries. This rich ethnic and cultural community provides London Business School with an exciting learning environment, a strong international alumni network and strong links to global business.

The quality of faculty research at London Business School was recently awarded the highest rating of 6* by the Higher Education Funding Council for England and a majority of the research produced by London Business School faculty is regarded as world-class. The School has achieved this distinction since the Research Assessment Exercise (RAE) began, reflecting its unerring commitment to academic excellence in research and teaching.

The School's excellence in business research fosters outstanding instruction providing students with the most current thinking available in management education. The School offers both full-time and executive MBA programmes, full-time and part-time Masters in Finance programmes, and a ten-month Masters in Science Sloan programme for experienced executives. One of the School's executive MBA programmes is offered in partnership with the Graduate School of Business at Columbia University and grants a degree from both institutions. London Business School offers more programme choices than any other top-ten business school, enabling students to choose the best option to match their interests, career goals, and preferences.

Regardless of the programme they choose, graduates of London Business School are highly regarded when they enter the global marketplace because of their classroom experience, their network of diverse and accomplished colleagues, and the level of practical experience they receive in our pro-

grammes. The School can boast the highest return on investment for two-year MBA programmes, as confirmed in a
recent Forbes magazine survey.

London Business School is also recognised as a leader in
the provision of Executive Education and has been ranked
seventh and eleventh in the world by *Business Week* and the
Financial Times respectively. Every year the School attracts
over 1,100 executives from around the world to its Open Programme portfolio and works with over 40 leading companies
in 10 different countries on its Custom Programmes, helping
to deliver tailored solutions to specific customer needs.

I am proud of what we achieve at London Business School,
and I think you will be proud of what you can achieve working with us. If you are considering a business education at
this point in your life, I recommend that you consider all of
the terrific options we offer.

UNIVERSITY OF PHOENIX IS THE LEADER OF "CONTINUING ADULT EDUCATION."

This university is focused on teaching people who are spurred on by
economic necessity and personal drive. They wish to quickly attain fresh
skills that lead to new jobs, better lives, and more income. Peter Drucker
noted more than twenty years ago that this market would become huge
during the twenty-first century. The founders of the University of
Phoenix spotted the opportunity and have become king of the new hill.
The university has gone public (APOL) and continues to grow during
both boom and bust economic times. The tide it is riding, continuing
adult education, shows no signs of dropping. Gene Ziegler, an expert in
e-learning and founder of Learning Technology Partners, impressed on
me how a new enterprise in the United States had captured the lead in
the market for on-line adult education.[4]

Example 28-4   New Market Leader: University of Phoenix

The web site of the University of Phoenix opens with a message
that is simple and crisp: it is the "University for Working Adults."[5]
Its positioning message is simple, clear, and stands out.

At University of Phoenix, you can earn your bachelor's, master's or doctoral degree any way you want to—on campus, online, or in certain areas using a combination of both, which we call FlexNet®. University of Phoenix has grown to be the nation's largest private university, specializing in the education of working adults by offering degree programs that are highly relevant, accessible, and efficient. With over 100 campuses and learning centers in the United States, Puerto Rico, Canada and via the Internet, you can complete your degree no matter where you live, what hours you work, or how often you travel or relocate.

That short message reflects the unfair advantage of the company. It is a message that is very difficult to write but is well worth the effort. It leaves the competition in a much weaker position.

Education is an old and very crowded market. Competition is intensive and global. Schools that appreciate the power of unfair advantage have used it to differentiate and rise to become king of the hill of the market categories they are focused on. They have left the envious competition at the bottom of the hill.

29

HOW COUNTRIES APPLY UNFAIR ADVANTAGE

Countries have learned to build and exploit unfair advantages. Some have recently lost theirs, while others are aggressively strengthening at the expense of rivals. Many governmental leaders cannot make up their minds about what an unfair advantage is for a country.

Countries compete. Like new enterprises, they seek ways to use local resources to construct healthy, growing economies. That most often succeeds when local entrepreneurs create new enterprises. Governmental success is based on creating an environment attractive to new businesses that become world-class. Company leaders and governments learn to cooperate to strengthen the competitive advantage of local businesses that create jobs and add tax revenues. The lures may be in the form of lower taxes or trained employees, weather or culture, resorts or cabins, fjords or mountains, beer or kiwis, cable cars or gondolas. Whatever the claims to fame, packages of attractive elements are offered to prospective businesses. Tourist departments and business development bureaus have become skilled at creating attractive messages that spread the good word. Once an unfair advantage is established, the country uses advanced marketing communications to spread the word, and the country becomes branded. Each country has some unfair advantage that can be exploited for economic differentiation and benefit. Countries that understand that can become economic gorillas.

COUNTRIES DOMINATE SPECIFIC INDUSTRIES.

Each country is known to be "the place to go to" for doing business in one or more industries, especially if you wanted to start such a related new business. Hollywood is the movie center of the world. High tech heaven is in Silicon Valley. China is leading light contract manufacturing with an economy expanding at one of the fastest rates in history. India is tops in several new outsourced services such as customer call centers and software programming.[1] Germany's companies use its revered talent pool of precision engineers to produce automobiles coveted for their driving performance. Japan uses its passion for quality to deliver automobiles respected for their manufactured superiority. Norway uses its fishing technology to dominate the world market for domesticated salmon. The list goes on and on.

After the competition to dominate new industries, a few countries emerge as gorillas.

Like new enterprises, countries end up ranked the same way: one world-class gorilla, a chimpanzee or two, and a dozen starving monkeys. That is why it is important for country leaders to understand how to build and use unfair advantage. If they do not, each of the lagging countries will be limited to the ranks of those who can only weakly follow, unable to become strong economically and culturally. They are like commodities, undistinguished.

Like entrepreneurs, countries spotting new market opportunities race for the top of the new hill.

Shrewd leaders of countries remain alert for new market opportunities. They know the early movers have the best chance to build unfair advantages that power them to domination of the new market and enjoy its expansion. The goal of countries is the same as that for entrepreneurs: to emerge as king of the hill of a new market category, not just a struggling me-too country. Taiwan quickly capitalized on doing outsourced semiconductor manufacturing for new enterprises in Silicon Valley. Hong Kong missed the same opportunity and today is still looking for an unfair advantage. Japan took the lead in advanced cell phone technology with DoCoMo's iMode, but ambitious underdog Korea has used CDMA technology to create the world's most advanced 3G wireless civilization, leapfrogging Japan and the rest of the world.

Focus is important for countries as well as for entrepreneurs.

Each country has a finite, very limited amount of resources. Like a new enterprise, a country cannot be outstanding by being a little good at a little bit of everything. Its leaders must choose what to become outstanding at and say no to the rest. Resources are finite. They must be focused. That is central to becoming outstanding. The trick is to decide what the role of the government should be. In the United States, business leaders want the least amount of help from the government in deciding how to conduct their businesses. In China and other Asian countries, the government is very closely directing where new investments are to be made. European socialistic governments exert close control over virtually all aspects of conduct for small and large businesses. Israel has found ways to support new businesses seeking to overcome their tiny size (local market) and disadvantaged location and become skilled at selling innovative products and services to a huge market: the United States and rest of the world. In all countries, the forces of private business and public politics are part of intensive struggles for leadership of new markets emerging around the world. The related issues of politics are not the topic of this book. I wish to simply make a point: government leaders who understand how to focus resources can build an unfair advantage that adds great value to the GDP and the well-being of its citizens.

A gorilla country continues to dominate by attacking itself.

It is tempting for a country dominating one industry to protect it when competition springs up from other countries. Corporate leaders who are the kings of their hills understand that is not wise. Instead, they know that in order to continue to win, the leaders must attack themselves, one of the principles of the defender strategy. The leading country should not protect; rather, it should spur on more innovation and more advances to keep its industry leadership ahead of competing countries. Like a good fitness program, that keeps local companies from becoming fat, out of competitive shape, and falling behind, it promotes healthy growth and competitive endurance. One of the tricks to managing the unfair advantage of a country is to recognize that human innovation and industrial competition are relentlessly changing the status quo of the marketplaces of the world. Countries that try to stand still, holding on and defending local industries, weaken their unfair advantage. Competition and innovation drive a never-ending game that is constantly in flux. As trade barriers continue to drop, globalization rises. More countries enter the World Trade Organization, and competition intensifies. Leaders of countries are compelled to change the unfair advantage that got the country to its current greatness but will hold its citizens back if not changed as fast as possible.

COUNTRIES: MOVE IT OR LOSE IT.

Countries that have not aggressively advanced their unfair advantages have lost what made them great. They are in pain.

Hong Kong envies Shanghai.

Hong Kong has a rich and colorful history of economic freedom that enabled entrepreneurs to grow from nothing to greatness. At the end of the last century, Hong Kong lost its unfair advantage when Great Britain left, and Hong Kong was returned to China. Shanghai took over leadership as the next great financial center of China. Hong Kong clung to the status quo, hoping to find a way to compete, but new financial service businesses continued to head for Shanghai. Similarly, Hong Kong lost its uniqueness as the democratic alternative to communistic China. Hong Kong returned to being governed by China under a mixture of democratic and one-party communistic methods of governing and economic management. No longer was it a place that ambitious refugees fled to, risking their lives, crossing guarded borders to get to freedom. No longer was there a steady addition to the pool of low-cost, hard-working labor, people free and determined to create a better life for themselves and their families. With the change in governments, wealthy Hong Kong entrepreneurs sold their properties and emigrated to Toronto and San Francisco. Today, skilled young people of many nationalities see less of an incentive to move to expensive Hong Kong. Instead, they see more exciting opportunities in Shanghai or Beijing, where hot new enterprises and name brand multinational corporations are eager to hire experienced multicultural thirty-somethings. Tourists and shoppers see Hong Kong as relatively expensive. For bargains, many travel instead to mainland China and southeastern Asian countries. Hong Kong has a big adjustment to make in order to recover and emerge as an invigorated competitor with a strong unfair advantage.

Germany lost it.

Germany lost its once-unequaled entrepreneurial zeal during the past fifty years. The capitalists flourished after 1945 in rebuilding war-ravaged

Germany. However, as affluence arrived, social forms of governments rose in popularity and emerged victorious. Voters had worked hard to recover from the rubble and wanted their successes—jobs and wealth and health programs and retirement—to be protected. By the 1960s, the social democratic movement had piled up job-protecting labor laws and paid for abundant social and pension benefits with higher taxation. Economic freedoms began to disappear, and the cost became prohibitive to fire or lay off unproductive employees. Germany increasingly stymied entrepreneurial companies that had made it one of the richest countries of the world. The middle-sized family businesses, *Mittlestand*, of Germany account for a huge portion of German exports (some calculations are as high as 80 percent) and hence contribute a large portion of the country's GDP. Yet those focused, small companies, founded by ambitious, hard-working entrepreneurs, face a bleak future. Youth are leaving the aging family-owned businesses, and it is up to aging parents to sell the assets or bring the small businesses to an end. Few youth in Europe today look to Germany as the land of promise for a new business. France has labor and tax laws similar to those of Germany. In both, youth are exiting in large numbers to seek their fortunes elsewhere. Some are starting new businesses in Eastern Europe, such as in Poland, the Czech Republic, and Hungary. Others head for the United States or Shanghai.

Today Germany is a country run by socialistic-thinking technocrats. It is also high on the list of countries in which not to start a new enterprise. The same goes for France. Big changes are not anticipated in the near future, but could happen if the voters recognize the power of (losing) an unfair advantage.

Japan's new business model creates new problems.

Japan's new business model succeeded in the postwar years but is central to its deep problems today. After World War II, Japan's entrepreneurs created many new enterprises and resurrected war-destroyed businesses. Many became world-class corporations. The government guided and supported Japanese corporate expansion through organizations such as MITI and a myriad of other structural benefits. The innovative government-business model of mutual cooperation became a powerful part of the country's unfair advantage. Many Japanese corporations arrived at the top of several new market segments and became world-class brands. But during the past decade, Japan's leaders found the once-attractive model was holding the country frozen in a decade-plus recession, unable to recover from a series of deep economic setbacks in the 1990s.

Today Japan is stuck with a system of government and culture that forms a business model that favors giant conglomerates known as *keiretsu*. This business model includes deep cultural roots that restrict rapid change and inhibit experimentation with new business models. Japan's leaders understand the deep problems and need for change. Alterations to laws and regulations, as well as shifts in social attitudes, are underway and are supported and promoted by the federal and local governments. However, the rate of change has been very slow compared with its Asian neighbors. With China growing so fast, the awakening giant neighbor could soon overtake Japan as the second wealthiest country in the world. China's annual growth rates of 6 to 7 percent will bring its GDP to a level challenging and then exceeding that of Japan sometime this century. That change will create a significant shift in economic benefits and political power. Even before the Internet boom, Japanese youth were looking outside the country for opportunities to begin their new businesses. The Japanese pool of venture capital is very small. Young adults who choose the way of the entrepreneur instead of a traditional job in a *keiretsu* or as a technocrat are frequently socially ostracized and even rejected by parents.

Japan's industries retain leadership in many markets but the competitive changes they are facing are happening very fast. There are few signs of significant shifts inside Japan that could quickly renew its once respected unfair advantage.

COUNTRIES RACE TO BECOME WORLD-CLASS ENTREPRENEURIAL CENTERS.

There are many encouraging examples of countries that are building unfair advantages and benefiting economically and socially.

China is racing to create jobs faster than workers are laid off from rusting, uncompetitive state-owned factories. Leaders are rushing to modernize and install the business infrastructure entrepreneurs need. For instance, commercial technocrats are drafting personal property laws. Under a Marxist economy, the laws did not exist. The list is very long of other supportive changes already begun by China's new, ambitious leadership. The proactive government is innovating and changing rapidly. More and more business freedoms in which entrepreneurs thrive are coming to pass. Time will tell how well the country's promising future is realized. So far it, is clear that China's leaders understand how to build unfair advantage.

India is beginning to tear down some of the barriers to new enterprises that its socialistic government has created. After gaining freedom from British colonial rule, India moved to a centralized economic system. It put up protective walls to protect fledgling new enterprises. The result was slow economic growth. Encouraging signs of change began during the 1990s. Barriers to competition began to fall, and local entrepreneurs worked with government to attract venture capital and start-up know-how. As in China, the Indian diaspora began returning home, eager to show how to convert ideas to world-class new enterprises and employ the well-educated technical students who emerged each year from local universities. India is strong with information technology and outsourced customer services, while China is strong with light manufacturing. The Indian government is showing encouraging signs of respecting the power of creating unfair advantages.

Singapore "hit wall," like a long-distance runner. It stalled after an astounding record of economic success during the past half-century. After nearly thirty years of expansion, the city-state found it harder and harder to find new growth opportunities. Fewer new multinationals chose Singapore as the preferred location to set up Asian headquarters and begin manufacturing. Other countries in Asia were lower cost. China was the more attractive market. Singapore was living on borrowed time. After hitting the economic crunch known as the Asian crisis of the 1990s, Singapore's technocrats moved swiftly and aimed to "redirect the metropolis into a citadel of the 'knowledge economy'" using entrepreneurship as the centerpiece of the new push to more greatness.[2] Their goal was to use new enterprises to counter losing a competitive edge for attracting new corporate business. By 2000, the government technocrats had begun a more aggressive swing to incentivize entrepreneurship. Changes began with more favorable laws for stock options, bankruptcies, residency, and immigration. More was added each year to attract world-class thinking entrepreneurs. By 2002, the Singapore government had decreed it important to begin educating all of its students about how new enterprises begin and grow.

South Korea has acted to encourage new enterprises as an alternative to the large family-owned industrial corporations, *chaebols,* that have brought the country so much wealth. The government is encouraging entrepreneurs, with high technology as the focus. In 2000

South Korea ranked fifth in the world for the number of trained scientists and engineers per capita. The government has established over 200 incubators for new businesses of all sizes. There is a local stock exchange for small, emerging companies. Laws are being modified to encourage start-ups. There is a pool of managers experienced in commercial competition throughout the world. South Korea's electronic and automotive enterprises sell products in most markets of the world. It's industrial construction and engineering corporations perform work in cities around the globe. The country is also promoting cultural changes. It understands that its citizens must also change socially if South Korea is to compete in the increasingly open markets of the world. Protection is being reduced for local businesses and labor unions in such industries as automobiles and finance. Subsidies for high technology companies are being reduced. English as a second language is promoted. There is much more to be done, but the changes show that the leaders of South Korea are determined to change so that local entrepreneurs can compete with the best in the world. South Korea's leaders understand how to assemble elements into an unfair advantage that grows stronger each year.

Those are a few examples of how leaders of countries have responded to the ambitions of entrepreneurs. The best understand how to assemble elements of local resources into an unfair advantage. Comparing countries to each other, there are remarkable differences in how deeply governments are involved. Most notable are the experiments with business models: they differ significantly among Asia, Europe, and the Americas. Time will tell who wins most during this century. The United States enters with a big lead, but other countries are ambitious and determined. My bet is that China surprises us all and sets a blistering pace as we enter what I call "The Century of the Asian." Also keep your eyes on Brazil. Fasten your seat belts. It's going to be a wild ride!

30

SPOTTING WEAKNESSES AND ADDING STRENGTHS

You move from an interesting plan to an unfair advantage by spotting the weaknesses in what appears to you to be a killer idea. Following are some practical tools for discovering weaknesses that are often repeated by first-time entrepreneurs. I have gathered them from my contacts with outstanding companies and their investors. The first is a list I use to audit the stories of entrepreneurs. The next, a checklist from an experienced and respected venture capitalist in Silicon Valley, contains examples of how it was applied in two real investment decisions.

JOHN'S CHECKLIST

My list contains weaknesses in the sequence I find most frequently cited by stakeholders in new enterprises. Use the list to test your story. Try scoring yourself using a 1 to 3 scale for each question, with 3 being the highest measure of weakness.

Table 30-1 John's Checklist of Weaknesses in Start-up Stories

---

1. The core team lacks the depth of experience (evidenced by mediocre track records) needed to get the job done for the next phase of the start-up.

2. Getting rich is more important to the core team than building a great company that solves a big problem and does great things well for many customers around the world.

3. The core team is incomplete. The following elements are missing: a leader who has run a business before, a marketing person who has invented and launched successful new products, and a technical leader skilled at converting ideas into hot-selling products.

4. The core team members have relied more on luck than on skill in their careers. They lack examples in their lives of having encountered recurring problems and successfully managed their way through them.

5. Hands-on experience with the related industry and technology is weak or missing in the core team. The core team lacks the required domain experience.

6. The idea does not address a big problem. It is a faster, better, cheaper alternative to existing solutions.

7. The target market segment is already crowded with me-too competitors struggling to stay alive. One company is already the new market leader and is outrunning the competition.

8. The idea for the business leans on a single thing to succeed (e.g., technology, or first-to-market, or faster speed).

9. The idea is for a single product, not a business.

10. The business model is an experiment. It adds to the risk of the new enterprise, rather than reduces it.

11. There is no plan for how strongly to compete with a me-too competitor.

12. The core team believes first to market and lots of patents are adequate defenses.

13. The initial unfair advantage cannot be advanced. After first product launch, late arrivals can easily copy and leapfrog.

14. The early products rely on features to win instead of psychological positioning in the minds of paying customers. Competitors can quickly copy the products once they are on the market.

15. The technology is looking for a market. Savvy competitors will leapfrog by starting with a big, compelling customer need and then will look for technology to help fill the need.

16. The wrong strategy is chosen to outmaneuver the market leader. Strategy is not well understood by the company's leaders.

17. It is a me-too business idea. There is nothing unique or original in it.

18. Focus is lacking. The marketing plan lacks sharp edges. The target market is too broadly defined.

19. There is little or no evidence that a lot of customers will be eager to purchase the first product. The core team has not done thorough customer surveys.

20. Detailed understanding is missing of how the end user will choose and use the first product. Generalizations expose weak market research and inadequate time spent talking with customers.

21. The technical problem is either too trivial or too hard to do. It can be quickly copied or is very likely to burn out the technical staff before they can complete the first product.

22. The business relies on "know-who" rather than "know-how" to win.

23. Strategic partners are mentioned, but a plan to use them intimately is missing. Large corporations and other new enterprises are not mentioned by name in the plan.

24. The first product depends on a contract or permission of a large corporation. There are several dependencies or hinge factors in the plan.

25. Channels to sell to customers are unknown or unclear. Even worse, the new company cannot easily access them.

26. Second products are not obvious. After the first one, there is only a vague plan for what can be next in a long line of fresh, exciting new products.

27. Sales are planned for the local market only. There is no plan to sell products around the world. Competitors can enter from other countries and attack head-on.

28. The sales are too small to get the company to IPO on NASDAQ.

29. There is only one exit for investors. The liquidity event alternatives are very constrained.

SOURCE: *Nesheim Group.*

ERIC'S CHECKLIST: WHAT A TOP VC FIRM LOOKS FOR

Eric Young of Canaan Partners, one of America's oldest and most respected venture firms, noted the following as an example of what he and his partners look for in the presentations of entrepreneurs. Included are two examples of how the criteria are applied to two real start-ups.

Table 30-2 VC Checklist for Unfair Advantage: Canaan Partners

---

Characteristics Canaan Looks for in Potential Investments

Product/market opportunity

Compelling value proposition

Easily recognizable and believable by potential customers

Customers will react with a sense of urgency

Channels to reach customer are definable and accessible

Competitively unique and different, a position that can be maintained

Opportunity is scalable after success in the initial target segment

---

People

Domain knowledge: know the customer and problems or solutions

Entrepreneurial: move aggressively; strong will to win

Technology base: uniqueness and barriers to competition

Experience: have overcome recurring challenges before

Team play: bond with investors for long-term benefit, ethics

Business model

Large potential enterprise value is primary goal: growth and profitability

Resource requirements and time: moderate amounts needed to meet milestones

How might the model need to change strategically (product line, channel, competition) as the business scales

Exit (liquidity) options: IPO and/or acquisition, when and likely for how much

Examples of How Canaan Applied These Characteristics to Real Companies

Why did Canaan invest particularly in NewcoOne?

Large degree of domain knowledge in founding team (finance and control in retailing)

Addressing a labor-intensive cost center in retailers and suppliers, not previously automated

Prospect for a discretely measurable (hard) ROI in meaningful amounts

Existing relationships among management team with potential customers; impressive beta customer committed

No prior start-up experience on the team but highly energized to succeed

No current competitors; prior efforts to do this by start-ups and existing ERP vendors have been unsuccessful

Success with initial functionality on a tactical level appears scalable over time into a higher-value strategic set of product capabilities for higher-level management

Intact engineering team that had worked together for some time

Could see a number of large potential acquirers with a strategic interest over time, as well as IPO

Why did Canaan invest particularly in NewcoTwo?

Consumer anxiety regarding privacy of personal information a recent phenomenon but growing rapidly; gathering significant press attention and is going to become a bigger problem before it gets solved

Different problem to solve from credit card fraud; requires collaboration among industry participants to be effective

Team was very credible, with excellent relations with potential customers based upon XYZoftware Inc. experience

Credit card fraud problem is analogous in many ways, which the team knows well from HNCorp.

Team had prior start-up experience, good leadership skills

Potential lock on a group of key technologists

Very attractive prospective business model: both product sale and long-term annuities

If successful, business model afforded significant barriers to entry

Reasonable capital requirements needed to execute plan

SOURCE: *Canaan Partners.*

WHAT A SERIAL ENTREPRENEUR LOOKS FOR

I asked Chao Lam, a serial entrepreneur from Singapore and Silicon Valley, what he looks for in presentations of ideas for new enterprises. He responded after listening to seven business plan presentations by students from Asia. The students had been challenged to create plans for real venture-backed businesses, beginning with an idea of their own. The work was completed in ten weeks. The projects were done while working full time at real start-ups. Here are the comments of an innovative entrepreneur who has seen a great deal from the real world of new enterprises.

Example 30-1   Start-up Plan Weaknesses: What a Serial
                Entrepreneur Observed

I greatly enjoyed listening to the students' presentations. Thanks
for involving me, although I have to admit my mind kind of wandered by the final presentations! I have a little more sympathy for
VCs now. I loved the energy, humor, and several innovative ideas
that the students presented. I thought I'd share with you some
observations. They are not meant to be critical, rather hopefully
helpful.

Competitive Analysis

- Competition is intense in almost all areas. There was a surreal
  quality to most of the competitive analysis sections, where
  almost all presentations claimed a unique position with no competitors. This is unrealistic. In several cases, a simple Google
  search would have resulted in at least a handful of competitors.
- In general, I would prefer a quick description of the landscape
  and zoom in much more detail on the close competitors and differentiation.

Unfair Advantage

- Unfair advantage is extremely difficult. The presentations made
  it sound cavalierly easy. I would focus on one advantage and
  really drill down on strategies to achieving advantage.
- Unfair advantage takes time and evolves over time. I think this is
  a key lesson from the chasm models. It is very difficult for start-
  ups to build brands; it is much harder to turn around an aircraft
  carrier than a speedboat. Only one team focused on the evolving
  nature of strategic advantage, and none focused on how advantage changes through the technology adoption life cycle.

Market Segments and Bowling Pin Strategy

- Several presentations focused on nabbing 1 percent of an unbe-
  lievably large market. This is a sure symptom that there has not
  been enough market segmentation homework done. It is much
  better to focus the company on nabbing 20 to 50 percent of a
  modest market than to talk amorphously about being in this
  incredibly large, emerging market.

- Selecting the right bowling pins is also very difficult. Reasons for choosing the first bowling pin and how this first pin will create a virtuous "domino effect" in attacking other bowling pin markets should be stated in much more detail.

Financials

- Perhaps it's the reality of the post-bubble world we live in, but I found the financials broadly unrealistic. Maybe a bottoms-up backing of the financials would help?
- A much clearer description of pricing and sales model would help too.

Lessons

- What are the lessons learned from the dot-com bubble? Several plans appear to have a pre-bubble flavor without acknowledging current sentiments and why such plans are very unlikely to be funded today.

Those are observations worth using to test the quality of any idea for a new enterprise. It implies how difficult it is to try to create a world-class unfair advantage in a few weeks.

31

CONCLUDING REMARKS AND CHALLENGES

*U*nfair advantage is the holy grail for organizations of all kinds. It is best learned by looking at new enterprises and uncovering the secrets of their remarkable successes. Governments, nonprofit organizations, and large corporations all need unfair advantages to win in this competitive world. Many have learned the secret. Even though very large, they behave with a freshness that reflects thinking like a new enterprise. Their leaders overcome adversity and intense competition with unfair advantages that lead to world-class benefits.

Organizations that desire to become king of the hill have learned to craft unfair advantage from selected elements and, like a house built with bricks, make it stronger day after day. They respect the adage that the only thing certain is change. That is how they win.

Winners are passionate about a singular goal: to become the dominant organization in a new market category. They remain focused on that singular desire while going through the unavoidably stressful process of giving birth to a new idea.

Converting an idea to a world-class new enterprise is a challenging process. The process is used by leaders to attain a singular goal: in five years or less, get your organization to dominate a new market. Determination and patience have their reward: it takes time—years—to study and become wise about the stages of birth of a new enterprise and how to move through each stage. When you understand that, you are ready to begin to craft your story about giving birth to a world-class idea.

Great new enterprises begin with great stories. They are crafted with intensive, hard work. The work is assembled into an outstanding business plan. It becomes a great plan when it excites the key stakeholders. Leaders with great stories get the best investors, the best employees, and best reports by the media. Great stories get people excited in seconds.

When you can state your unfair advantage in 30 seconds, you have an unfair advantage. Short is power. Short is very hard to do. It is the first test of how good the longer, complete story is.

A long version of your story is backed up by solid research. It stands up to the harshest scrutiny. It includes documented talks with real people who will use your product or service and with the potential customers who will send you money. It holds up during intense scrutiny by investors when they conduct due diligence investigations, employees who probe with tough questions during interviews, and reporters asking difficult questions. It reflects deliberate and patient construction aimed at getting it right before launching the new venture.

Patience is a distinctive mark of a great story. Being first to try to enter the new market is nearly certain death. It is far better to be first to get it right. Pioneers get a lot of arrows in their backs. That is not a pretty picture but is all too true.

Like creating a beautiful sculpture, the process of crafting the story takes a lot more time than most wish, requires a lot more resources than first thought necessary, and demands much more creativity than you imagined. It is very hard work. But the final result can be beautiful and exhilarating. When it is finished, you have discovered Grandmother's secret recipe: that special collection of ingredients that puts a "Wow!" on your lips every time you taste it. It is what gets your stakeholders excited. It is what thrills you. You feel as if you are soaring like a bird.

Unfair advantage stories are about how to ride waves to success. Leaders are excellent surfers of new opportunities. The waves are created by those constantly arriving disruptive technologies. Study the waves so you learn their phases. To enter the competition, modify your plan to take advantage of which phase the wave is in. One plan will not fit all the phases. Pick wisely so your chances are boosted of landing on the shore as a winner instead of crashing on the rocks.

Great worldwide corporations are born from new enterprises whose founding core team built and developed an unfair advantage. Countries and large cities also have unfair advantages that they use competitively to attract the best people and businesses. Universities and schools have recognized they are competing for stakeholders just like new enterprises: customers (students of all ages), suppliers (of just about everything), partners (from industry and government), investors (wealthy alumni, industry, and governments), employees (faculty, students, and administration), and the media (reporters, television, and so on). Each type of organization competes by innovatively using unique resources. Leaders who recognize this are passionate about altering and developing their unfair advantages. The organizations that do not will live lives of eternal struggle and mediocrity. They are undistinguished. They waste scarce resources. They live in frustration, sensing there is something out there that they could and should be doing with the resources they have. They intuitively know they have not yet crafted unfair advantages that could be used to transform them into world-class winners.

I vividly remember Johannes Hoech, a serial entrepreneur, telling me his lessons of the Internet era. He emphatically exclaimed, "Unfair advantage is everything to a new business. If you don't have it, go home. Don't even start to play the game!" I found investors at top venture firms agreed. So did Danny Lui cofounder of Legend Group, one of China's largest and wealthiest conglomerates. They are among the select few who have learned well in the new enterprise school of hard knocks. Others less fortunate include the founders of dead dot-coms and countless start-ups that expired trying to navigate through treacherous entrepreneurial mine fields without an unfair advantage. First-time entrepreneurs typically don't understand it, but serial entrepreneurs live by it. Deal-scarred venture capitalists eagerly seek it. Unfair advantage has become part of their souls.

PAST AND FUTURE

So where are we today? That's simple: another new wave is beginning as you read this, and other waves are peaking, while others are ending. They are always there. Pick the one you want to ride using your unfair advantage. And then, as Nike says, "Just do it!" No one has all the answers about how to create a new enterprise, so why not get started studying it right now?

During the 1990s a new chapter in formal business training began: entrepreneurship. Around the world, a new level of serious scrutiny by scholars and practitioners is revealing more and more about the behavior of new enterprises during the waves of the past three decades of high tech start-ups. In 2000 the London Business School began an entrepreneurship PhD program. In 2003, David BenDaniel noted that Cornell University offered forty-six entrepreneurship courses from eight schools taught by thirty-five faculty. Case studies about new enterprises are coming off the presses as fast as magazines.

All of us still have a lot to learn. This is a new science that is more art today than a well-studied science.

FROM RANDOM CHANCE TO MANAGED GAME

It seems as if everyone is acting, or trying to act, like new enterprises. Countries want fresh businesses to create new jobs, corporations seek entrepreneurial zeal because they want to grow faster, and schools aim to use courses about new enterprises to attract the best students. Each day we read and hear more about entrepreneurship.

This wave is part of an emerging story: how the world of the entrepreneur is shifting from a game of random chance to a managed game. The shift started toward the end of the past century. In 1985 Peter Drucker wrote, "The time has now come to do for entrepreneurship and innovation what I first did for management in general some thirty years ago: to develop the principles, the practice, and the discipline [of entrepreneurial management]. . . . [The] entrepreneur always searches for change, responds to it, and exploits it as an opportunity. Systematic innovation therefore consists in the purposeful and organized search for changes, and in the systematic analysis of the opportunities such as changes might offer for economic or social innovation. . . . And thus the discipline of innovation (and it is the knowledge base of entrepreneurship) is a diagnostic discipline: a systematic examination of the areas of change that typically offer entrepreneurial opportunities."[1] With that inspirational push, this book was created for leaders of the new enterprises of this century who want to manage change, not be managed by it.

PROGRESS

Perhaps your efforts will help advance this creative field. There are fascinating entrepreneurial issues outstanding, ones that need a lot more examination and scrutiny. Here are a few examples that veterans often discuss with religious fervor:

- How does an engineer burn out? How can the first product development process be better managed? What refresh cycles are needed to renew the original innovation and creative energy that enabled the first product launch? How do you keep technical staff from becoming bored?

- What can be done to make transitions of top managements more productive and less stressful? How can founders, professional managers, and executives in residence be used to increase the effectiveness of leadership changes?

- During boom times, how should investors play the game and win in the long run? What better investment strategies can be created that enable participation during the mania phase yet avoid its excesses?

- How can the Silicon Valley lessons be best transferred and modified in other geopolitical states and different cultures around the world? What can local new enterprises do with such modifications so they emerge as world-class competitors and become respected brands?

- What makes unfair advantage special for countries and large cities? How can their leaders better use unfair advantage to contribute to increasing healthy competitiveness and increased well-being of citizens?

- How does the cost of capital affect unfair advantages? What do investors actually do that increases or erodes unfair advantage? What are the special elements available to venture investors that a new enterprise can use in its struggle to greatness? Which ones are overtouted and useless?

- How important is the company culture to a strong unfair advantage? What elements of an organization's culture make the most difference in contributing to growing or shrinking unfair advantage?

- What can giant organizations do to better employ new enterprise methods in their plans to continue their greatness? How can they better participate when disruptive technologies set off waves of new opportunities?

- How should entrepreneurs play the new enterprise game when luck (good or bad) pops up? What should be done to anticipate and manage the results of unforeseen events that will affect the new enterprise?

- How can we generate a greater pool of outstanding people to be more useful members of boards of directors? Where should they come from, and how can they learn to transfer their wisdom from large, established organizations to fledgling new enterprises?

Those are but a few of the issues worth exploring. I am sure you can contribute more. It is a new world filled with opportunity for improvement, one I find exciting and fulfilling.

A WORD OF ENCOURAGEMENT

The best can happen to you. An entrepreneurial-sounding ancient writer put it this way over two thousand years ago. He wrote in the Bible in Ecclesiastes 9:11 the following (with my new enterprise additions in parentheses): "I again saw under the sun (in Silicon Valley) that the race is not to the swift, (microprocessors) and the battle is not to the warriors, (of start-ups) and neither is bread to the wise, (PhDs) nor wealth to the discerning, (venture capitalists) nor favor to men of ability, (leading new enterprises) for time and chance overtake them all."

A TIP FOR PERSONAL SUCCESS

There is a time for doing a start-up and a time not to try one. New enterprises can be very rewarding. And they can be very costly, personally. As I explained in Chapter 8 of *High Tech Start Up*, I found patterns and phases in the maturing of new enterprises, one of which might be just the right time for you to join a start-up (and others the worst time). But after you have committed to doing or joining a new enterprise, keep this in mind: Make it an adventure! What does that mean?

ADVENTURE!

Unknowns. The icons of the venture community tell me each time, "We do not know how this investment will turn out." They are the realists. They know the most likely result is a fire sale. They respect the small odds of success. They work hard to improve the chances of the companies they invest in. So do the serial entrepreneurs and their core teams who lead them.

Risks. Start-ups have lottery odds of fulfilling dreams (becoming king of a hill and going IPO). That is acknowledged by veterans of new enterprises. They plan and conduct their personal lives accordingly.

Treasure. Yes, there is wonderful reward to be gained in doing a start-up. But it is buried and hard to find. While searching for it, you will encounter a lot of surprises, good and bad. The treasure is more than fame and fortune, patents, and stock option wealth. It includes your soul. That encompasses character development, ethics and morals, and wisdom. It includes your health and family. When you discover your treasure, it is a wonderful, unforgettable moment.

Fun. Serial entrepreneurs know they have to have fun while doing a new enterprise. Venture investor Don Valentine says people in the business need a sense of humor. Scarred veterans of Silicon Valley put it this way: "When the start-up stops being fun, get out. It is time to go get a job." Hanging on for dear life to a dying organization is no fun. Fun has to remain in order to make it worth doing.

That's all folks. I wish you the best of success as you craft your unfair advantage, wherever you are!

APPENDIXES

- **Appendix A:**
  Business Plan Outline
- **Appendix B:**
  Scoring Sheet for Written Business Plan
- **Appendix C:**
  Scoring Sheet for Presentation of Business Plan
- **Appendix D:**
  Valuation Tables and Graphics
- **Appendix E:**
  Unfair Advantage in a Press Release
- **Appendix F:**
  Need and Opportunity of DataMed
- **Appendix G:**
  Famous Marketing Wars: Strategic Examples
- **Appendix H:**
  Marketing Compared with Selling

BUSINESS PLAN OUTLINE

*T*his is the classic business plan outline that has been most useful to the entrepreneurs with whom I have worked. Every story should be unique, so feel free to modify it to suit your needs. However, be sure to have a good reason for changing the outline. Make every change add to the impact of your story, your unfair advantage.

Appendix Table A-1 Detailed Business Plan Outline

(1) Executive Summary (maximum of four pages)
    (a) Purpose of this plan
        (i) Amount of funding desired
        (ii) Stage of company
        (iii) Milestone/goal after use of this round of funding
    (b) Customer Need and Business Opportunity
    (c) Solution: Product/service
    (d) Market: Size and Growth
    (e) Competition
    (f) Strategy
    (g) Business Model
    (h) Technology and Engineering
    (i) Management and Company Culture
    (j) Financial Summary
        1. Table: Summary for each year of five years:
        a. Sales

      b. Operating profit in $

      c. Operating profit in % of sales

      d. Head count

      e. Cumulative capital required

(2) Customer Need and Business Opportunity

    (a) Basic need/big problem waiting to be solved

    (b) Solution to fill need/fix big problem

      (i) Product/service

    (c) Who benefits

    (d) How it works

(3) Comparison with Competing Solutions

(4) Ideal Customer

    (a) Description: include numbers

      (i) End user who uses the product

      (ii) Customer who pays for the product

(5) Value Proposition (include numbers)

(6) Business Model

    (a) How to make money

    (b) Graphic picture of business model

(7) Business Strategy and Key Milestones

    (a) Competition

      (i) Market leader description

      (ii) Other competitors

      (iii) Competitive advantage of each company

      (iv) Plan to outmaneuver the competition

    (b) Major milestones

      (i) Table or Gantt chart: Show each major milestone with cumulative cash needed and head count

(8) Marketing, Sales, and Support Plan

    (a) Basic market size:

      (i) Total available market (TAM)

      (ii) Served available market (SAM): subset you will focus on

    (b) Market segmentation: "Bowling pins" (first and following market segments)

      (i) Ideal customer description for each bowling pin

    (c) Competition, positioning, and unfair advantage plan

      (i) Table: Comparison of your company against competitors

    (d) Branding/standard-setting plan

(e) Marketing communications plan (public relations and advertising and other)

(9) Sales
    (a) Sales model
        (i) Table with details for five years of sales
    (b) Size of markets
        (i) Table: Five-year sales forecast: TAM, SAM, SOM (share of market)
            1. Units
            2. Price per unit
            3. $Sales
                a. SAM as % of TAM
                b. SOM as % of SAM
    (c) Sales plan
        (i) Sales strategy and plans
        (ii) Channels of distribution
    (d) Possible upside to $ of sales

(10) Strategic Partners
    (a) Names, value propositions

(11) Customer Support Plan

(12) International/Global Plan (sales in countries other than home market)

(13) Operations Plan
    (a) Engineering plan
    (b) Manufacturing and outsourcing plan
    (c) Web site and information technology plan
    (d) Facilities and administration plan
    (e) Legal plan: Intellectual property
    (f) Management and key personnel
        (i) Core team and leadership (successor) plan
            1. Summaries of core team experience
            2. (Detailed résumés in appendix)
    (g) Organization chart
    (h) Staffing plan
        (i) Table: Head count projections for five years
        (ii) Recruiting plan
        (iii) Assumptions of recruiting costs in financial forecasts
        (iv) Incentive compensation program
    (i) Company culture plan

(14) Financial Forecast (words to explain the numbers)
   (a) Written overview of financial highlights
   (b) Income statement
      (i) Sales growth
         1. Sales model
      (ii) Expenses
      (iii) Profit margins
         1. Profitability breakeven date
      (iv) Head count
      (v) Sales per head count
      (vi) Key assumptions for balance sheet
      (vii) Cash flow and burn rate
      (viii) Positive cash flow date
      (ix) Financing plan: rounds of financing and any leasing and
      bank borrowing

(15) Valuation
   (a) Your company valuation (multiples of sales and net income)
   (b) Comparable companies for investors
      (i) Description
      (ii) Numbers (sales, head count)
      (iii) Comparable company valuations (multiples of sales and
      net income)

(16) Pages of Numbers: Five-Year Forecasts ($)
   (a) Sales model (one page)
   (b) Income statement
   (c) Balance sheet
   (d) Cash flow statement
   (e) Ownership
      (i) Percentage owned by participants
      (ii) ROI per year to investors
      (iii) Stock option pool

(17) Supporting Graphics
   (a) Sales and sales per head count
   (b) Sales and operating profit
   (c) Cash flow from operations and financing
   (d) Ownership (dilution) and return on investment for investors

(18) Appendix
   (a) Detailed résumés

SOURCE: *Nesheim Group.*

SCORING SHEET FOR WRITTEN BUSINESS PLAN

A written plan can be scored. The following is the score sheet I use for real companies and student projects. To make it fit life science new enterprises, extend the five-year time horizons to perhaps ten.

Date: Name of Judge:

Company Name:

Basic Idea:

	= TOTAL SCORE
SCORE	SCORE: 0 to 3 points per criteria, 1 is good, 2 is very good, 3 is outstanding. Maximum number of points is in parentheses.
	EXECUTIVE SUMMARY (2 × 3 = 6) Delivered a summary that was both complete and interesting to potential investors
	✓ Complete: A total mini business plan with all the needed paragraphs, including complete financial summary

	✓ Innovative: Included a compelling graphic and wording that stirred emotions based on unfair advantage
	BUSINESS IDEA (5 × 3 = 15)
	✓ Clear and detailed explanation
	✓ Opportunity: Saw a rising trend and or basic problem lacking a solution on which to build a viable business. Chance exits to dominate a new market segment/category
	✓ Need: Explained concisely what the ideal customer needs
	✓ Ideal Customer: Identified a crisp and focused first customer target and explained plausible follow-on customer targets ("bowling pins")
	✓ Customer Survey: Completed and documented a survey of ideal customers
	✓ Value Proposition: Made a clear, compelling, proposition of value to the ideal customer, including quantified justification (e.g. Return on investment) for price chosen
	STRATEGY and Milestones (4 × 3 = 12)
	✓ Strategy: Chose one of four basic strategies and applied it with convincing plan that suggests it could win
	✓ Competition: Comprehensive review of each competitor was made, including how to out-maneuver the market leader
	✓ Chart: Clear detailed understandable milestone chart
	✓ Positioning: Chose the market leader and created a clear competitive position

	MARKETING & SALES (10 × 3 =30)
	✓ Marketing: Used marketing techniques proven successful to contemporary companies and used them innovatively to strengthen unfair advantage
	✓ Sales: Made clear the pricing, units and sales channels to reach the customers and why they were chosen to boost unfair advantage
	✓ Customer Service: Presented department plan capable of supporting customer base with a specific level of quality service
	✓ Business Model: Graphics and words made it clear how the business could make money, including strategic partners
	✓ Strategic Partners: Selected compelling and powerful partners and how to use them to add to competitive advantage
	✓ Pricing: Chose and supported pricing plan and related strategy that fit value proposition and positioning of competing alternatives
	✓ Positioning: Used clear and compelling positioning statement and plan that support leadership (branding and standard setting) in the target market
	✓ PR, Ads and Marketing Communications: Created practical plan for communicating messages; used PR and other marketing communications correctly, with a wise role for any advertising; showed events timetable and expense budget
	✓ TAM SAM SOM Table: Included this five-year table and used it to explain size of targeted market and share of market for each of five years

	✓ World Market: Showed how to enter and prepare to compete in a global market
	OPERATIONS (6 × 3 = 18)
	✓ Technology: Applied and explained how to use technology to build a first product / service and to use it to strengthen unfair advantage; included headcounts, tasks and milestone chart
	✓ Web Site: Explained and showed mock exhibits of what and how the web site will operate and add to the unfair advantage.
	✓ Management: Explained and supported special expertise of each core team leader and included a pragmatic successor plan. Explained who the needed and missing personnel are and gave examples of who might be recruited citing people and companies by name.
	✓ Culture: Showed application of how to design and use company culture for attracting and retaining employees
	✓ Intellectual Property: Made a solid case for how to protect and use intellectual property for competitive advantage
	✓ Operations: Showed comprehensive understanding of what is needed to run the operations of a real business in their industry
	FINANCIAL (4 × 3 = 12)
	✓ Forecast: Used QuickUp™ or other spreadsheet model to forecast the financial statements and valuation of the company with forethought and without basic errors

	✓ Valuation: Produced equity sharing plan attractive to employees and investors for each of five years. IPO valuation supported by data from comparable public companies
	✓ Realism: Financial statements and support were realistic and believable and were supported by useful exhibits and graphs
	✓ Sales Model: Used detailed model to forecast units and prices and dollars, for multiple products and services, over each of five years
	UNFAIR ADVANTAGE (21) Demonstrated how to assemble a plausible, sustainable competitive advantage. Convincing opportunity to dominate a new market category. Killer Idea = 23 to 16, Good = 15 to 10, So-So = 9 to 4, Dud =3 to 0.
	PLAN OVERALL EFFORT (7 × 3 = 21)
	✓ Breadth: Completed all sections of the recommended outline for a business plan
	✓ Depth: Each section was well supported without unnecessary overlap and redundancy
	✓ Quality: Document used English well and showed care with the integration of the sections
	✓ Creativity: Demonstrated innovative application of lessons known to the start-up community (e.g. from books, magazines, guest speakers and school lectures.)
	✓ Names: Used names creatively to distinguish company, technology, product family and new market category

	✓ Leader: Presented a plan that had exciting chance of becoming the leader of a new category/market segment (see Management section below for scoring Leadership)
	✓ World-class: Plan represents a business that could be world-class and go to initial public offering within five years
	= TOTAL SCORE
	COMMENTS BY REVIEWER:

SOURCE: *Nesheim Group*

Appendix C

SCORING SHEET FOR PRESENTATION OF BUSINESS PLAN

A presentation of a plan can be scored. The good ones are based on a well-written business plan. The following scorecard is one I have used with good results.

You should have three versions of your presentation ready at all times:

- **Elevator pitch:** 30 seconds—everything important and exciting enough to get the investor (whom you ran into in the elevator) to ask you to step aside and tell you more.

- **3-minute pitch:** Start all over, and this time take breaths between sentences. Your goal is to get the investor interested enough to invite you to present for 30 minutes in his or her office.

- **30-minute pitch:** Start all over and now take about 7 minutes per slide to tell your exciting story.

Appendix Table C-1 Scoring Sheet for Presentation of Business Plan

Date:	Time of Start:	Time of End:

Name of Judge:	Company Name:

Basic Idea:

Score: 0 to 3, Highest = 3

	Score	Comments
1. Business Concept Clearly a presented viable business idea. 3 points Not a viable business idea as presented. 0 points		
2. Competition and Strategy Clearly did the research, knew the key competitors, understood the basics of why idea was better, and created a strategy with strong advantages that could win. 3 points Inadequate research, big gaps in understanding the business, appeared to have put in little effort. 0 points		

3. Demonstrated Market Need/Demand Convinced me that there is a real market need and that the plan could exploit it. Presented plan that could lead to domination of a new market segment. 3 points	Not clear why this product or service will sell; failed to consider key market issues; marketing techniques used in plan were inadequate. 0 points		
4. Business Model, Financials, and Valuation Clearly presented a viable way to make money for all the stakeholders. 3 points	No clear, viable way to make money for all stakeholders as presented. 0 points		
5. The Team Appear highly capable of succeeding as management team for this phase of the company. Wise choice of people for positions. Realistic CEO successor plan. 3 points	No one convinced me that they might be capable of managing the first phase of this company. Their ambitions as leaders are unrealistic. 0 points		

(Continued on next page)

Appendix Table C-1 (continued)

	Score	Comments
6. Presentation Each of the team presented. Clear, effective, enthusiastic, and made a strong impression. Creative use of presentation tools. 3 points	Presentation dominated by a few of the presenters. Confusing, left out key areas, failed to capture my interest. 0 points	
7. Unfair Advantage Demonstrated they have created a strong, sustainable competitive advantage. Applied lessons from real world, readings, lectures, and guest speakers. 3 points	Big gaps in understanding how to build an unfair advantage. Did not apply many lessons from real world, readings, lectures, and guest speakers. 0 points	

Total Points (0–21) =

SOURCE: *Nesheim Group.*

Appendix D

VALUATION TABLES AND GRAPHICS

The following are examples of tables and graphs used to build a financial plan to value your company.

Appendix Table D-1 Company Valuation Table

Company Valuation

	Year 1	Year 2	Year 3	Year 4	Year 5
Chosen company valuation ($M)	$4	$20	$65	$155	$225
SALES ($000)	$450	$7,500	$13,000	$25,200	$44,000
Multiple of sales	4.0	4.0	4.0	4.0	4.0
Company valuation ($M)	$2	$30	$52	$101	$176
NET INCOME ($000)	($4,190)	($888)	($2,776)	($821)	$3,093
Multiple of net income	33	33	33	33	33
Company valuation ($M)	($138)	($29)	($92)	($27)	$102

SOURCE: *QuickUp.*

Appendix Table D-2 Ownership Table

Company Ownership

	Year 1	Year 2	Year 3	Year 4	Year 5
Number of Shares					
Total investors	1,000	2,100	3,600	4,500	4,500
Total noninvestors	2,015	3,380	3,930	4,430	5,130
Total company shares	3,015	5,480	7,530	8,930	9,630
Investors					
Preferred Series A	1,000	1,000	1,000	1,000	1,000
Preferred Series B		1,100	1,100	1,100	1,100
Preferred Series C			1,500	1,500	1,500
Preferred Series D				900	900
Total investors	1,000	2,100	3,600	4,500	4,500
Noninvestors					
Founders	2,000	2,000	2,000	2,000	2,000
Vice presidents and other executives		900	1,100	1,200	1,300
Directors		300	400	500	600
Managers		100	200	300	400
Employees		50	200	400	800
Total management and employees	2,000	3,350	3,900	4,400	5,100
Contractors	5	10	10	10	10
Support services	5	10	10	10	10
Other noninvestors	5	10	10	10	10
Total nonmanagement and employees	15	30	30	30	30
Total noninvestors	2,015	3,380	3,930	4,430	5,130

Portion Owned					
Total investors	33.2%	38.3%	47.8%	50.4%	46.7%
Total noninvestors	66.8%	61.7%	52.2%	49.6%	53.3%
Total company	100.0%	100.0%	100.0%	100.0%	100.0%
Investors					
Preferred Series A	33.2%	18.2%	13.3%	11.2%	10.4%
Preferred Series B	0.0%	20.1%	14.6%	12.3%	11.4%
Preferred Series C	0.0%	0.0%	19.9%	16.8%	15.6%
Preferred Series D	0.0%	0.0%	0.0%	10.1%	9.3%
Total Investors	33.2%	38.3%	47.8%	50.4%	46.7%
Noninvestors					
Founders	66.3%	36.5%	26.6%	22.4%	20.8%
Vice presidents and other executives	0.0%	16.4%	14.6%	13.4%	13.5%
Directors	0.0%	5.5%	5.3%	5.6%	6.2%
Managers	0.0%	1.8%	2.7%	3.4%	4.2%
Employees	0.0%	0.9%	2.7%	4.5%	8.3%
Total management and employees	66.3%	61.1%	51.8%	49.3%	53.0%
Contractors	0.2%	0.2%	0.1%	0.1%	0.1%
Support services	0.2%	0.2%	0.1%	0.1%	0.1%
Other noninvestors	0.2%	0.2%	0.1%	0.1%	0.1%
Total nonmanagement and employees	0.5%	0.5%	0.4%	0.3%	0.3%
Total noninvestors	66.8%	61.7%	52.2%	49.6%	53.3%

SOURCE: *QuickUp from Nesheim Group.*

Appendix Table D-3 Wealth Table

	Year 1	Year 2	Year 3	Year 4	Year 5
Chosen company valuation ($M)	$4	$20	$65	$155	$225
Total Number of Shares, company	3,015	5,480	7,530	8,930	9,630
Company value / shares fully diluted	$1.33	$3.65	$8.63	$17.36	$23.36
WEALTH					
Total investors	$1,327	$7,664	$31,076	$78,108	$105,140
Total noninvestors	$2,673	$12,336	$33,924	$76,892	$119,860
Total company shares	$4,000	$20,000	$65,000	$155,000	$225,000
Investors					
Preferred Series A	$1,327	$3,650	$8,632	$17,357	$23,364
Preferred Series B	$0	$4,015	$9,495	$19,093	$25,701
Preferred Series C	$0	$0	$12,948	$26,036	$35,047
Preferred Series D	$0	$0	$0	$15,622	$21,028
Total Investors	$1,327	$7,664	$31,076	$78,108	$105,140
Non-Investors					
Founders	$2,653	$7,299	$17,264	$34,714	$46,729
Vice presidents and other executives	$0	$3,285	$9,495	$20,829	$30,374
Directors	$0	$1,095	$3,453	$8,679	$14,019
Managers	$0	$365	$1,726	$5,207	$9,346
Employees	$0	$182	$1,726	$6,943	$18,692
Total management and employees	$2,653	$12,226	$33,665	$76,372	$119,159
Contractors	$7	$36	$86	$174	$234
Support services	$7	$36	$86	$174	$234
Other noninvestors	$7	$36	$86	$174	$234

Total nonmanagement and employees	$20	$109	$259	$521	$701
Total noninvestors	$2,673	$12,336	$33,924	$76,892	$119,860

SOURCE: *QuickUp from Nesheim Group.*

Appendix Table D-4 Investors' Return on Investment Table

	Year 1	Year 2	Year 3	Year 4	Year 5
Sales ($000)	$450	$7,500	$13,000	$25,200	$44,000
Equity capital ($000)	$500	$2,000	$6,000	$10,000	$0
Chosen company valuation ($M)	$4	$20	$65	$155	$225
Total company shares	3,015	5,480	7,530	8,930	9,630
Company value / share fully diluted	$1.33	$3.65	$8.63	$17.36	$23.36
Investors' multiple and risk curve (investors' multiple = (Year 5 $/share)/(this Years' $/share); 1$ invested this year will grow X times to = $/share in Year 5)	17.6	6.4	2.7	1.3	1.0
Investors' ROI ($1 grows to Year 5 $/share at this interest rate per year)	105%	86%	65%	35%	

SOURCE: *QuickUp from Nesheim Group.*

Appendix E

UNFAIR ADVANTAGE IN A PRESS RELEASE

Note how the following press release mentions several elements of an unfair advantage. How many can you spot in the press release?

Appendix Example E-1   Press Release Includes Unfair Advantage: ArcSight

2002 Wednesday April 10, 8:04 am Eastern Time

Press Release

Source: ArcSight

INDUSTRY MOMENTUM INCREASES FOR ARCSIGHT WITH FUNDING FROM KLEINER PERKINS

Second-Round Funding Validates Vision and Value to the Market-place for Provider of Enterprise Security Management Software

SUNNYVALE, Calif., April 10 /PRNewswire/—ArcSight, a leading provider of enterprise security management solutions, today announced $9.5 million in second-round funding led by the premier venture capital firm, Kleiner Perkins Caufield & Byers. In addition, SVIC, which led the first round of funding, will be participating in the second round along with Integral Capital. This brings the total amount raised by ArcSight to $25.5 million.

Kleiner Perkins has deep experience in helping build industry-leading security and network management companies, and has backed a number of highly successful companies including Internet Security Systems, Symantec, VeriSign, and Tivoli. ArcSight's new round of funding will enable the company to increase the momentum for the industry's first comprehensive, enterprise-level solution that enables large organizations to manage security as a critical business process, satisfying senior management's need to protect vital information assets and functions. Once security is managed as a business process, continuous improvement is available and business managers can make better decisions regarding risk and investment.

ArcSight's software improves the efficiency and effectiveness of enterprise security by integrating and automating the monitoring, correlation, investigation, resolution, and reporting of threats and attacks. As the market enters its high-growth phase, ArcSight will use the funds to support further product development, add to its talent base, and expand its sales and marketing efforts.

"Enterprise security is now a senior management issue, and our customers and strategic partners have embraced the ArcSight vision and technology. Now, this additional investment provides both the validation and resources to aggressively attack the market," says Robert Shaw, ArcSight CEO and president. "To pass the Kleiner Perkins standard for investment is very exciting and gratifying."

TED SCHLEIN JOINS ARCSIGHT BOARD OF DIRECTORS

As part of Kleiner Perkins' commitment, partner Ted Schlein joins ArcSight's Board of Directors. Schlein's areas of expertise include security, enterprise applications, infrastructure, and services. Prior to joining Kleiner Perkins, Schlein served as vice president of Networking and Client Server Technology at Symantec Corporation, and is credited for his role in establishing the company as a leader in both the utilities and antivirus markets.

"I expect enterprise security management to quickly become a core business application with ArcSight leading the way. As the number and type of security threats continue to outpace the ability of most organizations to protect their assets, the ArcSight solution brings enormous value to the current suite of enterprise IT solutions," says Schlein. "Kleiner Perkins chose to invest in ArcSight based on the strength of its team, superior technology, and focus on a large, high-growth market. I look forward to collaborating with the company as it brings to market a solution that can quickly eradicate many problems associated with securing corporate information."

ABOUT ARCSIGHT

ArcSight is a leading provider of enterprise software solutions that integrate and optimize the management of diverse security devices deployed across a network. By delivering complete monitoring, correlation, investigation, resolution, and reporting—all within a single solution—ArcSight provides a coordinated infrastructure that maximizes security results while decreasing overall costs. ArcSight's intelligence and workflow transform information security into a well-understood, effective, and efficiently managed business process directly linked to business goals and objectives. More information can be found at *http://www.arcsight.com*.

ABOUT KLEINER PERKINS CAUFIELD & BYERS

Kleiner Perkins Caufield & Byers (*www.kpcb.com*) is a leading venture capital partnership headquartered in Menlo Park, Calif. The firm has backed many industry-leading companies including AOL, Compaq, Genentech, Hybritech, IDEC, Intuit, Juniper Networks, Netscape, Sun Microsystems, and Verisign.

NOTE: ArcSight and the ArcSight logo are registered trademarks of ArcSight. All other companies, products, and services mentioned herein are the property of their respective owners and should be treated as such.

How many elements of an unfair advantage did you see in the press release? There are many. Now try writing a similar press release for your own start-up as it announces the seed round of its first funding. That will tell you much about how unfair your advantage is so far.

NEED AND OPPORTUNITY OF DATAMED

*T*he following is from the business plan of DataMed. It is the section explaining what the company will offer, the need, and business opportunity.

Need and Opportunity of DataMed

DataMed Local Data Repository is a local database within hospitals that stores patient records which constitute: diagnosis by doctors, observations by nurses, medication taken, laboratory reports, radiology reports, detailed patients' medical history, billing, insurance information.

DataMed Chart is the main feature of DataMed's products. It streamlines the workflow process into one desktop application that provides access to the functions that support the electronic medical record. DataMed Chart is a clinician's desktop solution for viewing, ordering and documenting the electronic medical record, which is maintained in the DataMed Local data repository. With the electronic version, doctors and nurses use the Personal Data Assistant (PDA) to input patients' data at the site of care.

In order to achieve the goal of providing a complete IT solution for hospitals, DataMed also offers the DataMed Hospital Automation Plan. This plan is an optional feature within DataMed's Architecture. It excels in its flexibility and compatibility. Hospitals can install only the feature they want or install the entire integrated EMR system. Our system is readily compatible with most of the existing EMR systems; therefore, hospitals do not need to worry about having to change their entire system when installing our product.

DataMed Hospital Automation Plan is an internal hospital IT system. It automates the clinical processes within hospitals and the physician's practice—it collects, refines, organizes, and evaluates detailed clinical and management data. The system also enables the entire care team to plan and manage individual activities and plans, as well as measure outcomes and goals. Our plan is divided into specific sub-packages that can be installed separately. The division specific sub-packages include the Laboratory Pack, the Radiology Pack, the Emergency Room Pack, the Pharmacy Pack, the Registration Pack, Financial and Operational Management Systems, the Materials Management System, and the Surgery Unit Pack.

Apart from this, DataMed also offers the option for our customers to link with other regional hospitals for the purpose of referrals and sharing medical records. This is done through DataMed Link that connects community-based physicians to health systems for referrals, authorizations, claims, eligibility, and reporting.

After setting up two or more local data repositories, DataMed will proceed to establish a central database called the DataMed Central Data Repository (DCDR). This centralized database will link the patient's record from all affiliated hospitals within the DataMed Medical Network. This system makes the patient's record retrievable anywhere, anytime.

DataMed Central Data Repository is a database that periodically synchronizes itself with all the DataMed Local Data Repositories. The DLDRs contain each hospital's own database. Normally, when a doctor or a nurse retrieves information from DLDR, it will only retrieve information that is currently in the DLDR. The DLDR will not automatically synchronize with the centralized database. The centralized database will be accessed only upon the doctor's request and the patient's agreement in order to protect the patient's privacy. Once the doctor has requested data from the central database through DataMed Chart, the DLDR will synchronize that particular patient's data with DCDR. This is set up to make sure that all patients' records are the most updated, even when the patient has gone to other hospitals. Doctors and hospitals do not directly access this central database; they use DataMed Chart to access patient records from DLDR.

After setting up the DataMed Central Data Repository, DataMed will launch the E-DataMed Chart. It is an electronic version of DataMed Chart. Through E-DataMed Chart, patients can securely retrieve their medical information online. They can also enter and track health information through a record keeper that helps organize and build a complete family health record. The system also allows users to complete health assessment surveys and receive follow-up through preventive care programs and results monitoring, as well as to access a medications guide to promote safe use of prescribed and over-the-counter medications. On top of all these, patients can utilize a health calendar with reminders to track and manage health-related appointments and activities

Finally, DataMed will develop a Statistical Analysis package that sorts the data in the DataMed Central Data Repository. The only data to be analyzed will be specific to each patient's reactions to different drugs.

DataMed's solutions emphasize flexibility. Our products can be acquired individually or as a fully integrated health information system.

VALUE PROPOSITION

DataMed creates value for health care professionals, health institutions, patients and pharmaceutical companies.

Health Care Professionals

Health care professionals, at the forefront of the most sacred profession, have the responsibility to ensure patients receive the best possible care in the most efficient manner. Specifically, our product provides them with the following value:

Reduced error rate—doctors' reputation is protected

DataMed Chart, with its user-friendly interface, drop down lists using predefined menu items, and spell check using a comprehensive medical dictionary, significantly reduces the error rate in data input. According to a study, hospitals usually lose 3% to 8% of information during the transfer of information by humans. Installing a fully automated medical record system will greatly reduce the amount of information error and loss; this can translate into savings of several million dollars in large hospitals. This will protect the doctor's reputation against faults in data.

Convenient information retrieval—no more waiting time

There are customized views that allow related data to be displayed as a summary format. Our DataMed Local Database Servers at each hospital ensures speedy connection.

Secure information storage—no information is tampered

Our DataMed Central Database Server acts as a backup storage device that ensures medical records are never lost. Together with the SSL technology that we employ, our system is tampering safe. Therefore, once the doctor has made a diagnosis and prescription, that information will not be altered or viewed by unauthorized personnel.

Convenient patient referral—utilization of local medical resources

With DataMed Link, hospitals can refer patients to one another and synchronize patient data using DataMed Central Database Server.

Medical advice—reminders of consequences that doctors missed.

We also have intelligent agents that provide treatment suggestions and warnings on drug conflicts and side effects by using a drug information database and our proprietary statistical analysis package.

Hospital Administration

Hospital Administrators want to increase efficiency, decrease operations costs, and eliminate all errors involved in human transfer of information. DataMed can help achieve this goal by automating workflow and integrating the various departments such as billing, inventory control, laboratory, etc. As processes become automated, hospital staffs can save time in transferring information, and human errors are minimized. Using PDA technology, doctors and nurses can become more efficient in recording patient data. In this way, DataMed can reduce the number of inpatient deaths each year due to inefficient medical care and the transfer of inaccurate medical records to the doctors. As mentioned previously, a report shows that an upgraded IT system can save approximately 36 lives each year in each hospital. For the patient and his family, this is an incalculable saving. For the hospitals and doctors, this can reduce their malpractice rate and the insurance premium.

Pharmaceutical Companies and Research Institutions

Each year, drug companies spend a large amount of money to collect medical data for research on new drugs. Much of the expense is in data correction. Currently, no company is specialized in collecting data concerning patients' reaction to drugs. Since DataMed automates the input and the storage of medical data, we guarantee that we can provide accurate information for the drug companies. Our statistical analysis package allows them to see trends and relationships between drug, treatment, symptoms, and outcomes. In this way, they will save millions of dollars in terms of research. Also, since they need less time to research the data, they can release their new drug into the market much sooner; this increase in efficiency will bring significant increases in profit for them.

Individual Patients

We can provide patients with the ability to see their own records anytime and anywhere. We can also assure them by stressing our security that their confidentiality is protected.

FAMOUS MARKETING WARS: STRATEGIC EXAMPLES

The following are examples of the use of the four basic strategies in famous marketing wars.

EXAMPLE: Flanking followed by Offensive

MARKET: Spreadsheets

Who is the market leader? Visicalc = Visicalc Inc.

Who are the attackers? 1-2-3 = Lotus; Excel = Microsoft

Battle 1: The first spreadsheet was Visicalc, invented by Dan Bricklin and Bob Frankston in 1979. It worked on the Apple II personal computer. Together they made history. Visicalc was a "killer app." It boosted the Apple II to the top of the sales charts. Visicalc became the market leader of a new market segment: software spreadsheets. Visicalc Corp became king of the spreadsheet hill.

Battle 2: IBM introduces its own version of the personal computer, the IBM Personal Computer. Microsoft introduces the DOS operating system for it. A Boston start-up called Lotus introduces a spreadsheet for the PC called 1-2-3. Management of the Visicalc company hesitated and waited to see if the PC would be a success. The company does not respond quickly enough. It leaves the PC base uncovered. It does not develop a spreadsheet for the PC. 1-2-3 rockets to success along with the PC. Lotus becomes the new spreadsheet market leader. This is a classic example of a flanking move that created—almost overnight— the new king of the spreadsheet hill: Lotus Corp. with its 1-2-3.

Battle 3: Microsoft decides it is time to introduce a spreadsheet. What was its name? No, it was not Excel. It was Multiplan. It was so poor, so buggy and clunky, that it got zeros in some product reviews. It was bad. So was the strategy chosen by Microsoft. It attempted to use the offensive strategy, attacking 1-2-3 head-on. It did not work. Blood flowed in red ink losses everywhere Microsoft turned. After a brief and bloody first attempt, Microsoft stopped selling Multiplan and crawled back to Redmond with stumps instead of hands, blood flowing all the way. 1-2-3 easily won that battle and remained king of the PC spreadsheet hill. Meanwhile, food fights in the Visicalc boardroom were tearing the company apart. The PC had zoomed way ahead of the Apple computers, leaving Visicalc stuck with a tiny Apple II user market.

Battle 4: Apple introduces the Macintosh computer. It has no spreadsheet. No company had created one for it by the time it is introduced. It is hard to write software applications for the Mac. Months after the Mac's introduction, Visicalc, the Apple II defender, has not responded, nor has Lotus with its 1-2-3 for the PC. Both defenders choose not to respond. Meanwhile, Microsoft is copying the Mac operating system (software that will later emerge as Windows). Microsoft decides to design a spreadsheet for the Mac. It names it Excel. It moves into an overlooked market segment. Excel works well, gets good product reviews. The flanking move wins. Excel becomes king of the Mac spreadsheet hill. Visicalc begins to settle into the sunset along with the Apple II. Lotus focuses on the PC.

Battle 5: By now Microsoft has done its homework. It has learned painfully the weaknesses in 1-2-3 and by now has added the power of intimate knowledge of the next PC operating system (from Microsoft). Carefully picking its timing, Microsoft launches Excel for the PC. This offensive move by Microsoft is aimed at the weaknesses of the defender (Lotus 1-2-3's). In a short number of months the sales of Excel for the PC begin rising. In a few years 1-2-3 is relegated to history. Excel becomes the new king of the PC spreadsheet hill and thus dominates the software spreadsheet market. Flanking moves are powerful. They can win, big time.

Appendix Example G-2   After the IBM PC: Start-ups Compaq and Dell

EXAMPLE: Flanking

MARKET: Personal computers: Early battles for a new market

Who is the market leader? IBM—Personal computers

Who are the Newcomers? Compaq—"Luggable PC" sold only through retail dealers; Dell—PCs sold directly to consumers and businesses

Battle 1: IBM leads the new PC market and uses its vast worldwide sales army to sell directly to businesses. Austin, Texas, engineers and Dallas venture capitalists shape a plan for a new PC that is portable. It will be sold exclusively through a new sales channel: retail computer stores. Compaq is created. Its PC is portable. It also has noticeable weight and suitcase size. The market quickly attaches an affectionate name to it: "The luggable PC." IBM the Defender does not respond. Compaq becomes king of the portable PC hill.

Battle 2: An enterprising student finds new retail stores eager to sell PCs to him at wholesale prices. The stores have to find buyers for their over-ordered (to get deep discounts) quantities of PCs. The student, Michael Dell, starts to sell at attractive prices to his budget-minded university friends in Austin, Texas. Soon he recognizes that no large PC companies or retail stores are organized to sell directly to consumers. He drops out of school to focus his fledgling business on doing that. IBM and Compaq do not respond. Dell becomes king of the direct-to-consumer PC hill.

Appendix Example G-3   From Sun Workstations to Networked Computers

EXAMPLE: Responsive strategic move from Defensive to Flanking

MARKET: Networked Computers: Moving the playing field

Who is the market leader? Sun Microsystems

Who are the attackers? IBM, DEC, HP in low- to middle-market workstations; Silicon Graphics in high-end workstations

Battle 1: The start-up, Sun Microsystems, emerges as the gorilla Defender of workstations after the first rounds of the new market workstation war are over. However, Sun's success with revolutionary UNIX-based workstations quickly attracts giants from other markets (IBM from mainframes and Digital Equipment Corporation (DEC) from minicomputers). The giants arrive in full battle gear determined to engage Sun and overcome its lead. The multinational companies view tiny Sun as a pesky upstart that has upset the status quo and should be gotten rid of as soon as possible. Hewlett-Packard (HP) quietly responds with its predictable style of close follower. Sun finds itself facing attack by three determined giants with huge resources. What is tiny Sun to do? Defend at all costs, to the last dollar?

Battle 2: Founder CEO Scott McNealy and crew surprise the competition. "The network is the computer" becomes their new battle cry. They redefine the market and move into position as the leader of a new market segment. Sun becomes king of the hill of networked computers. Sun's management knows the power of this adage: "When under attack by giants, move the battlefield to a fresh area where your smaller company can defend with more strength." That is another example of dynamic strategy: Action 1 → Reaction 2 → Re-Reaction 3.

Battle 3: Sun's attackers are left behind, fighting among themselves to gain the coveted position of leader of the workstation market. The three giants—IBM, DEC, and HP—rely on the loyalty of their existing customers for business. They spend tens of millions of dollars continuing to attack each other in order to try to grab a sliver of market share at the others' expense.

Battle 4: Silicon Graphics, which has become king of the hill of the high end of the workstation market, begins to be eaten alive from attacks on its exposed lower belly: middle- and low-priced and ever-more-powerful small workstations. Like a slow whale attacked by a pod of killer sharks from below, Silicon Graphics responds with more of the same: it touts its revered technology—"on the bleeding edge"—in a desperate attempt to stay ahead of the oncoming herd of stampeding giants. Silicon Graphics changes its marketing message to try to differentiate further from the workstation masses: "3-dimensional computing for exotic uses." Silicon Graphics eventually bleeds to near death and becomes an afterthought.

In the end, Sun survives and even thrives during the early 1990s. Its moves noted above include one of the principles of a guerrilla strategy: "Be prepared to bug out at a moment's notice." Moving the battlefield was a brilliant innovation.

Appendix Example G-4   RealNetworks the Start-Up

EXAMPLE: Guerrilla

MARKET: Internet audio

Who is the market leader? No one (yet)

Who are the attackers? Fresh industry = no market leader exists (yet)

Battle 1: The 1990s Internet boom is hot, with thousands of new enterprises attempting to create products to sell to exciting new e-commerce companies. Microsoft is booming, making many employees into millionaires. Some leave to start new enterprises. They often are seed-funded with wealth from their own stock options. One group decides to form a company they name RealNetworks. Its business model will be to give away proprietary Internet audio players to consumers and make money selling RealNetworks servers to e-commerce corporations.

Who is the market leader (when there is no industry yet)? In this case it is "how we are doing things today." Since there is no Internet player-server industry yet, there is no Internet audio being played. That gives an open field for RealNetworks to enter. That is good news because the king of the hill has not yet been determined. It is also bad news for RealNetworks because as soon as it launches its first product, the world will wake up and the attack will begin, first from the me-too start-ups and then from established corporations.

RealNetworks launches and quickly becomes the king of the Internet audio hill.

Appendix Example G-5   RealNetworks Attacked by Microsoft

EXAMPLE: Defending

MARKET: Internet audio

Who is the market leader? RealNetworks

Who are the attackers? Me-too start-ups; Microsoft

Battle 2: RealNetworks quickly succeeds and becomes the industry standard. The company's products become "the audio player format of choice." Soon RealNetworks dominates the new market segment. Industry media acknowledge it as king of the Internet audio hill.

Me-too start-ups attempt to attack RealNetworks head on but are wiped out by it. Their blood flows all over the carpet.

Then, just as the battle seemed over and Real appeared to have won, out of the dark came what pundits have dubbed "The Evil Empire": Microsoft. Real management gets a message from Microsoft: "Come on over for a talk." The Real boys from Redmond, Washington, sense that a dark cloud is coming to rain on the party of RealNetworks. After all, they are Microsoft veterans and know how the giant plays the competitive game.

Upon arriving at their former employer, they sit down to listen. They are not surprised to hear Microsoft people calmly announce that the giant would like to purchase a one-year license from RealNetworks, but in about a year Microsoft will introduce its own version of an Internet audio player-server system not compatible with RealNetworks. Take it or leave it.

RealNetworks takes the license (and Microsoft's money) and returns home to change its immediate plans. The leaders realize they are the Defender. It is up to them to craft the wisest response to the Offensive attacker, Microsoft. This comes in the form of a series of rapid new product introductions, followed by strategic partner moves. RealNetworks ends its neutral stance on the monopolistic practices of Microsoft and quickly joins the Microsoft antitrust coalition. RealNetworks is still king of the hill, but under attack by an Offensive giant willing to lose lots of money in order to try to capture leadership of the Internet audio business.

And in 2003 Apple launched a for-fee audio music listening service with many of the Internet features RealNetworks offers and then Apple launched the iPod. Keep watching to see what happens next in this segment of the expanding Internet audio market. RealNetworks has a long war ahead of it as we leave the exciting saga unfinished.

Appendix Example G-6   Solectron Leads Outsourced Electronic
Manufacturing

EXAMPLE: Guerrilla to Flanking to Defender

MARKET: Outsourced computer manufacturing (also known as electronic manufacturing services, EMS)

Who is the market leader? In-house manufacturing departments, no market exists yet

Who are the attackers? Defenders = In-house manufacturing departments; Me-too start-ups

Battle 1: A mathematician from IBM, Winston H. Chen, passionate about quality, purchases a tiny printed circuit board company and names it Solectron. Wave 1 begins with Solectron creating a way of "getting our foot into the door, a beachhead we can defend." It creates a focused and unfair advantage mixing a combination of elements: (1) supply lower component cost (buy in larger quantities at deeper discounts than the in-house manufacturing departments of its customers), (2) deliver better quality, (3) ensure more on-time delivery (than in-house manufacturing), and (4) focus on doing pesky low-volume rush jobs of builds of fast turnarounds of high-performance computer prototypes (referred to as Beta builds). In-house manufacturing departments hate such work ("It disrupts our long production runs and raises our costs per unit!"). Solectron becomes king of this special (unwanted and tiny) hill.

Running against the negative opinions of the doubters, Solectron's plan for Wave 1 succeeds! Business booms, and so do the new markets for workstations and personal computers. And of course the boom attracts the first me-too competitors, trying to copy Solectron's success.

Battle 2: What does Solectron do now? Wave 2 is put into action. Solectron announces it will compete for the American national quality championship, the new, coveted Baldrige Quality Award. The growing start-up thinks that even just competing will separate it from the me-too competitors that have a less-than-best image. It is trying to get a share of the EMS market by simply cutting prices. Again Solectron is laughed at by observers. And once again, Solectron does the impossible: tiny Solectron wins the revered Baldrige Award for its class! Respect takes over where doubt stood. Believers begin to eagerly contract for the special services of Solectron.

Wave 2 is over. Solectron emerges as king of a now well-known (and growing) hill.

Battle 3: Even more competitors arrive. They try harder to copy Solectron. Solectron puts Wave 3 into action. It has seen what is about to become the next advance in electronic manufacturing. It amounts to a revolution: surface-mounted semiconductors that require a huge new investment in new manufacturing equipment (numerical process control), a vast information technology system (track every step so quality can be controlled in minute detail), and intensive and expensive training of production employees.

This move by Solectron wipes out competition from many large in-house manufacturing departments. "Leave it to Solectron" becomes the response from presidents of many companies. "Outsourcing" begins to appear in media stories. Meanwhile, those tiny prototype contract jobs have converted into long production runs of standard products that are being delivered in large quantities by the growing and accelerating Solectron. Me-too competition is falling further behind.

Battle 4: Not sitting on its hands, Solectron puts Wave 4 into action. Acting like the Defender, Solectron competes again for the Baldrige Award and wins a second time! The competition stops trying to compete for the award, settling instead for meeting ISO standards. Solectron expands geographically into Asia and Europe. It gains economic benefits of large economies of scale. It adds even more volume discounts to its competitive advantage. It now gets first pick of scarce electronic processors and rare new components. Solectron starts purchasing factories that are about to be abandoned by its growing list of giant customers. Solectron has become number one in the world. It goes public. It has become the undisputed king of the hill of electronic manufacturing services.

MARKETING COMPARED WITH SELLING

Start-up marketing and selling are often mixed up in the minds of first-time entrepreneurs. In start-ups marketing and sales do different things than in large public corporations. Here are some ways to avoid getting confused as you seek to use them to build unfair advantage: *Marketing* is the function that creates *customers*. *Selling* is the function that converts customers to *invoices*.

Marketing asks questions like these:

- What is going on out there (in the marketplace)?

- What should we (the company) do about that?

- Who are our most likely customers?

- How many are there in each category?

- How do they behave?

- What gets them excited?

- How should we reach them, get their attention, get our message to them about our products?

- What else could we sell to those customers?

- With whom out there are we going to be competing?

- How will we win against competitors?

Those are key questions your vice president of marketing should be able to answer. They are also very good questions to use during interviews of employee candidates.

Salespeople focus on these questions:

- Where can we sell the most?

- How can we get orders fastest?

- How can we explain our own advantages so that we expose the disadvantages of our competition?

- Which steps are involved in the sales process?

- How can we find a valid argument to justify a premium price?

- How do we quickly and accurately qualify if a customer represents a real business opportunity?

- Who has the decision power in the customer's organization?

- What can we do to boost the customer's perception of support and service from us?

MARKETING BUILDS PLANS AND WORKS ON COMPETITIVE MANEUVERS.

Marketing's objective is to capture the most market share, a percentage of the target market segment. Its tool is a blueprint, a strategic battle plan of how people think, work, and choose new products. It believes action means outmaneuvering the competition by moving around a battlefield. Its leaders see themselves as strategic commanders in a war room—people who plan as deliberately as possible the company's competitive moves so the salespeople win the most deals. Marketing gets its information from external market research work and from streams of facts and rumors from the front lines, especially via emails and phone calls from sales personnel in the field. The marketing person has a time horizon of three to five years.

SALES BUILDS CHANNELS AND WORKS TO CLOSE ORDERS.

Those in sales want to reach the customer (through selling channels) and close on an order (get a signed purchase order) in the shortest possible time. Their tool is a sales plan, a tactical map of customers (real people with names and locations and contact information and behavior and likes and dislikes). They think action is moving down the pipe (channel) to reach the customer and then closing on the deal (getting the purchase order signed) as fast as possible. Their leaders see themselves as hands-on tactical commanders in the front lines, feeding information back to the home office. Their time horizon is a few weeks to several months (twelve months at the most).

MARKETING AND SALES WORK TOGETHER AND YET CONFLICT CONSTRUCTIVELY.

Both want the start-up to win big, very big. But similar to sibling rivalries, they see weaknesses in each other and are not afraid to be heard critiquing the other function. Marketing complains, "Sales thinks mostly about their commissions" while sales moans that "marketing can't create a product that leaps off the shelf." Both think they could do the other's job much better. CEOs have learned that neither can do the other's job better, and thus the CEO must constantly work to get the two departments focused on executing their specialty in harmony with each other.

Next let's focus on examining new enterprise marketing tools and how to use them to build an unfair advantage for a new enterprise like yours.

INCLUDED IN MARKETING

Marketing involves a *complex process* using many tools, including these:

- Names of the company, technology, market segment, and business
- Choice of what product or service to sell
- Methods of manufacturing or servicing
- Colors, sizes, shapes
- Packaging
- Location of business
- Advertising
- Public relations
- Market research and analysis

- Measure of market size and projected growth

- Business model of how to make money

- Sales training

- Solutions to problems facing customers

- Lists and analysis of competitors

- Plans for working with strategic partners

- Growth plan for three to five years

- Follow-up and feedback from the customers

- Income statement and profit

Marketing is a game for thinkers. It is a cerebral function. Marketing people hold a lot of meetings, coordinating the many departments in the company working on new products. They talk a lot with people outside the company about emerging markets, rumors about competitors, and the wars of marketing. Marketing is a very powerful function. Employees find their morale lifted by messages send out by the marketing department and are depressed when the messages are weak and not inspiring. Success is measured by how large a portion of the target market is owned by the company. Marketing people see themselves as the brain center of the company, strategically critical. People good at marketing have a lot of competitive passion and inspire other departments.

INCLUDED IN SALES

Sales includes everything you need to close orders for your business. *Sales* is an *intensive process* with many tools, including these:

- Sales collateral materials

- Monthly forecast of likely sales outcome over next twelve months

- People-intensive contact

- Negotiating and persuading

- Pushing to close on orders

- Motivational compensation such as quotas and goals

- Organizational savvy

- Sales presentations

- Sales-rallying meetings

- Telephone inquiries

- Sales and cash collections from customers

- Qualifying customers

- Preparing quotations

- Planning sales activities based on forecasted sales

Sales is a game for people who need to "go out there and do something." They hate meetings (unless related to closing an order). Sales is a very emotional function. Employees get excited when orders arrive at headquarters and depressed when they don't. The media most often measure the growth of a new enterprise by the size of sales. Salespeople commonly see themselves as the energy center of the company, the heartbeat of the entire corpus, all-important. People good at selling have a lot of energy and excite other departments.

Try not to get sales and marketing confused with each other. They are related but very different. That is why most new enterprises I speak to have one vice president for each of the two functions. Marketing helps create business opportunities. Sales then picks up leads (also called *suspects*) and qualify them as prospective customers (also called *prospects*) and takes them through the sales process. The sooner you know your customers' buying patterns, the sooner you will be able to match your sales process to fit those buying patterns.

ENDNOTES

Introduction

1 *San Jose Mercury News*, July 6, 2003 p. 25A, referring to an interview in *Playboy*, January 1988.

Chapter 1 What Is an Unfair Advantage?

1 This is based on the pioneering thinking of Kevin Coyne, "Sustainable Competitive Advantage—What It Is, What It Isn't," *Business Horizons*, January–February 1986, 27–43.

2 "A Terrible Panic Among Private Companies," *Business Week*, January 13, 2003.

3 Geoffrey A. Moore, *Inside the Tornado* (New York: Harper Business, 1995).

4 Geoffrey A. Moore, *The Gorilla Game* (New York: Harper Business, 1999).

5 "A Global Pill Factory," *Far Eastern Economic Review*, September 26, 2002, p. 63.

6 Thanks for use of this idea go to Sarah Keim, Brian Kim, Jordan Patti, and Nikhil Swaminathan.

7 *San Jose Mercury News*, July 28, 2003.

Chapter 2 What Are the Parts of an Unfair Advantage?

1 *San Jose Mercury News*, February 20, 2003.

2 Peter Drucker, "The Next Society," *Economist*, November 3, 2001.

3 Bob Nelson, *1001 Ways to Reward Employees* (New York: Workman Publishing, 1994).

4 Kenneth H. Blanchard and Spencer Johnson, *The One Minute Manager* (New York: Berkley, 1983).

5 Drucker, "The Next Society."

Chapter 3 Building Business Plans with Unfair Advantages

1 Geoffrey A. Moore, *Crossing the Chasm—and Beyond* (New York: Harper Business, 1995), p. 25.

2 Robert X. Cringely, *Accidental Empires* (New York: Harper Business, 1996).

3 "Venture Wire Summary," *Venture Wire*, February 7, 2002.

Chapter 4 How to Assemble an Unfair Advantage

1 "Talk About Scary," *Wall Street Journal*, June 20, 2002.

Chapter 6 Customer Need and Business Opportunity

1 Gene G. Marcial, "Staying at Home—with Karaoke?" *Business Week*, June 10, 2002.

2 Guy Kawasaki, *The Art of the Start* (New York: Portfolio Penguin Group, 2004).

3 "CelPay Puts Africa on Wireless Map," *Wall Street Journal*, December 2, 2002.

4 Thanks to Wilfred Lam, Alison Lau, Jorge Tseng Lee, David Wang, and Samson Yao for use of their business plan for DataMed Corp.

Chapter 7 The New Enterprise Strategic Mind

1 Al Ries and Jack Trout, *Marketing Warfare* (New York: McGraw-Hill, 1986).

2 Al Ries and Laura Ries, *The Fall of Advertising and The Rise of PR* (New York: Harper Business, 2002).

Chapter 9 Types of Strategies

1 Carl von Clausewitz, *On War* (New York: Knopf, 1993).

2 Al Ries and Jack Trout, *Marketing Warfare* (New York: McGraw-Hill, 1986).

3 Clayton M. Christensen, *The Innovator's Dilemma* (Boston: Harvard Business School Press, 1997).

4 Peter Drucker, *Innovation and Entrepreneurship* (New York: Harper & Row, 1985).

5 "The return of von Clausewitz," *Economist*, March 7, 2002.

6 Geoffrey A. Moore, *Inside the Tornado* (New York: Harper Business, 1995), pp. 68–72.

7 Lisa Brausten, "Start-Up Good Technology Tackles Top Sellers of Hand-Held Devices," *Wall Street Journal*, May 9, 2002.

8 Gene G. Marcial, "Staying at Home—with Karaoke?" *Business Week*, June 10, 2002.

9 Web site of Dolby Laboratories, www.dolby.com, February 2003.

Chapter 10 Marketing

1 Regis McKenna, "Marketing Is Everything," *Harvard Business Review,* January 1991, 65–79.

2 Sony USA web site, www.sony.com, March 2003.

3 Notiva web site, www.notiva.com, March 2003.

4 Al Ries and Laura Ries, *The Fall of Advertising and the Rise of PR* (New York: Harper Business, 2002).

Chapter 13 Strategic Partners

1 Thanks to Manish Kathuria, Caoyu Jing, Lesley Lu, and Colin Soh for this idea.

Chapter 14 Customer Support

1 Siebel Systems web site, www.siebel.com, February 2003.

Chapter 15 Engineering and Technology

1 *Silicon Valley Business Journal,* July 26, 2002; *Wall Street Journal,* February 4, 2003.

Chapter 20 Facilities and Administration

1 *The American Heritage Dictionary of the English Language,* 4th ed. (Boston: Houghton Mifflin, 2003).

Chapter 21 Financial Plan

1 *High Tech Start Up,* Chapter 3.

Chapter 23 Surfing Disruptive Technology Waves

1 Charles P. Kindleberger, *Manias, Panics, and Crashes: A History of Financial Crises* (New York: Wiley, 2000).

Chapter 24 Going World-Class

1 Web site of Telephone Systems International, www.telsysint.com, February 2003.

Chapter 26 Venture Capital Firms Apply Unfair Advantage

1 Web site of Sequoia Capital, www.sequoiacap.com, February 2003.

2 Web site of Kleiner Perkins Caufield & Byers, www.kpcb.com, February 2003.

3 Web site of Nokia Venture Partners, www.nokiaventurepartners.com, February 2003.

4 Web site for Alliance Venture Partners, www.allianceventure.com, February 2002.

Chapter 27 Giant Corporations Apply Unfair Advantage

1 In November 1971, Intel publicly introduced the world's first single chip microprocessor, the Intel 4004, invented by Intel engineers Federico Faggin, Ted Hoff, and Stan Mazor.

2 Robert Levering, Milton Moskowitz, and Michael Katz, *The One Hundred Best Companies to Work For in America* (New York: Addison-Wesley, 1984).

Chapter 28 MBA Schools Apply Unfair Advantage

1 Web site of Harvard Business School, www.hbs.edu, February 2003.

2 Web site of National University of Singapore, www.nus.edu, February 2003.

3 Web site of London Business School, www.london.edu, February 2003.

4 http://www.geneziegler.com/contact.shtml.

5 Web site of the University of Phoenix, www.uopxonline.com, April 2003.

Chapter 29 How Countries Apply Unfair Advantage

1 "Outsourcing to India: Backroom Deals," *Economist*, February 22, 2003.

2 "Face Value: Whither Singapore Inc?" *Economist*, November 30, 2002.

Chapter 31 Concluding Remarks and Challenges

1 Peter Drucker, *Innovation and Entrepreneurship* (New York: Harper & Row, 1985).

BIBLIOGRAPHY

Blanchard, Kenneth H., and Spencer Johnson. *The One Minute Manager.* New York: Berkley, 1983

Christensen, Clayton M. *The Innovator's Dilemma: When New Technologies Cause Great Firms to Fail.* Boston: Harvard Business School Press, 1997.

Clausewitz, Carl von. *On War.* New York: Knopf, 1993.

Cringely, Robert X. *Accidental Empires.* New York: Harper Business, 1996.

Drucker, Peter. *Innovation and Entrepreneurship.* New York: Harper & Row, 1985.

Kawasaki, Guy. *The Art of the Start.* New York: Portfolio Penguin Group, 2004.

Kindleberger, Charles P. *Manias, Panics, and Crashes: A History of Financial Crises.* New York: Wiley, 2000.

Moore, Geoffrey A. *Crossing The Chasm—And Beyond, Rev. Ed.* New York: Harper Business, 2002.

———. *The Gorilla Game.* New York: Harper Business, 1999.

———. *Inside the Tornado.* New York: Harper Business, 1995.

Nelson, Bob. *1001 Ways to Reward Employees.* New York: Workman Publishing, 1994.

Ries, Al, and Ries, Laura. *The Fall of Advertising and the Rise of PR.* New York: Harper Business, 2002.

Ries, Al, and Trout, Jack. *Marketing Warfare.* New York: McGraw-Hill, 1986.

EXAMPLES

FIGURES

TABLES

ACKNOWLEDGMENTS

My mission in this book—to boost the chances of success for new enterprises—is built on the experiences of risk takers from around the world. These include the many people who sent emails and shared their life experiences. I have also been fascinated and inspired by:

- Dick Barker for sharing his living example of how to remain a world-class competitor and retain one's integrity and wit

- David BenDaniel whose special entrepreneurial mind continues to contribute innovative insight to so many of us in the real world

- Clayton Christensen who finally expressed what we did not know how to say about why new enterprises outrun the giants

- Kim Cushing for her frank, insightful comments about how Silicon Valley thinks and behaves

- Peter Drucker who painted this century's fresh pathway for new enterprises and challenged entrepreneurs and scholars to follow it

- Gert Kindgren for his special view of the latest thinking about new enterprises in Europe

- Danny Lui for his patient explanations of how the Asian entrepreneurial mind works, particularly in China

- David MacMillan for sharing how he sets the new enterprise strategy bar to the world-class level and shows entrepreneurs how to reach it

- Geoffrey Moore for his pioneering documentation of the process of how high tech new enterprises develop

- Shannon Murray for his special view of how first-time entrepreneurs interpret and misinterpret lessons from serial entrepreneurs

- David Rex for his keen insight about how the real entrepreneurial process is working beyond Silicon Valley

- Al Ries for his courage and innovative explanations about what makes a few consumer marketing ideas outstanding and the rest also-rans

- Ken Tidwell for sharing the inside story of how the entrepreneurial technical mind-set really works

- Don Valentine for his sense of humor and wisdom about what it takes to make world-class enterprises out of nothing

- Bob Wallace whose keen sense of the business mind and editorial wizardry kept me optimistic about finishing this book

- My wife, Gisela, whose special view of the world makes my life a delight

John L. Nesheim
john@nesheimgroup.com

INDEX

ABOUT THE AUTHOR

JOHN NESHEIM is one of the world's best-known entrepreneurial advisors. He coaches CEOs planning to build world-class new enterprises from original ideas. John has assisted more than three hundred ventures that raised over $2 billion in financing. His seminal work, *High Tech Start Up*, is the handbook used by entrepreneurs, corporations, schools, and governments to apply the best practices for creating fresh businesses. John is CEO of the new enterprise research firm, Nesheim Group, www.nesheimgroup.com. He teaches entrepreneurship for Cornell University and the University of Singapore and conducts his workshop, *14 Steps to IPO*, in countries around the world. John lives with his wife, Gisela, in Carmel, California.

Printed in the United States
By Bookmasters